Praise for
Managing the Professional Service Firm

by

David Maister

"The more attention my colleagues and I pay to what Maister says, the better our company performs."
—John Beardsley, Chairman and Chief Executive Officer, Padilla Speer Beardsley

"David Maister is, quite simply, the clearest, wittiest, smartest law firm strategist ever. And reading or listening to him is about as much fun as it is productive."
—Steven Brill, Former Chairman and Chief Executive Officer, American Lawyer Media, L.P.

"David Maister's name is synonymous with the latest thinking in professional service firm management. This book suggests why."
—James L. Heskett, Professor, Harvard Business School; co-author of *The Service Profit Chain*

"David Maister's work is not only intellectually stimulating and inspiring for professional practice leaders, but his articles are always practical, down-to-earth and readily implementable. I have personally profited from David Maister's advice, and I am convinced that his articles are most valuable to those who manage a professional firm anywhere in the world."
—Egon P. S. Zehnder, Former Chairman, Egon Zehnder & Partner Inc.

"David Maister's material is not only thought-provoking, it is action-provoking. Golin/Harris has been a fan and a follower for years. This collection is a valuable resource for everyone in public relations."
—Rich Jernstedt, President and Chief Executive Officer, Golin/Harris

"David Maister's thoughts and writings apply original strategic insight combined with practical management advice to the difficult area of professional service management. I can think of no higher compliment than that his thinking and advice are being used on a daily basis in practice management across Europe."
—Willem Brocker, PriceWaterhouseCoopers.

"David Maister has, over the years, been a very thoughtful observer of how professional firms govern themselves. This collection is important reading, not just for managing partners, but new associates."
—Frederick W. Gluck, Former Managing Director, McKinsey & Co.

"David Maister understands the keys to success in professional service companies like no other. His insights are precise and his recommendations manage to be both original and down to earth. Even the most successful managers of professional companies can learn from his writings."
—Jon Moynihan, Group Chief Executive, PA Consulting Group (UK)

MANAGING the PROFESSIONAL SERVICE FIRM

DAVID MAISTER

FREE PRESS
BUSINESS

TO KATHY

AS THE YEARS GO BY, MY LOVE

This paperback edition first published by
Simon & Schuster UK Ltd, 2003
A CBS COMPANY

7 9 10 8 6

Simon & Schuster UK Ltd
Africa House
64–78 Kingsway
London WC2B 6AH

www.simonsays.co.uk

Simon & Schuster Australia
Sydney

A CIP catalogue record for this book is available
from the British Library

ISBN 0–7432–3156–2

Printed and bound in Great Britain by CPI Bath

CREDITS

Chapter 1: "A Question of Balance." An earlier version of this chapter was published under the title, "Balancing the Professional Service Firm," by David H. Maister, in the Fall 1982 issue of the *Sloan Management Review* (Volume 24, no.1), reprinted by permission of the publisher. Copyright 1982 by the Sloan Management Review Association. All rights reserved.

Chapter 2: "The Professional Firm Lifecycle." An earlier version of this article was published under the title, "The Three E's of Professional Life," by David H. Maister, in the *Journal of Management Consulting*, Vol. 3, No.2, pp.39–44(1986). Copyright 1986 the *Journal of Management Consulting*.

Chapter 3: "Profitability: Health and Hygiene." First published in the July 1991 issue of the *International Accounting Bulletin*. Copyright 1991 David H. Maister.

Chapter 4: "Solving the Underdelegation Problem." First published in the January 1991 issue of the *International Accounting Bulletin*. Copyright 1991 David H. Maister.

Chapter 5: "The Practice Development Package." First published in the April 1993 issue of *The American Lawyer*. Copyright 1993 David H. Maister.

Chapter 6: "Listening to Clients," by David H. Maister. Reprinted by permission of *Business Quarterly*, published by the Western Business School, The University of Western Ontario, London, Ontario, Canada. Spring 1989 issue.

Chapter 7: "Quality Work Doesn't Mean Quality Service." David H. Maister is a contributing author for *The American Lawyer*. This article is reprinted from the April 1984 issue of the *American Lawyer*. © 1984 *The American Lawyer*.

Chapter 8: "A Service Quality Program." A version of this chapter appeared in the October 1992 issue of *The American Lawyer*, under the title, "Turning Talk into Action." Copyright 1992 David H. Maister.

Chapter 9: "Marketing to Existing Clients." First published in the *Journal of Management Consulting*, Vol. 5, No.2, pp. 25–32 (1989). Copyright 1989 *Journal of Management Consulting*.

Chapter 10: "How Clients Choose." First published in *The American Lawyer*, October 1991. Copyright 1991 David H. Maister.

Chapter 11: "Attracting New Clients." First published in November and December 1992 issues of *The American Lawyer*. Copyright 1992 David H. Maister.

Chapter 12: "Managing the Marketing Effort." First published in the *International Accounting Bulletin*, January 1992. Copyright 1992 David H. Maister.

Chapter 14: "How to Build Human Capital." David H. Maister is a contributing author for *The American Lawyer*. This article is reprinted with permission from the June 1984 issue of *The American Lawyer*. © 1984 *The American Lawyer*.

Chapter 15: "The Motivation Crisis." David H. Maister is a contributing author for *The American Lawyer*. This article is reprinted with permission from the December 1985 issue of *The American Lawyer*. © 1985 *The American Lawyer*.

Chapter 16: "On the Importance of Scheduling." An earlier version of this chapter was published under the title, "Job Scheduling Sets the Pace in Professional Firms," by David H. Maister, in the *Journal of Management Consulting*, vol. 1, No. 1 (1982). Copyright 1982 *Journal of Management Consulting*.

Chapter 17: "On the Meaning of Partnership." David H. Maister is a contributing author for *The American Lawyer*. This article is reprinted with permission from the October 1983 issue of *The American Lawyer*. © 1983 *The American Lawyer*.

Chapter 19: "How Practice Leaders Add Value." This chapter is an extensively rewritten version of two earlier articles: "The Power of Practice Leadership," published in the March 1993 issue of *The American Lawyer*, and "The Management Strain," published in *The Counselor*, Vol. 22, No.2 (1986). Copyright 1993 David H. Maister.

Chapter 20: "How to Create a Strategy." First published in the April 1990 issue of *The American Lawyer*. Copyright 1990 David H. Maister.

Chapter 23: "The Art of Partner Compensation." David H. Maister is a contributing author for *The American Lawyer*. This article is reprinted with permission from the November 1984 issue of *The American Lawyer*. © 1994 *The American Lawyer*.

Chapter 24: First published in the January/February 1993 issue of *The American Lawyer*. Copyright 1993 David H. Master

Chapter 25: "Pie-Splitting." David H. Maister is a contributing author for *The American Lawyer*. This article is reprinted with permission from the March 1984 issue of *The American Lawyer*. © 1984 *The American Lawyer*.

Chapter 26: "Partnership Governance." A portion of this chapter first appeared under the title, "Partnership Politics," in the October 1984 issue of *The American Lawyer*.

Chapter 27: Reprinted from "The One-Firm Firm," by David H. Maister, *Sloan Management Review* (Fall 1985) by permission of publisher. Copyright 1985 by the Sloan Management Review Association. All rights reserved.

Chapter 29: "Making the Network Work." First published in *Eurobusiness*, March 1989. Copyright 1989 *Eurobusiness*.

Chapter 30: "Creating the Collaborative Firm." First published in the *International Accounting Bulletin*, April 1991. Copyright 1991 David H. Maister.

Chapter 31: "Coordinating Industry Specialty Groups." First published as "Industry Specialization: Essential but Hard to Manage," in the *Journal of Management Consulting*, Vol. 2, No.1 (Winter 1984/1985), pp.50–55. Copyright 1984 *Journal of Management Consulting.*

Chapter 32: "Asset Management." First published under the title, "Managing Your Firm's Balance Sheet" in *Management Consulting '90*, Kennedy Publications. Copyright 1990 David H. Maister.

CONTENTS

ACKNOWLEDGMENTS

This book attempts to serve managers of professional service firms by presenting both new ways of looking at the various issues faced by such firms and by offering practical advice for their resolution. The chapters of this book are, in the main, made up of articles published separately over the last ten years. I owe a debt of gratitude to the many journals that provided an outlet for my work (see Credits at the front of the book.) However, special mention must be given to Steve Brill and *The American Lawyer*, where I am currently a contributing author. Not only did the magazine publish much of my early (and recent) work, but Steve has always acted both as a source of encouragement to stick with the terrifying task of writing and as an archenemy of sloppy thinking. I am grateful to all at *The American Lawyer* for their support.

Two people have played an essential role not only in this work, but also in all of the research and consulting that led to it. They are Kathy Maister, my wife, and Julie MacDonald O'Leary, my business manager. To both, I offer my gratitude and unending loyalty. A wise philosopher once said that "All theory is autobiography," and many of my views have been formed from my own experience in running a small professional enterprise. Kathy, apart from being an outstanding and supportive coach, has taught me much about relationships and partnership. She has always been an invaluable sounding board. Julie is the consummate professional—talented, dedicated, flexible, and always eager to take on more responsibility. I shudder to think about what I would have done without her.

In 1991–92 our team was enhanced by the addition of Cliff Farrah who helped to make the rest of us more effective at what we do. We follow his career with interest and high expectations.

Naturally, nothing in this book could have been developed without the support of the many clients who gave me the opportunity to work with them in developing, implementing, and revising new approaches to professional firm management. I am grateful to those of my clients who had the courage to seek out and experiment with disruptive, provocative, and challenging ideas.

INTRODUCTION TO

The reception accorded to this book since its initial publication in 1993 has been very gratifying. It has gone through numerous printings in hardcover, 10 printings in paperback, sold in excess of 250,000 copies, and has been translated into Dutch, French, Spanish, Japanese, Polish and Serbo-Croatian. It has been referred to as the 'bible' of professional service firms in many disciplines and, according to Amazon.com and Amazon.co.uk, received 5-star evaluations from readers from as far afield as Italy, the US, the UK, Russia, Norway, Hong Kong and Brazil.

In writing the book, I tried to capture the core principles of good management across a variety of professions and, I hoped, across time, avoiding topics likely to be influenced by fashion and fad. Naturally, the book omits some topics that could have been addressed, and includes many subjects that I could have explored in greater depth. Many of these omissions of coverage and depth were addressed in my later books.

However as I review these pages, I am confident that there is nothing that I would remove or amend. In spite of all the turbulent changes that the professions have undergone, I stand by the analyses and views expressed here. Many of the topics addressed here have seen significant changes in practice: client service and an emphasis on marketing to existing clients are much more common than they were ten years ago. The forthcoming 'people crisis' that I wrote about then received a great deal of attention as the 'war for talent' became palpably real. The one-firm corporation model is a goal pursued by many more firms now than it was back then.

There is, nevertheless, work still to be done. The very concept of management remains troublesome in many professions; it is still true that group leaders and others in managerial roles are expected to be 'players' first and foremost, and 'coaches' only second. Training for managerial roles remains the exception rather than the rule. Similarly, the notion that success is achieved by paying attention to energizing, exciting and enthusing people is a concept that receives more lip service than day-to-day action.

The biggest change in management made by professional firms in the last ten years has been a much greater degree of financial discipline, and the results have been clearly positive. However, in the language I introduced in this book, much of this improvement has been in the area of 'hygiene.' The questions of long-run 'health' remain a constant challenge, and, as noted, I am encouraged that many individuals and firms still turn to this work as a source of ideas on how to get on the path to achieve that long-run success.

David Maister
Boston, MA
January 2003
www.davidmaister.com
david@davidmaister.com

PART ONE

BASIC MATTERS

CHAPTER 1

A QUESTION OF BALANCE

One of the most interesting discoveries in my consulting work has been the fact that (apparently) every professional service firm in the world has the same mission statement, regardless of the firm's size, specific profession, or country of operation. With varying refinements of language, the mission of most professional firms is:

> To deliver outstanding client service; to provide fulfilling careers and professional satisfaction for our people; and to achieve financial success so that we can reward ourselves and grow.

The commonality of this mission does not detract from its value. Simply put, every professional firm *must* satisfy these three goals of "service, satisfaction, and success" if it is to survive (see Figure 1–1). Management of a professional firm requires a delicate balancing act between the demands of the client marketplace, the realities of the people marketplace (the market for staff), and the firm's economic ambitions.

Many factors play a role in bringing these goals into harmony, but one has a preeminent position: the ratio of junior, middle-level, and senior staff in the firm's organization, referred to here as the firm's leverage. To see the importance of this factor, we shall briefly examine, in turn, its relation to the three goals of the firm.

3

FIGURE 1–1

The Three Goals

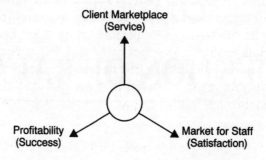

LEVERAGE AND THE CLIENT MARKETPLACE

The required shape of the organization (the relative mix of juniors, managers, and seniors) is primarily determined by (or rather, as we shall see, *should* be determined by) the skill requirements of its work: the mix of senior-level, middle-level, and junior-level tasks involved in the projects that the firm undertakes. Consider three kinds of client work: Brains, Grey Hair, and Procedure projects.

In the first type (Brains), the client's problem is at the forefront of professional or technical knowledge, or at least is of extreme complexity. The key elements of this type of professional service are creativity, innovation, and the pioneering of new approaches, concepts or techniques: in effect, new solutions to new problems. The firm that targets this market will be attempting to sell its services on the basis of the high professional craft of its staff. In essence, their appeal to their market is, "Hire us because we're smart."

Brains projects usually involve highly skilled and highly paid professionals. Few procedures are routinizable: Each project is "one-off." Accordingly, the opportunities for leveraging the top professionals with juniors are relatively limited. Even though such projects may involve significant data collection and analysis activities (normally performed by juniors), even these activities cannot be clearly specified in advance and require the active involvement of at least middle-level (project management) professionals on a continuous basis. Consequently, the ratio of junior time to middle-level and senior time on Brains projects tends to be low.

Grey Hair projects, while they may require a highly customized "output" in meeting the clients' needs, involve a lesser degree of innovation and creativity in the actual performance of the work than would a Brains project. The general nature of the problem to be addressed is not unfamiliar, and the activities necessary to complete the project may be similar to those performed on other projects. Clients with Grey Hair problems seek out firms with experience in their particular type of problem. In turn, the firm sells its knowledge, its experience, and its judgment. In effect, they are saying, "Hire us because we have been through this before; we have practice at solving this type of problem."

Since for Grey Hair-type projects the problems to be addressed are somewhat more familiar, at least some of the tasks to be performed (particularly the early ones) are known in advance and can be specified and delegated. The opportunity is thus provided to employ more juniors to accomplish these tasks.

The third type of project, the Procedure project, usually involves a well-recognized and familiar type of problem. While there is still a need to customize to some degree, the steps necessary to accomplish this are somewhat programmatic. The client may have the ability and resources to perform the work itself, but turns to the professional firm because the firm can perform the service more efficiently, because the firm is an outsider, or because the client's own staff capabilities to perform the activity are somewhat constrained and are better used elsewhere. In essence, the professional firm is selling its procedures, its efficiency, its availability: "Hire us because we know how to do this and can deliver it effectively."

Procedure projects usually involve the highest proportion of junior time relative to senior time (and hence imply a different organizational shape for firms that specialize in such projects). The problems to be addressed in such projects, and the steps necessary to complete the analysis, diagnosis, and conclusions are usually so sufficiently well established that they can be easily delegated (under supervision) to junior staff. For Procedure projects the range of possible outcomes for some steps may be so well known that the appropriate responses may be "programmed."

The three categories described here are, of course, only points along a spectrum of project types. However, it is usually a simple task in any profession to identify types of problems that fit these categories. The choice that the firm makes in its mix of project types is one of the most important variables it has available to balance the firm. The choice of project types influences significantly, as we shall see, the economic and organizational structures of the firm.

Consider what will happen if a firm brings in a mix of client work such that its "proper" staffing requirements would be for a slightly higher mix of juniors, and a lesser mix of seniors than it has (i.e., the work is slightly more procedural than the firm would normally expect). What will happen?

As Figure 1–2 suggests, the short-run consequence will be that higher priced people will end up performing lower-value tasks (probably at lower fees), and there will be an underutilization of senior personnel. The firm will make less money than it should be making.

The opposite problem is no less real. If a firm brings in work that has skill requirements of a higher percentage of seniors and a lesser percentage of juniors (Figure 1–3), the consequences will be at least equally adverse: a shortfall of qualified staff to perform the tasks, and a consequent quality risk.

As these simple examples show, matching the skills required by the work to the skills available in the firm (i.e., managing the leverage structure) is central to keeping the firm in balance.

LEVERAGE AND THE PEOPLE MARKETPLACE

The connection between a firm's leverage structure (its ratio of junior to senior professional staff) and the people marketplace can be captured in a single sentence: People do not join professional firms for *jobs,* but for *careers.* They have strong expectations of progressing through the organization at some pace agreed to (explicitly or implicitly) in advance.

FIGURE 1–2

The Consequences of Too Much Procedural Work

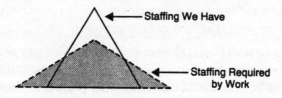

FIGURE 1–3

The Consequences of Too Much Brains Work

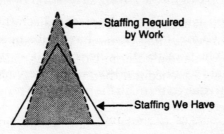

The professional service firm may be viewed as the modern embodiment of the medieval craftsman's shop, with its apprentices, journeymen, and master craftsmen. The early years of an individual's association with a professional service firm are, indeed, usually viewed as an apprenticeship, and the relation between juniors and seniors the same: The senior craftsmen repay the hard work and assistance of the juniors by teaching them their craft.

The archetypal structure of the professional service firm is an organization containing three professional levels. In a consulting organization, these levels might be labeled junior consultant, manager, and vice president. In a CPA firm they might be referred to as staff, manager, and partner. Law firms tend to have only two levels, associate and partner, although there is an increasing tendency in large law firms to recognize formally what has long been an informal distinction between junior and senior partners.

Responsibility for the organization's three primary tasks is allocated to these three levels of the organization: seniors (partners or vice presidents) are responsible for marketing and client relations, managers for the day-to-day supervision and coordination of projects, and juniors for the many technical tasks necessary to complete the study. The three levels are traditionally referred to as "the finders," "the minders," and "the grinders" of the business. The mix of each that the firm requires (i.e., its ratio of senior to junior professionals) is primarily determined by the mix of client work, and in turn crucially determines the career paths that the firm can offer.

While the pace of progress may not be a rigid one ("up or out in five years"), both the individual and the organization usually share strong norms about what constitutes a reasonable period of time for each stage of the career path. Individuals who are not promoted within this period will seek greener pastures elsewhere, either by their own choice or career ambitions, or at the strong suggestion of the firm.

This promotion system serves an essential screening function for the firm. Not all young professionals hired subsequently develop the managerial and client relations skills required at the higher levels. While good initial recruiting procedures may serve to reduce the degree of screening required through the promotion process, it can rarely eliminate the need for the promotion process to serve this important function. The existence of a "risk of not making it" also serves the firm in that it constitutes a degree of pressure on junior personnel to work hard and succeed.

The promotion incentive is directly influenced by two key dimensions: the normal amount of time spent at each level before being considered for promotion, and the "odds of making it" (the proportion promoted). These factors are clearly linked to a firm's leverage structure (and its growth). For any given rate of growth, a highly leveraged firm (one with a high ratio of juniors to seniors) will offer a lower probability of "making it" to the top, since there are many juniors seeking to rise and relatively few senior slots opening up. A less leveraged firm, at the same rate of growth, will need to "bring along" a higher percentage of its juniors, thus providing a greater promotion incentive.

LEVERAGE AND PROFITABILITY

A professional service firm's leverage is also central to its economics. The "rewards of partnership" (the high levels of compensation attained by senior partners) come only in part from the high hourly (or daily) rates that the top professionals can charge for their own time. Profits also come, in large part, from the firm's ability, through its project team structure, to leverage the professional skills of the seniors with the efforts of juniors.

The successful leveraging of top professionals is at the heart of the success of the professional firm. As demonstrated below, a significant portion of partnership profits derives from the surplus generated from hiring staff at a given salary and billing them out at multiples of that salary. By leveraging its high-cost seniors with low-cost juniors, the professional firm can lower its effective hourly rate and thus reduce its cost to clients while simultaneously generating additional profit for the partners.

FIGURE 1–4

Linking the Three Goals

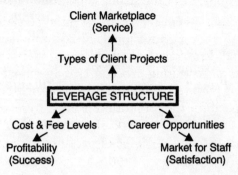

The market for the firm's services will determine the fees it can command for a given project; its costs will be determined by the firm's abilities to deliver the service with a cost-effective mix of junior, manager, and senior time. If the firm can find a way to deliver its services with a higher proportion of juniors to seniors, it will be able to achieve lower service delivery costs. The project team structure of the firm is therefore an important component of firm profitability.

The relationship between a firm's leverage structure and its three goals is illustrated in Figure 1–4, which shows the principal forces tying these elements together.

GURU ASSOCIATES: A NUMERICAL EXAMPLE

To explore further how these items interrelate, let us consider a numerical example (Table 1–1). Guru Associates, which engages in a variety of projects, nevertheless has a typical project which requires 50 percent of a senior's time, 100 percent of a middle-level person's time, and the full-time efforts of three juniors. No one is expected to bill 100 percent of each's available time. Nevertheless, if the firm is to meet its economic goals, it will require that seniors and managers are engaged in billable work for 75 percent of their time, and juniors 90 percent.

Guru Associates currently has four seniors. If it is to meet its target of 75 percent billed senior time, its available senior time will be four times 75 percent, or the equivalent of three seniors working full-time. This implies six projects, if the typical project requires 50 percent of a senior's time.

TABLE 1–1

Level	Requirements for Average Project	Target Utiliza- tion	Required Staffing for 6 Projects @ Target Utilization	Required Staffing for 12 Projects @ Target Utilization
Senior	50% of 1 person	75%	4	8
Middle	1 person	75%	8	16
Junior	3 people	90%	20	40

With six projects, the firm needs the equivalent of six full-time middle-level staff, according to the project team structure. (Each project requires 100 percent of a middle-level person). At 75 percent target utilization (billed hours divided by available hours), this means that the firm must have eight middle-level staff. Similarly, at three juniors per project, the firm needs eighteen full-time juniors, or at 90 percent billability, twenty juniors.

Simple calculations such as these show that, with eight seniors, the firm would need sixteen managers and forty juniors. The proportions remain constant: one senior to every two managers, to every five juniors. Unless there is a change in either the project team structure (i.e., the types of projects the firm undertakes), or the target utilization (matters which will be discussed below), the firm must keep these ratios constant as it grows.

This seemingly simpleminded calculation, relating the staffing mix requirements of the work to the staffing levels existing in the firm, is in fact of extreme importance.

If we know the salaries of the staff members and their billing rates, we can construct the pro forma income statement of this firm at full utilization. The role of leverage is amply illustrated by Guru Associates (Table 1–2). The four seniors (partners) personally bill a total of $1.2 million, or $300,000 apiece. At per-professional overhead costs of $40,000 (including the costs of all secretaries, administrative staff,

TABLE 1–2
The Economics of Guru Associates

Level	No.	Target Utilization	Target Billable Hours @ 2,000 Hours per Person per Year	Billing Rate	Fees	Salary per Individual	Total Salaries
Senior	4	75%	6,000	$200	$1,200,000		$600,000
Middle	8	75%	12,000	$100	$1,200,000	$75,000	$600,000
Junior	20	90%	36,000	$50	$1,800,000	$32,000	$640,000
TOTALS					$4,200,000		$1,240,000

Fees	$4,200,000
Salaries	(1,240,000)
Contributions	$2,960,000
Overhead*	$1,280,000
Partner Profits	$1,680,000
Per Partner	$ 420,000

* Assume overhead costs of $40,000 per professional

space, supplies, etc.), this would result in a per-partner profit of $260,000 if these seniors were totally unleveraged.

With a healthy seven staff members per senior, partner profits now total $420,000 apiece. About 60 percent of each partner's profit comes not from what he or she bills, but from the profit generated by the nonpartner group. Thus the benefits of leverage!

(It should be immediately stressed that high leverage is not *always* good. As we have already observed, having high leverage is completely inappropriate if the firm has a high level of Brains work. What we can say is that leverage should be as high as the requirements of the work allow).

We now turn to Guru Associates' position in the market for staff. Guru Associates has the following promotion policies. It considers that it requires four years for a junior to acquire the expertise and experience to perform the middle-level function, and it expects to promote 80 percent of its candidates to this position. A lower percentage would be insufficient to attract new juniors, and a higher percentage would imply that insufficient "screening" was taking place (i.e., that there was no room for "hiring mistakes"). From middle-level to senior is also expected to take four years; but because fewer candidates develop the critical client relations skills that Guru Associates requires, on average only 50 percent of candidates make it.

We shall now trace the evolution of Guru Associates over time. Among the eight middle-level staff, we may assume that, since it takes four years to make senior, one quarter of them (i.e., two) are in their final year as middle-level staff. If Guru Associates is to abide by its promotion policies, then it can expect to promote 50 percent, (i.e., one candidate). Whether by firm policy or by the personal decision of the individual, the nonpromoted candidate will leave the firm. (Note that this result tends to happen in most professional service firms regardless of whether the firm has an up-or-out policy. Middle-level staff may, if allowed, hang on for another year or two, but most eventually leave if not promoted. As we shall see, there is a strong incentive for the firm to encourage them to leave, since they are occupying slots eagerly sought by the juniors coming up behind them.)

Counting both those promoted and those leaving we have reduced the number of middle-level staff by two; and increased the number of seniors by one. Since we now have five seniors, we require ten middle-level staff (unless the mix of project types changes) and have six remaining. We must seek out four new middle-level staff from among our juniors. Of the twenty in the firm, we assume one quarter (five) will be in their final year as juniors. Since our expectation (or policy) is to promote 80 percent at this level, we will, indeed, promote four out of the five to fill our four available slots. (The fact that these figures match is not, of course, fortuitous. The percentage that can be promoted at a lower level is determined by the shape of the professional pyramid.) Like the "passed over" middle-level staff person, the fifth junior may reasonably be assumed to leave the firm.

We now have fifteen juniors left. However, with five seniors, and ten managers, the firm requires twenty-five juniors: it must hire ten. These changes are summarized in Table 1–3, which follows the same logic for years 1 through 9.

In year 5, the first batch of middle-level staff that were promoted from junior in year 1 will be ready to be considered for promotion to senior. It will be recalled that there are four of them. If promotion opportunities are to be maintained, then two will be promoted (i.e., 50 percent) and two will leave. This creates a total of ten seniors. With a total of ten seniors in year 5, twenty middle-level staff are required. Of the sixteen in the firm the previous year, four have been promoted or have left, meaning that a total of eight juniors must be promoted. Fortunately (but not fortuitously) ten juniors who were hired in year 1 are to be considered for promotion. The expected 80 percent target may be maintained!

What must be stressed at this point is that we have arrived at these staffing levels solely by considering the interaction of the firm's leverage structure with the promotion incentives (career opportunities) that the firm promises. What we have discovered by performing these calculations is that the interaction of these two forces determines a target (or required) growth rate for the firm. As Table 1–3 shows, Guru Associates must double in size every four years solely to preserve its promotion incentives. If it grows at a lower rate than this, then either it will remove much of the incentive in the firm, or it will end up with an "unbalanced factory" (too many seniors and not enough juniors) with a consequent deleterious effect upon the firm's economics.

If the firm attempts to grow faster than target rate, it will be placed in the position of either having to promote a higher proportion of juniors, or to promote them in a shorter period of time. Without corresponding adjustments, this could have a significant impact on the quality of services that the firm provides.

We have seen that the leverage structure and the promotion policies together determine a target (required) growth rate. It should be acknowledged, however, that there is another way of looking at the relationship between these variables. An equivalent way of stating the relationship would be to observe that if given a growth rate and a leverage structure, the promotion incentives that result can be specified. We may see this by examining Table 1–3 once more. Suppose that we had constructed this by specifying the growth rate and the project team structure. We would then have discovered that we could afford to promote only four out of five juniors and one out of two managers. We would also have discovered that we would have a "built-in," or target, turnover rate averaging over 4 percent (two resignations per year for the first four years while the average number of nonsenior staff was 45.5).

TABLE 1–3

The Consequences of Guru Associates' Promotion Policies

	Staff Numbers									
	0	1	2	3	4	5	6	7	8	9
Senior	4	5	6	7	8	10	12	14	16	20
Middle	8	10	12	14	16	20	24	28	32	40
Junior	20	25	30	35	40	50	60	70	80	100
TOTAL	32	40	48	56	64	80	96	112	128	160
New Hires		10	10	10	10	20	20	20	20	40
Resignations		2	2	2	2	4	4	4	4	8
Annual % Growth in Staff		25	20	17	14	25	20	17	14	25

In this example, Guru Associates can achieve what would be considered an extremely low target turnover rate if it achieves its optimal growth. However, the norm in many professional firms is a much higher rate than this, often reaching as high as 20 to 25 percent (for example in some CPA firms). The key point to note here is that, given a growth rate and an organizational structure, the target turnover rate of the firm can be specified. (This does not, of course, tell us what the actual turnover experience of the firm will be. We are considering here the turnover that the firm requires to keep itself in balance. While it may be able, through its promotion system, to ensure that the actual rate does not get too low, it may have to use other devices to ensure that the actual turnover rate does not get too high through too many people quitting.)

In most professions, one or more firms can be identified that have clearly chosen a high target rate of turnover. Partners (or shareholders) can routinely earn a surplus value from the juniors without having to "repay" them in the form of promotion. This high turnover rate also allows a significant degree of screening so that only the "best" stay in the organization. Not surprisingly, firms following this strategy tend to be among the most prestigious in their industry.

This last comment gives us the clue as to why such firms are able to maintain this strategy over time. Individuals continue to join these organizations, knowing that the odds of "making it" are very low. In the eyes of many potential recruits, the experience, training, and association with the prestigious firms in the industry make the poor promotion opportunities at such firms worthwhile.

Young professionals view a short period of time at such firms as a form of "post-postgraduate" degree, and often leave for prime positions they could not have achieved as quickly by another route. Indeed, most of the prestige firms following this strategy not only encourage this but provide active "outplacement" assistance. Apart from the beneficial effects that such activities provide in recruiting the next generation of juniors, such alumni are often the source of future business for the firm when they recommend to their corporate employers hiring their old firm (which they know and understand) over other competitors.

The ability to place ex-staff in prestigious positions is thus one of the prerequisites of a successful churning strategy. (An exception might be provided by those professions where legal requirements such as professional certification necessitate that juniors spend time in a firm. However, even here the prestige firms provide active outplacement assistance.)

GROWTH AND PROFITABILITY

Before we leave the topic of growth, we should take a quick peek back at Guru Associates. How did its growth contribute to its profitability? Let us perform our analysis on the basis of constant (year 0) dollars, to remove the effect of inflation. By implication, this means that the salaries and billing rates at each staff level remain the same. What does the firms' profit and loss statement now look like? Table 1–4 repeats the analysis of Table 1–2, using year 5 staffing levels instead of year 0.

The result? Per-partner profits have not increased! In fact, they have remained *precisely* the same!

What this simple example shows is that there is no necessary relationship between growth and profits. As we have seen, growth in a professional firm is driven primarily by the need to attract and retain staff, and is critical for that reason, but is not a guarantee of higher per-partner profits.

Why is this so? We shall explore the reasoning in greater detail in subsequent chapters, but the basic fact is this. If a firm grows subject to two conditions, as Guru Associates has, whereby: (a) the mix of client projects (and hence fee levels) remains the same; and (b) the project staffing (or leverage) is such that the same *proportion* of senior or partner time is required to handle each project; then the number of seniors or partners that the firm requires will correspond *exactly* to the growth rate. In consequence of this, the profit pool may increase because of the higher volume, but it must be shared among a correspondingly increased number of partners.

If per-partner profits are to increase, then one of the two conditions must be broken. Either the firm must bring in a different mix of business commanding higher billing rates (i.e., find higher-value work for its people to do), or it must find ways to serve the same kinds of work with an ever increasing proportion of junior time, and a declining proportion of senior time.

It is interesting to note that few prominent professional firms act as

TABLE 1-4
The Economics of Guru Associates
(Year 5 in constant dollars)

Level	No.	Target Utilization	Target Billable Hours @ 2,000 Hours per Person per Year	Billing Rate	Fees	Salary per Individual	Total Salaries
Senior	10	75%	15,000	$200	$3,000,000		
Middle	20	75%	30,000	$100	$3,000,000	$75,000	$1,500,000
Junior	50	90%	90,000	$50	$4,500,000	$32,000	$1,600,000
TOTALS					$10,500,000		$3,100,000

Fees	$10,500,000
Salaries	(3,100,000)
Contributions	$7,400,000
Overhead*	$3,200,000
Partner Profits	$4,200,000
Per Partner	$420,000

*Assume overhead costs of $40,000 per professional

17

if growth were profit neutral. Indeed, rapid growth is often listed as a primary goal of the firm, and advances in top-line growth are used as a primary internal and external measure of success. If justified in the name of providing career opportunities for staff, this indeed makes sense. However, if desired on profitability grounds, it would appear that many professional firms are fooling themselves!

SUMMARY: THE KEY ROLE OF LEVERAGE

Perhaps the most significant management variable to be disclosed by the previous analysis is the choice of the mix of projects undertaken, and the implications this has for the (average) project team (i.e., leverage) structure. As we have seen, this latter variable is a significant force in influencing the economics of the firm, its organizational structure, and its positioning in the client and people markets. The leverage structure, in the sense used in this book—as the average or typical proportion of time required from professionals at different levels— has not been a variable that is routinely monitored by firm management. However, as we have shown, its role in balancing the firm is critical.

It is possible, and not uncommon, for the firm's project team structure to change over time. If it is possible to deliver the firm's services with a greater proportion of juniors, this will in general reduce the costs of the project. Competition in the market for the firm's services will, over time, require the firm to seek out lower costs for projects of a particular type, and there will often be opportunities for an increasing proportion of juniors to be used on projects that, in the past, required a high proportion of senior time. What in past years had the characteristics of a Brains or Grey Hair project may, in future years, be accomplishable as a Procedure project.

When considering new projects to undertake, it is usually more profitable for the firm to engage in one similar to that recently performed for a previous client. The knowledge, expertise, and basic approaches to the problem that have already been developed (often through a significant personal and financial investment) can be capitalized upon by bringing them to bear on a similar or related problem. Frequently the second project can be billed out to the client at a similar (or only slightly lower) cost, since the client perceives (and receives) something equally custom-tailored: the solution to his problem. However, the savings in costs incurred by the firm in delivering this customization are not all shared with the client (if, indeed, any are). The firm thus makes its most money by "leading the market": being able to sell as a fully customized service (at a fully customized price) what increasingly becomes a service with reproducible, standardized elements.

While it is in the best interests of the firm that similar or repetitive engagements be undertaken, this is often not in accord with the desires of the individuals involved. Most individuals that join professional firms do so out of the desire for professional challenge and variety and the avoidance of routine and repetition. While they may be content to undertake a similar project for the second or third time, they will not be for the fourth or sixth or eighth.

The solution, of course, is to convert the past experience and expertise of the individual into the expertise of the firm by accepting the similar project, but utilizing a greater proportion of juniors on second- or third-time projects. Apart from requiring a lesser commitment of time from the experienced seniors, this device serves the admirable purpose of training the juniors.

For all these reasons, we might suspect that, over time, the proportion of juniors to seniors required by the firm in a particular practice area will tend to increase. If this is allowed to proceed without corresponding adjustments in the range of practice areas, the basic project team structure of the firm will alter, with significant impacts on the economics and organization of the firm. The dangers of failing to monitor the project team structure are thus clearly revealed.

Examples of failure in this regard abound in many professions. One consulting firm which learned how to utilize junior professionals increasingly in serving its clients aggressively began to hire new junior staff. After what all concerned considered the reasonable period of time for the promotion decision, the firm realized that, at the rate it had been growing, it could not promote its normal proportion of candidates: It did not need as many partners and managers in relation to the number of juniors it now had. Morale in the junior ranks suffered, as did productivity. (This latter impact was not surprising: there is a close connection between morale, commitment, and productivity in professional service firms.)

An investment banking firm discovered that, over a period of years, it had so increased the range of analyses and services it provided in advising its clients that it, too, needed more juniors on each project. Successfully integrating this new project team structure required major changes in all of the firm's administrative procedures, particularly its human resource and professional development activities. For these firms, as for all professional service firms, successful management became a question of balance.

CHAPTER 2

THE PROFESSIONAL FIRM LIFECYCLE

In any professional service there are three key benefits that clients seek: expertise, experience, and efficiency. However, even within the same practice area, the relative priority that a given client places on these elements can vary dramatically. A client with a large, complex, high-risk, and unusual problem will appropriately seek out the most creative, talented, or innovative individual or firm he can find—at almost any cost. Prior experience in the clients' industry, or past exposure to problems of a similar type, may be useful but are secondary to the client's need for frontier expertise.

While many professionals would like to believe that all client needs fall into this Brain Surgeon category, such clients represent only a small proportion of the aggregate fees spent in any given practice area. A much larger client base exists for what I term Grey Hair approaches to practice. These types of client recognize that their problems have probably been faced and dealt with by other companies, require less complete customization, and are probably not crisis issues. Accordingly, they will be shopping less for the sheer brain power of critical individuals and more for an organization that can bring past experience to bear in solving these problems. A high level of expertise is still required, and efficiency is not irrelevant, but extensive experience with similar problems is worth more to the client than an extra degree of intellect or a few dollars of savings.

21

There will also exist within the same practice area a third group of clients, who have problems that they know can be handled competently by a broad range of firms. Rather than looking for the highest possible expertise, or the most prior experience, these clients will be seeking out a professional firm that can meet their needs for a prompt start, quick disposition, and low cost: They will seek the efficient firm.

Since clients of each of these types exist within every practice area, it would be tempting for a practice group to try and respond to all of these various needs, particularly in these competitive days when professional firms are hungry for increased revenues. However, accommodating the varying needs of these different types of clients within a single practice group is an almost impossible task. A group that wishes to attract the "high expertise" engagements must organize its affairs and methods of doing business in such a way that will make it an unlikely candidate to be chosen by a client who places most emphasis on efficiency and, of course, vice versa.

Rather than discrete categories, the expertise, experience, and efficiency labels are obviously meant to describe only points along a spectrum of practice (see Figure 2–1). However, as we shall see below, every aspect of a practice group's affairs, from practice development to hiring, from economic structure to governance, will be affected by its relative positioning on this spectrum. Increasingly, firms will have

FIGURE 2–1

Spectrum of Practice

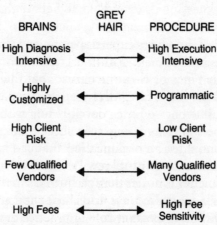

to decide which type of client need they are attempting to serve, and organize their affairs appropriately.

THE EXPERTISE PRACTICE

To justify this conclusion, we shall examine, in turn, the optimal forms of management for each of the three types of practice. First, imagine a professional practice group (or firm) that focuses its attentions on serving the needs of clients with frontier problems. How would you run such a practice?

True to the professions' traditional self-image of being elite practitioners, the staffing requirements of this "expertise-based" practice would be such that the firm would need to seek out and attract only the top percentile graduates from the best schools, in order to generate top-notch apprentices who could meet the quality needs of the frontier practice. Training would best be accomplished through an informal apprenticeship system and, since standards would be high, a rigorous up-or-out promotion system would ensure that the firm retained only the best and the brightest.

While some large-scale engagements might require large numbers of junior professionals to draft documents, perform analyses, or conduct client interviews, most expertise engagements would tend to require a high percentage of senior professional time, due to the high diagnostic component in the work. Accordingly, we would expect the expertise practice area to be relatively unleveraged, with low fixed costs and high margins. The firm would make its profits through high billing rates or some form of value billing, justifiable and sustainable because of the criticality, complexity, and risk in the client engagement.

Optimal marketing of an expertise practice matches closely the forms of practice development traditional in the professions. Since for this type of critical engagement the client would be seeking the best available talent, prominence and reputation would be the keys to winning clients. The best practice development techniques would be writing articles or books, giving speeches or being quoted in the appropriate media, thus establishing credentials as an "expert." Practice development would tend to revolve more around building the reputation of individuals rather than the firm, as in the common client comment "I hire lawyers, not law firms." Reputation within the profession would play an important role in practice development.

Since few clients would have regular ongoing needs for top-flight critical expertise, the client mix of professionals practicing in this area would tend to be diverse, and constantly shifting. With relatively low leverage and an up-or-out system, the internal pressure for growth would be less than in other practice area types and (appropriately) growth would not be a major goal for the firm.

As in all aspects of firm management, the best form of governance in an expertise-based practice area would fit the traditional professional mold: a collegial partnership of peers headed (if at all) by a leader who symbolizes the firm's commitment to high standards. Decision making would be by consensus, and management (to the extent that it existed) would largely be accomplished by inspiration. The autonomy of the individual partner would be among the most supreme virtues in the firm, with little use made of formal internal structurings. No individual or group of individuals could be said to "own" the firm. Rights to participation in the firm's future profits would be "given away" by senior professionals in order to retain top talent.

THE EXPERIENCE-BASED PRACTICE

Now consider a firm whose practice-mix was made up predominantly of clients who, rather than needing the profession's most creative talent, wanted to find a firm that had accumulated experience in handling certain types of problems, and would not take an expensive "start with a blank sheet of paper" approach to the problem. The marketing task of such a firm would be different. Rather than relying on individual talents, the firm would need to create more of an institutional reputation, based not only on the "raw" talent of key individuals but on the ability of the firm to bring to bear its collective knowledge derived from past engagements.

For such firms, practice development would involve identifying, documenting, and promoting their specialized knowledge, through brochures describing previous engagements, client newsletters, or special seminars on topics related to the firm's particular area of experience. Experience based practice areas would tend to have a more clearly focused and stable mix of clients, with steady relationships becoming increasingly important.

In contrast to the "frontier practitioners," the work content of the typical engagement would require less time spent on diagnosis and more on executing increasingly predictable (if still technically demanding) tasks. Accordingly, the ratio of junior to senior professional time would increase, with profits from increased leverage offsetting the generally lower billing rates. It is in this middle experience stage of practice area maturity that time-and-expenses billing practices would be (and are) most relevant and common in all professions.

The firm's hiring needs would expand to include a major role for less skilled professionals and more paraprofessionals, since the increased structuring of familiar engagement types would allow the firm to employ an increasing degree of systems and procedures and hence require less mature talent. Training approaches would become increasingly formal with greater use of out-of-hours classroom sessions and practice manuals.

Since individuals who had worked in the firm for any period of time and absorbed the knowledge and skills of the firm would remain productive and marketable team members even if they did not have the abilities to progress to the top rank, there would be less need for the firm to enforce an up-or-out system, and it could make use of a system of "permanent associates." While the need for senior talent would remain high, the group could accommodate a broader array of talents since it would have the ability to empower an individual by supplementing his or her talents with the experience base of the firm. Hiring could not only be more broad based (the group would not have to restrict its attentions purely to the upper reaches of the grade-point average), but could accommodate increasing numbers of lateral experienced hires. Training would need to become a little more formal and structured in order to capture and disseminate internally the firm's experience base.

Because of a greater requirement for team approaches in delivering services, the need to disseminate internally and organize the firm's collective experience and knowledge, professionals in the firm would become more interdependent and there would be a greater need for formally recognized departments and areas of specialization. The managerial task of focusing the collective efforts of the firm's principals around carefully chosen areas of experience would become increasingly important, and firm management, a more clearly delineated position, more formally recognized.

While growth might still be controlled, there would be increasing pressure to provide career opportunities to the proportionately larger number of junior professionals who had accumulated valuable experience that the firm could ill afford to lose. Since the value added that the firm brings to its clients would be less embedded in individual people and more in the firm's collective experience, a greater sense of equity ownership would prevail, and new partners or shareholders might be required to buy their future participation in firm profits by contributing to partnership capital or, in some instances, purchasing shares.

THE EFFICIENCY-BASED PRACTICE

Finally, let us consider a practice area that had a high preponderance of clients who were mostly interested in the efficiency with which the firm dealt with low-risk, familiar types of problems. The firm would be squarely in the business of demonstrating that it had established systems and procedures to handle specific types of problems. Cost, reliability, speed, and other such characteristics would come to the fore, and practice development tactics would involve highly targeted and specialized brochures, competitive presentations and, as in some professions today (including accounting, medicine, architecture, and investment banking), selected use of advertisements promoting specific services. The client mix in such practices would tend to be focused around a core of high volume clients.

Client fee sensitivity would require that engagements be staffed at the most junior level possible, including maximum possible use of paraprofessionals and increasing use of technology to substitute for professional labor. Fee pressures would be offset by increasing use of staff and technology leverage; and pricing would increasingly become a matter of fixed-price contracts or bids. As yet infrequent in some professions (such as law), fixed-price contracts or bids are increasingly common in investment banking, medicine, consulting, and architecture.

Efficiency practices, with their relatively high fixed cost structure and many juniors, would need to take a more studied, planned approach to growth in order to capture the volume necessary to offset lower margins. The needs for both management and administration would increase, in order to devise optimum ways of dealing with familiar engagement types and to monitor and supervise the project teams to ensure that the best procedure is indeed being followed. Rather than the heavy use of judgment employed in expertise-based practices, efficiency practices have high needs for short-interval measurement systems both for quality assurance and productivity. Rather than inspirational leadership styles, efficiency based practices would need managers who are disciplined, organized, and detail oriented.

Since the value-added of the firm would be more solidly based in its operating systems, procedures, and marketing programs, rather than on the individual talents of the professionals, ownership would tend to be closely guarded. Indeed, in a wide variety of professions, there are an increasing number of efficiency-based practices formally organized as corporations, with equity ownership held by a small group. Transfers of ownership are accomplished by selling stock, internally or externally, at fair market value.

OTHER DIFFERENCES

In the analysis above, we have found significant and incompatible differences between the three "ideal" practice types in marketing, pricing, leverage structure, hiring needs, promotion structure, ownership structure, and leadership styles. Yet these are not the only differences to which one can point. For example, as one examines a variety of professions, it is also possible to identify different location strategies across the spectrum of practice types. Expertise-based practices, as a generalization, tend to be based in a single location relying on the development of a national or regional reputation to attract clients. As the practice matures through experience to efficiency-based practices, it is more common to find multiple-location firms, frequently organized into profit centers. This evolution is to be expected, since the essence of a multiple-location strategy is to enhance the ability of the individual office to serve clients by drawing upon the experience base and systems of the network.

Compensation approaches also vary significantly over the practice life cycle. At the expertise end, it is appropriate (and not uncommon) to find profit-sharing and bonus pool systems for junior professionals, while in experience-based practices greater use is made of straight salary, with increases deriving from seniority and the accumulation of increasing amounts of experience. At the efficiency stage, salary structures can frequently be found (for example, in accounting and engineering firms) which are, in essence, better described as wage systems, with provisions for overtime payments for the most junior personnel.

Not only do the tactics of marketing change over the professional life cycle, but so does the organizational responsibility for practice development. In expertise practice areas, business development tends to be a personal responsibility of each partner (or partner equivalent). As the practice area matures, the firm needs to develop more structured, organizationally based approaches to market. In some professions (including actuarial services, engineering, and medicine), certain service areas have evolved to the point that they require the equivalent of an in-house marketing department, headed by a marketing specialist from outside the profession.

IMPLICATIONS

The degree to which professional marketplaces have already recognized and embodied the overwhelming differences between expertise, experience, and efficiency practices varies significantly. In some, such as architecture, consulting, or public relations, where competition has been intense, differences between firms practicing at different parts of the spectrum are readily identifiable. In other professions, the differences are only now beginning to emerge.

Two trends in the professions make understanding (and implementing) the distinctions between expertise, experience, and efficiency practices critical to the success of the professional service firm. First, greater sophistication of clients means that they are increasingly able to analyze their true needs in different types of engagements and distinguish between firms whose style of practice matches the specific benefit they seek. Second, the evolution of practice areas through the stages of the spectrum is becoming very rapid. In every profession, one can point to practice areas that, in only a few short years, moved rapidly from being frontier activities handled only by a handful of innovative firms to high-volume practices offered by increasingly large numbers of competent firms.

As this evolution takes place, firms are continually confronted with a basic dilemma. On the one hand, they can choose to follow a practice area down its life cycle, adapting organization structures, staffing strategies, pricing, leadership styles, and all else we have discussed above to the new requirements of the marketplace. Of course, in so doing they will be transforming the fundamental nature of their firm. The life cycle of the practice becomes a life cycle for the firm. On the other hand, they can choose to gradually abandon maturing practice areas in order to maintain stability in firm culture and management, requiring them to move into new practice areas that more closely match the basic approach of the firm.

The third available (and most frequently selected) option—maintaining a firm with diverse practices at various stages of the life-cycle spectrum—is a challenging managerial task. The conflicting economic, behavioral, and managerial requirements of different practice areas are sufficiently great to create severe internal tensions and stress as firms struggle to establish firmwide management philosophies to accommodate these diverse needs.

The most common, and successful, approach to resolving these tensions is through the use of departments and divisions: in effect establishing "Chinese walls" between operating groups, allowing each to evolve its own management approaches, appropriate to the marketplace it serves. As potentially divisive as this may sound, it is frequently a more sensible solution than the attempt to impose increasingly inappropriate management practices on a firmwide basis. A classic illustration of this approach is given by some large accounting firms who allow variations in various management practices between their accounting, tax, and consulting divisions. One can even observe elements of this approach inside law firms where litigation, corporate, tax, mergers & acquisitions groups, and others appear to be run (appropriately) on very different bases.

In firms that take this approach, it is important to ensure that the aggregate mix of practice area "maturities" remains reasonably stable, and evolves gradually, if at all. Even if a firm has a diverse mixture, there nevertheless remain certain aspects of firm management that must be addressed at the firm level. How these are decided is heavily influenced by the relative proportions of expertise, experience, and efficiency practices that make up the firm. A firm cannot be run smoothly if one year its practice is dominated by fees from expertise services and the next year efficiency services are in greatest demand.

For many firms the greater course of wisdom may be to reach for some internal consistency between and among its practice areas, so that a single approach to management practice can be devised. Such consistency would provide not only internal benefits, but also a common identity in the marketplace. Experience has shown that it is difficult, if not impossible, for one part of the firm to create a strong "frontier expertise" reputation when the firm is already well known as a low-cost provider. Similarly, a firm with a national reputation as being on the cutting edge is unlikely to be able to create and sustain a group going after the mature marketplace segments. In most professions, a consistent image in the marketplace is a valuable asset, which can be rapidly compromised if the firm attempts to serve too diverse a set of client needs. Few firms, in my experience, have a clear picture of their true positioning along the expertise, experience, efficiency spectrum. Indeed, given the diversity of practices contained inside many professional firms, no single answer could be derived. It is this reason above all that has led to the failure of so many strategic planning and firmwide marketing efforts inside professional firms.

A second problem for firms attempting to understand their true market positioning is the natural temptation of all professionals to underestimate the progress of a practice area down the life cycle. In numerous (anonymous) surveys I have conducted inside professional firms, I have been consistently surprised at how high a proportion of their personal work professionals at all levels report could be done by more junior staff. (Firmwide averages sometimes exceed 30 or 40 percent.) Even allowing for some client preferences to deal with high level professionals, these results show that many practice groups continue to maintain expertise-based approaches to running their affairs when their marketplace is probably closer to the efficiency stage.

Given the broad array and diversity of client needs, there is plenty of room in the professions for firms and practices of all types. There will always be a need for expertise-based firms, experience-based firms, and efficiency-based firms, any one of which, if managed appropriately, can be as successful as any other. However, we will increasingly see these firms being run in very different ways. The message is simple: Match management practices to the practice.

CHAPTER 3

PROFITABILITY: HEALTH AND HYGIENE

In a partnership, the ultimate measure of profitability is (or should be) profit per partner, which is driven by three main factors, *margin, productivity*, and *leverage*.

As Figure 3–1 shows, "profit per partner" should be viewed as the professional firm equivalent of "return on equity." The time and efforts of the partners (who have a claim on the profits of the firm) can be seen as the firm's equity investment (often called "sweat equity"). The total assets employed in the business are the sum of the (partner) equity investment, and the nonpartner staff, whose salaries are comparable to assets financed by debt, at a fixed interest rate.

In managing a professional firm, as with any business with multiple products or service lines, or multiple locations, it is a mistake to place too much stress on one of these three subfactors (margin, productivity, or leverage). Different operating units can and do achieve high profit per partner in different ways. Some offices, practice units, or even individual partners, will achieve it by being in high margin businesses, perhaps with modest leverage. Alternately, another office, practice unit, or partner may achieve an equally high profit per partner with thin margins and modest productivity but high leverage.

31

FIGURE 3–1

Profitability Formulas

$$\boxed{\text{The Dupont formula for industrial companies:}}$$

$$\frac{\text{Profits}}{\text{Equity}} = \frac{\text{Profits}}{\text{Sales}} \times \frac{\text{Sales}}{\text{Assets}} \times \frac{\text{Assets}}{\text{Equity}}$$

$$= \text{Margin} \times \text{Productivity} \times \text{Leverage}$$

$$\boxed{\text{The formula for professional firms:}}$$

$$\frac{\text{Profits}}{\text{Partner}} = \frac{\text{Profits}}{\text{Fees}} \times \frac{\text{Fees}}{\text{Staff}} \times \frac{\text{Staff}}{\text{Partners}}$$

Unfortunately, in many firms, the reporting systems do not provide equitably for these varying paths to profitability. For example, chargeability and realization reports are circulated more frequently and more broadly than reports showing how well partners leverage themselves. Consequently, an individual partner who fails to leverage himself but has high personal chargeability and high realization (i.e., good productivity) will show up "better" in the firm's reporting systems than one who is less personally chargeable and commands a lower hourly fee, but keeps five juniors busy. However, the leveraged partner's activities may "throw off" more cash into partnership profits than the unleveraged partner.

Rather than establish firmwide goals for margins, productivity, or leverage, firms should hold each practice (or partner) accountable for a profit per partner target and let the practice (or partner) figure out the best mixture of margin, productivity, and leverage necessary to achieve this goal.

This simple prescription is not commonly followed in professional firms today. Few use net profit per partner as their main method for regular reporting of practice economics. Yet it is only by understanding the profit per partner of different practices, services (and even engagements) that the firm can manage its "equity investments" (partner time) wisely.

HEALTH AND HYGIENE

The reason so many firms have control systems that emphasize only parts of the profitability formula is that their control systems are designed to focus on short-term profitability (what I term "hygiene"), and ignore the issue of "health" (i.e., increasing the fundamental profit potential of the organization).

To test this for your firm, I offer a quiz, one you may wish to circulate among your partners. Shown in Figure 3–2 is a list of possible profitability improvement tactics for a professional service firm.

If your firm is like many others, you'll discover something like this: The list of quick-impact profitability improvement tactics is very different from your list of permanent- impact tactics. And you probably score your firm best on the short-run tactics, and least well on the permanent improvement tactics.

What this reveals is that improving profitability has two distinct management components. Some elements (predominantly short-run "hygiene" issues) get overmanaged, and many (long-run "health" issues) are undermanaged. To see which is which, let's discuss each of the items in our original profit formula.

MANAGING MARGINS

Many professional firms, in comparing the profitability of different practices, place particular emphasis on the margins achieved. This is always misleading and often dangerous. In my experience, many low-margin practices are more profitable, on a profit-per-partner basis, than higher margin practices with low leverage because of the effective use of leverage. This does not mean that high leverage is always good, or always appropriate. But it does mean that, in the month-to-month control of the firm, submeasures like margin are insufficient indicators of profitability.

There is a second reason to avoid placing too much stress on margins in managing a practice: The margin that a practice achieves is mostly a consequence of what is accomplished with productivity and leverage. Consider, for example, a practice that has high productivity (i.e., high revenue per person). By definition, this means it will have a low number of people per dollar of revenue. Since the overwhelming

FIGURE 3–2

A Profitability Quiz

You are asked to rate the items on this list in three ways. First, rank the items from 1 to 19 according to which action will have the quickest impact on profitability. Then rank the items according to which will have the most permanent, long-lasting impact on profitability. Finally, for each item, rank your firm's performance on a scale of 1 to 5 (1=we've really got this one under control, 2=we do well on this, 3=we need to improve, 4=we're weak at this, 5=we're not working on this).

		Rank for Quick Impact	Rank for Permanent Impact	Rank for Performance
a	Justify higher fees (specialize, innovate, add more value)			
b	Increase utilization (billable hours per person)			
c	Find ways to use juniors more in the delivery of services			
d	Drop unprofitable services			
e	Drop unprofitable clients			
f	Improve speed of billing			
g	Improve speed of collections			
h	Use marketing to get "better" work, not just more work			
i	Invest in new (higher value) services			
j	Develop methodologies to eliminate duplication of effort on engagements			
k	Help engagement leaders improve project management skills and performance			
l	Speed up skill-building process in staff			
m	Make greater use of paraprofessionals			
n	Reduce space and equipment costs			
o	Reduce support staff costs			
p	Deal with underperformers (partners)			
q	Deal with underperformers (non-partners)			
r	Other (specify)			
s	Other (specify)			

proportion of costs in a professional practice is related to the number of people on staff, costs will be low and margins good. Margins will have been automatically improved through productivity improvement.

Some factors affecting margins *are* distinct from productivity and leverage—for example, space costs, equipment, and the like. These costs are hygiene factors. It is critical to avoid waste: we must not have too much excess space, too many computers, too many support staff. But once the "hygienic level" is achieved, it would be unwise to pursue profit improvement by pushing for even less space, even fewer computers, even less support staff. Beyond the hygiene level, such cost cutting would improve short-term profits, but would not represent a smart long-term profitability improvement strategy (i.e., would not improve the health of the organization). Margin management is short-run management.

MANAGING PRODUCTIVITY

As Figure 3–3 shows, a firm's productivity is the simple multiplication of its utilization times the average (realized) fee per hour. Again, we need to make the distinction between hygiene and health. A firm's average chargeability (or utilization), which most firms appropriately monitor very carefully, is predominantly a short-run issue. Each year, this is one of the first things the firm must take care of, like good hygiene. If the firm is below a "reasonable" chargeability, there is no point talking about long-run strategy.

However, once a "target" chargeability is attained, we are unlikely to raise the firm's long-run profit per partner by looking for year-on-year increases in utilization. While firms could make more money by having people work Sundays, it is not the most creative of profit-improvement strategies. The real challenge is to figure out how to make more money without having to work so hard!

If they are to achieve high productivity, firms must raise their net realized fee per hour (or value). A firm that can do this is being more than hygienic, it is building the fundamental health of the business. Of course, this means more than just raising the firm's prices: It means that the firm must do those things (skill-building, specialization, innovation, value-added services) that will make clients willing to pay more for the firm's services.

FIGURE 3–3
Productivity

$$\text{Productivity} = \frac{\text{Fees}}{\text{Staff}} = \frac{\text{Fees}}{\text{Hours}} \times \frac{\text{Hours}}{\text{Staff}}$$

$$= \text{Value} \times \text{Utilization}$$

MANAGING LEVERAGE

Returning to our formula, one factor remains for discussion: leverage. This, like fee levels, is a fundamental "health" issue. Once overheads and utilization are in the hygiene range, only an improvement in fee levels or leverage will change the basic economics of the business. But what should the right amount of leverage be?

The appropriate leverage for any practice is determined by one thing, and one thing alone: the nature of the services the practice is engaged in. A practice that specializes in cutting-edge, high-client risk ("brain surgery") work will inevitably need to be staffed with a high partner-to-junior ratio: lower level people will not be able to deliver the quality of services required. On the other hand, practices that deal with more procedural "nonemergency" needs will be inefficient if they do not have high leverage, since high-priced people should not be doing low-value tasks.

"Managing" leverage means one thing: ensuring that the mix of skill levels on a project matches the true skill requirements of the engagement. Unfortunately, this is not often done well. (See Chapter 4, Solving the Underdelegation Problem.)

PROFITABILITY AND GROWTH

It is interesting to note that, in the formula for profitability, growth and size do not appear. Of course, it is essential that professional firms grow in order to motivate and retain the firm's best staff. Without growth, much of the dynamism of the practice will be lost, and morale will suffer. Having said this, the question of the relationship between growth and profitability is unclear.

Imagine, for example, that a firm successfully grew the practice by 25 percent in a given year, but grew it in such a way that (a) the mix of business (and hence the realized fee rates) remained the same; and (b) the firm's method of serving that additional volume of business used the same staff-to-partner ratio currently existing. In this scenario, the firm would need 25 percent more partners to handle that volume, and if the realization rates were the same as the firm's existing business, the net profit per partner would remain the same (see Chapter 1).

Growing by 25 percent and adding 25 percent more partners is not a bad result but it does not further the goal of improving profit per partner. To do that , we must break one of the two conditions imposed; either bring in work that has higher fee levels than the firm's current average, or find ways to service the firm's work with higher leverage. This is the same conclusion as that reached before: Only increased fee levels or leverage move the firm forward. All else is hygiene. It is the nature of the work brought in, not just its volume, that contributes to profit health.

Yet this is not how most firms control their practice development efforts. Many firms are revenue driven, or "top-line" oriented, taking the view that "any new business is good business." This is patently false. A new $100,000 engagement can be very profitable, or be one that loses the firm a lot of money. Yet many firms reward partners for the volume of fees (top-line) that they bring in, not whether or not they bring in profitable work.

In large part, they do this for the very reason we have been discussing: the lack of a good profitability reporting system that allows them to know which work is truly profitable and which is not. If you never measure profitability at the engagement level (or do so with misleading indicators such as margin or realization alone), it is hard to guide and reward partners' practice development activities properly. If profits are to improve, this will only be done by improving how profitably engagements are run: proper staffing, proper delegation, efficient use of people's time. Project leaders should be held accountable for engagement success, considering revenues *and* the costs of resources consumed (including the costs of partner time).

The effects of this have been shown in firm after firm that have begun to examine (either as a special study or as a new method of reporting) the profit per partner-hour of different engagements. It is quite common for firms to discover that 125 percent of their profits are made from 80 percent of their engagements, and that 20 percent of their engagements lose 25 percent of their profits. This would not be bad if these were conscious, strategic investment decisions. But, in firm after firm, it is revealed that engagements that "looked profitable" when judged by margin or realization show up as poor investments when the profit is related to the amount of partner time invested to generate that profit.

As a consequence, many firms cannot "fix underperformers" as a profit improvement tactic because their financial reporting systems do not reveal where the real underperformers (assignments, service lines, clients, or partners) really are.

Fixing underperformers can be both a hygiene *and* health issue. By eliminating loss-making activities, profits can be improved in the

TABLE 3–1

Profitability Tactics
(In descending order of impact on profit health

ONE: RAISE PRICES (i.e., FEE LEVELS)
- Earn higher fees through specialization, innovation, adding more value
- Use marketing to get "better" work
- Speed up skill-building process in staff
- Invest in new (higher-value) services

TWO: LOWER VARIABLE COSTS (DELIVERY COST FOR EACH ENGAGEMENT
- Improve engagement management performance
- Increase leverage in the delivery of services
- Make greater use of paraprofessionals
- Develop methodologies to avoid duplication of effort

THREE: FIX UNDERPERFORMERS
- Deal with underperformers
- Drop unprofitable services
- Drop unprofitable clients

FOUR: INCREASE VOLUME
- Increase utilization (billable hours per person)

FIVE: LOWER OVERHEAD COSTS
- Improve speed of billing
- Improve speed of collections
- Reduce space and equipment costs
- Reduce support staff costs

---

short-run. In addition, by freeing up resources (particularly partner time) locked up in low-profit areas, the potential is created to deploy these resources in more productive areas. No one, as a short-run issue, wants to drop unprofitable clients or services, but if low profitability cannot be fixed through more efficient staffing (i.e., leverage) then working to replace low-profitability work with high-profitability work is critical to long-run success.

PUTTING IT ALL TOGETHER

The list of tactics given in Figure 3–2 (the profitability quiz) can be grouped into five categories, which represent the basic approaches in improving the profitability of any business (see Table 3–1). These are (in order of impact on profit health):

1. Raise prices (fee levels)
2. Lower variable (delivery) costs
3. Fix underperformers
4. Increase volume
5. Lower overhead costs

As we have seen, the first two categories are the keys to health, and the middle category (underperformers) has the potential to be so. The last two categories are hygiene areas which are critical for the short term, but limited in their ability to bring about a fundamental transformation in profit potential. Profitability will not come from managing hygiene factors alone: Future profitability depends on health as well—and firms' methods of measuring, reporting, and managing need to reflect both.

CHAPTER 4

SOLVING THE UNDERDELEGATION PROBLEM

Like all human beings, professional service firms could be a great deal healthier if they eliminated their bad habits. This chapter focuses on a single bad habit that reduces profitability, adversely affects motivation and morale, reduces a firm's competitive capabilities, and *in addition* prevents senior professionals from spending more time with clients and investing in the future of the firm.

This bad habit is called *systemic underdelegation*.

Imagine that a questionnaire was sent to each and every professional in your firm, top-to-bottom, asking the following single question:

What percentage of your professional work time is spent doing things that a more junior person could do, if we got organized and trained the junior to handle it *with quality*?

(Obviously, do not include in this calculation that work which the *client insists* you perform yourself, since the client must get what he asks for.)

Imagine that each person answered honestly, and the responses were tabulated to calculate the firmwide average.

My research shows that, for the typical professional service firm, the firmwide average is *frequently* as high as 40 or 50 percent, and

41

sometimes more. This is equivalent to saying that, of the firm's entire productive capacity, 40 or 50 percent is consumed with a higher-priced person performing a lower-value task. Obviously, this is not a wonderful situation.

If one examined a manufacturing company and discovered that, of all the resources used to produce the company's output, some 40 or 50 percent were more expensive than necessary to achieve the same level of quality, one would be tempted to use words like "inefficient," "unproductive," "wasteful." The same words, I believe, can be applied to most firms' methods of operation.

WHY IT'S A PROBLEM

Before addressing why this situation exists, and what can be done about it, we should examine the four primary ways in which this systemic underdelegation hurts the firm:

PROFITABILITY

By definition, systemic underdelegation means that the firm has a high-cost delivery system: It costs the firm more to do a project than if it used trained juniors to handle that part of the project they could do with quality. In the short run, this may not hurt the firm: If the clients are willing to pay us higher fees to be inefficient, why change?

There *is* a reason to change. It is called "competition." As the professions get more competitive, and fee resistance more common, high delivery costs will lead to marketing problems and a competitive disadvantage. There is also a reason to change before fee pressures force it: profitability. If the clients are happy with the fees, but we staff the project in a high-cost way, we are reducing the amount of profit that can be brought to the bottom line.

SKILL BUILDING

By having higher-priced people busy with lower-value tasks, the firm loses the skill building (development) of the people not delegating and also gets less rapid skill building of juniors. Professional firms do not sell time (although they often bill that way). Rather, their stock-in-trade is skill. Anything that compromises the rate of skill building (which systemic underdelegation does) hurts the firm.

MORALE, MOTIVATION, SATISFACTION, AND EXCITEMENT

If underdelegation exists, that is, if juniors are being given additional responsibilities less rapidly than they are capable of handling with good training and supervision, the result will be poor morale and motivation. My research shows that, if left untreated, the lack of challenging ("growing") work will be *the* single biggest contributor to turnover/retention problems. My research also reveals that if senior people are spending 50 percent of their time doing what a junior could do, *their* morale and motivation is also reduced.

UNDERINVESTMENT IN THE FUTURE

Last, but definitely not least, underdelegation causes senior people to neglect high-value tasks that are of critical importance to the future success of the firm. In firm after firm, I encounter senior professionals who know the importance of client service, business development, supervision and coaching, methodology-building, and personal development. In all of these cases, however, they report that they are not doing as much as they would like because they are "too busy"—and they are.

But too busy doing what? If, with 50 percent of their time, they are too busy doing things that, with appropriate training, someone at a half or two-thirds their salary could do, it would seem that some bad trade-offs are being made in the allocation of these valuable people's time.

THE CAUSES OF THE PROBLEM

Reduced profitability. Compromised skill building. Lessened morale. Neglect of investment activities. This is a serious list of negatives. Why, then, is this situation so common?

While there clearly are a variety of personal factors at work ("I prefer to do it myself" or "I have more confidence it will be done correctly if I do it"), I have learned that a bigger explanation is provided by the measurement and reward systems of most firms (hence the name *systemic* underdelegation).

First, an excessive pressure on personal billability (or chargeability) at senior levels can lead to inefficiencies in staffing. If a partner feels that he or she is *primarily* held accountable for personal billable hours (rather than, say, the profitability of the engagements that partner is responsible for), then he or she is likely to hoard work rather than be active in looking for operating efficiencies.

This will be particularly true, and is particularly dysfunctional, if the firm is having a weak year. In a weak year the firm would be better served if the partners pushed more work down and spent the time in the marketplace generating new work, instead of attempting to protect their position by staying busy on work that the underutilized juniors could do and avoiding marketing efforts. (Yet in various countries experiencing a recession, this is the exact behavior I have observed.)

A second cause derived from the firm's management systems is that in few firms are engagement leaders held responsible for seeking out ways to reduce the *costs* of delivering the engagement. Amazingly, some firms do not track the profitability of their work engagement by engagement. Even among those who do, the primary measure of engagement-level profitability that most firms use is the realization rate—that is, the percentages of the standard rates of the personnel used on the engagement that are collected from the client. As critical as this factor is, my research shows that it does not provide an adequate incentive to look for opportunities to increase leverage (i.e., delegation) on the engagement. When there is no particular incentive for a partner to find ways to increase the leverage on his or her client project, underdelegation is sure to result. Partners must be held responsible not only for the revenues they collect on an engagement, but also the precise costs to the firm that they incur by the way they get the engagement done.

A third reason for underdelegation to develop is that there is a reluctance to invest in the coaching and supervision time necessary to achieve successful delegation. On any single engagement, it will always be *more* costly, not less, to spend the time to get a junior involved: It will take a junior longer to do it than doing it yourself, and you'll have to spend time supervising. Consequently, even though more supervised delegation and coaching will reduce costs over time, they increase costs in the short run. This is the old Catch-22. Using the junior person "on this one" is more costly because we haven't previously trained him or her, so we end up not training the person on this one either. Thus firms tend to underinvest in good coaching, even though they preach it fervently. The problem is that few firms currently have any mechanism to track, on a real-time basis, whether or not good coaching (and hence potential delegation) is being done. Without such a system, short-term thinking and underdelegation result.

A fourth cause is the individual partner's (understandable?) concern about what the partner will have to do if he or she does push the work down: pay more attention to marketing, client service, coaching, seeking out and working on truly partner-level client work. A systematic effort to push down work that rightfully can and should be pushed down will, if successful, result in a need to find replacement activities for the firm's partners that truly match their skill and experience level. Fear that it does not exist, or is less comfortable to pursue than staying chargeable on any available work, is, I have learned, a prime contributor to the problem.

A push on operating efficiencies (better matching of work tasks to appropriate skill levels) will require renewed attention to a marketing program that focuses on high-value-added new business. It could be argued (and has been by many partners) that in some markets such work does not exist, or cannot be obtained in sufficient volume to replace the basic work pushed down.

This very well may be the case, but this is not an argument to continue with inefficient staffing. Rather it suggests that in certain areas of practice the firm may be overpartnered. The appropriate response would be to help such partners find ways to increase their value on the marketplace, redeploy them, or as a final resort help them find alternate careers. Having high-priced partners doing too much low-value work is a recipe for disaster.

SOLVING THE PROBLEM

The diet and exercise program to solve the bad habit of underdelegation is not necessarily a pleasant one. In fact, it is tough. It is designed to make bad habits very visible when they occur, and to make each partner accountable for eliminating them in his or her practice.

There are three essential elements to the program, and some additional options.

STEP ONE: ENGAGEMENT-LEVEL PROFITABILITY MEASURES

The first essential step is to modify the partner performance appraisal system to place less emphasis on the partners' personal efforts (i.e., chargeable hours) and to make partners primarily accountable for the net income per partner (or net income per partner hour) of each engagement.

In most firms, computer records are kept on the revenue attributable to any engagement and the number of hours worked on that engagement by specified individuals. It is, therefore, a relatively simple task to calculate, using latest salary and compensation data, the cost to the firm of the resources consumed in performing the engagement.

By considering both revenue and costs, firms will get a better fix on which engagements are truly most profitable, and which represent opportunities for efficiency improvements through better staffing, increased delegation, and leverage.

Once this information system is in place, firms will be in a position to hold partners accountable for engagement profitability, encouraging them to identify opportunities to improve operating efficiencies on the engagement.

STEP TWO: TRACKING AND REWARDING COACHING ACTIVITIES

To overcome the problem of "deferred maintenance" in the coaching area (and the resulting lack of delegation), firms should introduce a system whereby all staff on an engagement complete an evaluation form (see Figure 4–1), rating their engagement experience, at the end of every engagement.

These forms are sent to the managing partner, and the scores accumulated through the year. At year-end, the *aggregate* score for each partner (i.e., the evaluations of all staff members on all work supervised by that partner) are compared to the aggregate scores for the office (and firm) as a whole.

In this way, an encouragement and accountability for delegation, good engagement management, and skill transfer will be accomplished. By establishing a measurable monitoring system, behavior in

FIGURE 4–1

Rate Your Engagement Experience

Please rate your engagement experience on a scale of 1 (strongly disagree) to 5 (strongly agree) on the following:

My work made good use of my knowledge and ability.	1	2	3	4	5
This engagement helped me learn and grow.	1	2	3	4	5
My work was interesting and challenging.	1	2	3	4	5
When tasks and projects were assigned to me, I understood thoroughly what was expected of me.	1	2	3	4	5
When they were assigned, I understood how my tasks fit into the overall objectives for the engagement.	1	2	3	4	5
Help was available when I needed to have questions answered.	1	2	3	4	5
I received PROMPT feedback on my work, good or bad.	1	2	3	4	5
When I was corrected for something I did or failed to do, it was done in a constructive way.	1	2	3	4	5
I received good coaching to help me improve my performance.	1	2	3	4	5
I was kept informed about the things I needed to know to do my job properly.	1	2	3	4	5
I was actively encouraged to volunteer new ideas and make suggestions for improvement.	1	2	3	4	5
I had the freedom to make the necessary decisions to do my work properly.	1	2	3	4	5
Team meetings were conducted in a way that built trust and mutual respect.	1	2	3	4	5
I am proud of the quality of work I did on this engagement.	1	2	3	4	5
In this engagement we set very high standards for performance.	1	2	3	4	5
I felt that I was a member of a well-functioning team.	1	2	3	4	5

Instructions: *To promote your honest comments, you are not asked to identify yourself on this form. However, we ask that you send it, in a sealed envelope, to the practice head's secretary who will aggregate your comments with others who worked on this engagement and with other engagements so that we can track our* overall *performance. In order to encourage response, we ask that you write on the* outside *of the sealed envelope your name and project number, so that the practice head's secretary can monitor what responses have been received.*

QUESTIONS FOR CODING PURPOSES:
(a)   What is the project number of this engagement?
(b)   What is your level/title?
(c)   How many hours did you work on this engagement? _____
(d)   Who was your immediate supervisor on this project?

this area can be influenced in a way that no amount of speeches, mission statements, and training programs can accomplish.

STEP THREE: THE SCHEDULING PROCESS

In tackling the issue of staffing efficiency on engagements, no activity in the office surpasses in importance good management of the scheduling process.

Once it has been decided how an engagement is to be staffed (who is assigned, and what portion of the engagement each is scheduled to do), the engagement's leverage structure is in place. Staffing decisions also clearly play a significant role in determining the amount (and character) of skill building. Most of the skill building that takes place in the firm's practice comes from the types of engagements its people are sent on, and what part of the engagement they are given to perform.

As we have noted, many studies have shown that motivation, morale, and ultimately retention are affected by nothing as much as the pattern of work that the staff is given to perform. Accordingly, the scheduling process is where most of the real *managerial* decisions in running the practice are taken. It is the place where the real strategic trade-offs between short-term profitability, client service, skill building, and retention are made.

High-level attention to this area by practice managers offers a significant opportunity to correct the underdelegation problem. Unfortunately, in many firms scheduling is viewed as an administrative or tactical function, which it is not. It should be the time when powerful practice managers challenge equally powerful partners to defend why they have staffed their engagement in the way they have; to explain why they really need the people they have requested. Only in the to-and-fro of such discussions will the (often hidden) underdelegation problems be revealed. (For more on this topic, see Chapter 16, On the Importance of Scheduling.)

ADDITIONAL TACTICS TO SOLVE THE PROBLEM

In addition to the approaches listed above (but rarely as a substitute for them), some firms have had success in tackling the underdelegation problem by being more aggressive in raising the fee rates of the firm's more senior or experienced people, setting these billing rates individual by individual, and not by group criteria such as seniority. In effect, they are constantly testing the value of each of the firm's senior people in the marketplace.

This has a number of positive effects. First, it induces the firm's senior people to "stretch" for more higher-value tasks, and not meet their obligations to the firm too easily by remaining billable at rates below their true worth. Second, by being aggressive on senior rates, the firm addresses the underdelegation issue by causing such people to reflect more carefully on what portion of the work they should perform, and what they should pass down.

Other firms have used their annual partner performance evaluation system to "challenge" the partners' use of their time, and to help the partners set personal growth goals for themselves. The theory behind this is that if the partner has a clear vision of how he or she can "move on" to higher value activities, the partner will be more willing (even eager) to "pass on" existing activities that can successfully be done by others. If the partner has no "personal strategic plan," then there will be a reluctance to delegate the current activities. In some cases, it has been necessary for firm management to "protect" those who delegate until they find replacement activities, making it less risky for individuals to take on new tasks.

In other firms, in order to assist individual partners in achieving operating efficiencies through better delegation, practice committees have been formed to study the firm's methodologies and perform an "industrial engineering" study. By closely examining what skill levels are truly required to perform designated tasks, such studies can provide ready-made methodologies (and training manuals) for individual partners to use in their delivery of the firm's services.

CONCLUSION

Solving the underdelegation problem is not easy. The problem is, in my experience, endemic to the professions. And the diet requires taking a fresh look at some important management systems of the firm.

The reader should ask the following questions:

- Does underdelegation exist in my firm?
- What benefits would accrue if we could eliminate it, even partially?

- Can we use some of the approaches described in this chapter?
- If not, what else will solve the problem?
- What happens if we do nothing?

My experience suggests that most firms will discover not only that they have opportunities in this area, but that the pain of the diet will be more than outweighed by the benefits flowing from the renewed health and vigor of the organization.

PART TWO

CLIENT MATTERS

CHAPTER 5

THE PRACTICE DEVELOPMENT PACKAGE

Say the word "marketing" to a room full of professionals, and different individuals will think of very different things. Some will think, "All you have to do is satisfy your current clients and business will come." Others will reply, "A stream of new clients is essential to the health of any firm." Some will offer the view that "The key is to manage your client relationships," while others will reflect that "We need to get out into the community and meet new people."

The truth is that every one of these comments is valid, but none of them represents the answer by itself. Professional firms must execute a full *package* of practice development steps covering five main categories of activity:

Broadcasting
Courting
Superpleasing
Nurturing
Listening.

None of these categories may be neglected—only the complete package will work.

Broadcasting includes all those activities that generate leads, enquiries, and opportunities with new clients. By definition, broadcasting activities, which include such things as seminars, articles, newsletters, and speeches, have more than one person in the audience. The firm broadcasts a message to its target market in the hope of generating contacts, enquiries, and, in some cases, requests for proposals. (A discussion of these tactics is presented in Chapter 11, Attracting New Clients.)

Once a specific opportunity with a specific new prospect emerges, a new activity is called for—*courting*. The firm is no longer addressing a *group* of potential buyers, but a single, specific prospect. This activity is traditionally called selling and proposing, but such words fail to capture what is truly required. When a client hires a professional, or a professional firm, he or she must make the decision to enter into a relationship, and the process is best understood as a courtship. (Some ideas on how to do well in this phase are contained in Chapter 10, How Clients Choose.)

Both of the preceding categories describe explicit efforts to win *new* clients. However, there is great truth in the old adage that there is no more effective practice development than outstanding "word of mouth." Accordingly, a major component of practice development is *superpleasing* existing clients on existing matters. This means much more than doing outstanding technical work and more than servicing the client in such a way that he or she is just "satisfied." Effective word of mouth only results when the client is *delighted* and eager to work with the individual again. Since good word of mouth has to be earned, firms and individuals must invest in this area. (See Chapter 7, Quality Work Doesn't Mean Quality Service, and Chapter 8, A Service Quality Program.)

Paying attention to the client on the current matter is a necessary condition for winning a client's future business, but not a sufficient one. Relationships, to remain strong, must be *nurtured*, and future business must be earned. Clients do not like to be taken for granted, and they expect their "suppliers" to invest visibly in the relationship to earn future business. They expect firms to invest their own (non-reimbursed) time in getting to know the clients' business, earning future business by bringing new ideas, being willing to spend time with the client "off the clock" discussing future issues, and so on. This process requires a planned program of "marketing to existing clients" (Chapter 9).

The fifth and final category needed to round out the practice development package is *listening* to the market, otherwise known as "gathering market intelligence." The better the firm's understanding of how clients think (and what they're thinking about lately), the more effective it will be able to market itself. Any firm that fails to make this investment will be severely handicapped, having to market itself based upon what it "guesses" or "assumes" clients want. A firm that is willing to make the investment will easily obtain an in-depth understanding of how clients think, what they want, and how they choose. All it has to do is to be organized and systematic about going to the horse's mouth and asking the client, through such devices as client panels, senior partner visits, and attending client industry meetings to listen (not to talk or sell) (Chapter 6).

HOW MUCH TIME FOR EACH?

You may want to estimate what percentage of your firm's total practice development effort is spent on each of the five categories. (See Figure 5–1) What would you consider a balanced package? Do you currently overemphasize one or two areas at the expense of the others? You might also reflect on how effectively your firm performs each of the five phases of the practice development effort. What grade would you give yourself for each of the five?

My observation of professional firms in general is that they tend to overinvest their nonbillable practice development time in categories mentioned first on my list (broadcasting and courting) and, as a rule, underinvest in those activities lower on my list (superpleasing, nurturing, and listening). In large part, I have learned, this is because firms tend to assume that the last three categories all occur "naturally" during the conduct of matters (i.e., on billable time) and hence do not warrant any extra investment of nonbillable effort. This, in my experience, is an incorrect assumption.

Take, for example, listening activities. I may pay close attention to my clients while working with them, and think that I understand them. However, while working on current matters with clients there is a strong need to stick to the matter at hand and to focus on getting the job done rather than getting the client to talk about other things. But if I invite the client to dinner or to my offices to talk, not about the current matter, but about what's going on in his or her business, I can (and will) learn a great deal that will be useful to my future practice

FIGURE 5–1

Where Does the Time Go?

	Percent of non-billable practice development time spent	Evaluation of how well this is done now (1 = We're terrific at this part of practice development; 5 = We don't do this very well at all)
Broadcasting (generating leads and enquiries)		
Courting (selling and proposing		
Superpleasing (ensuring client delight with current matter)		
Nurturing (marketing to existing clients)		
Listening (gathering market intelligence)		
	100%	

development efforts. If I attempt to sell that client something without having previously listened, my practice development efforts will be less effective.

This is not an aesthetic or moral point ("You *ought* to pay more attention to existing clients and listen more"), but a simple matter of effective business practice: Which investments will give a good return for each non-billable practice development hour? Consider, for example, Table 5–1 which gives another way of looking at the alternatives of where an individual professional or firm can put its practice development investment. There are two sets of alternatives. The first choice available is whether to invest in marketing to existing clients or marketing to prospects, and the second is whether to market to those

TABLE 5-1

	Existing Client	*Prospective Client*
Aware of a new need	Superpleasing (Highest ROI)	Courting
Not aware of a new need	Nurturing	Broadcasting (Lowest ROI)

clients or prospects who are already aware of a new need versus those who are not currently aware of a need.

Where on this grid will a firm get its highest return on investment (ROI) for its first nonbillable practice development hour? For most firms, the answer will be in the top left-hand corner—making sure that your existing clients who are aware of a new need (which they may or may not have previously told you about) give the work to you. Are your existing clients already giving you all (or a high percentage) of their business as new needs emerge? If the answer is yes, then you can assume that this part of the practice development package is covered, and deserves no extra effort. If, however, you have only a portion of your clients' total work, then this area deserves your top priority, and an investment of nonbillable practice development time. Unless something is seriously wrong with your relationships, it should be easier to get more of an existing client's business than the first matter from a new client. Since the ROI in this practice development activity is so high, it would be sensible for any firm's practice development plans to begin with the following simple questions:

Which of our existing clients have additional work to give us?
What level of nonbillable investment makes sense to ensure that we get that work?
What activities will increase the probability that this client will want to give us future work?

Where on the grid is the *lowest* ROI practice development activities? Again, there can be no doubt about the answer—it is the bottom right hand corner—a nonclient, not aware of a new need. Yet if you were to walk into the typical law firm and ask about their practice development activities, you would hear a great deal about attempts to go out into the community and try to contact people with whom there is no current relationship, who are not currently aware of a need, and trying to sell them something! Firms must do *some* of this—a stream of new clients is essential to the continued success of any professional firm. However, the issue is one of balance. This is the most time-intensive form of building the practice, and should be used as "fill-up" rather than the leading component of the practice development plan.

Which of the two remaining boxes has the higher ROI? Here we can be less definitive, but we can certainly describe two very different practice development tasks. The top right-hand corner describes a situation where the prospective client is aware of a new need, but we have no existing relationship with that company. We can be confident that a new matter will be forthcoming—they're going to hire somebody—and our task is to make sure that it's us they choose. Our main task here is courting, a relatively time-intensive activity. To be selected, we need to get to know the client's business from scratch, begin to develop a relationship with the key decision makers, invest in preparing presentations and (possibly) proposals, and engage in a sequence of meetings before a decision is made. And all of this is probably taking place in a competitive environment, since the nonclient is aware of a need and is probably talking to more than one firm.

By way of contrast, the lower left-hand corner represents an existing client who is not currently aware of a new need, but with whom we do have a relationship. Investing time here is a bet—a gamble that if we spend time with client executives exploring their business issues, we may uncover something that they're not aware of but should be. (How likely is it that if you take the time to learn more about the client's affairs you will, indeed, uncover something? In most cases, this is a good bet). Once something has been uncovered, the practice development task is to bring it to the attention of the relevant decision makers (whom you probably already know). This is not a lengthy time-consuming task, and the ROI should be good.

This analysis suggests that the second highest ROI of nonbillable practice development time is likely to be spending time with existing clients who are not currently aware of a need, with competitive efforts in chasing nonclients aware of a new need coming third. It must be stressed one more time that this discussion is not meant to suggest that one box is more important than another, or that any may be neglected. In fact, quite the opposite is true—they must all be accommodated.

Moreover, there *is* a logical order to these practice development activities. First comes listening. Do this well, and all that follows will be easier. Next comes superpleasing. The better we can do there, the easier it will be both to win existing clients' future business and to win new clients through word of mouth. Third, it makes sense to ensure that you capture the new business of existing clients before tackling the more difficult area of winning new clients. Finally, it makes sense to ensure that you are good at turning enquiries into signed deals before you improve your success at generating enquiries.

What balance, then, would I give to the competing activities? Roughly this. I would begin by designing an effective listening program so that the firm regularly, consistently gets input from its marketplace, and I would invest as much as it takes to do this well. Let's say 10 to 15 percent of all practice development time for this.

Then, I would turn to superpleasing, and consider how much nonbillable time I would need to spend with current clients on current matters to leave them truly delighted and not just satisfied. I could probably "satisfy" them on billable time, but if a little extra non-reimbursed effort would delight them, I would consider it a wise place to put my nonbillable practice development effort. Let's say that a planned program of superpleasing would require 10 to 15 percent of my total practice development time.

Next, I would turn to the nurturing category and ask whether any of my existing clients had additional matters that I might earn by investing in the relationship. Probably, I would find a number of high ROI opportunities here, deserving of 30 to 35 percent of my efforts.

Only then would I turn to the new client side, with a total of 35 to 50 percent of available time. Between broadcasting and courting, it is clear that courting (which involves, among other things, winning a prospect's trust and confidence) is the more time intensive. Accordingly, I would try to limit my "lead generation" (broadcasting) activities to about 10 percent, leaving 25 to 40 percent for courting specific prospects.

Are these percentages cast in stone? Clearly not. Newly emerging practices will require a different balance than mature ones, and firms in different stages of practice development maturity will need to re-stress some of the categories more than others. But balance there must be, and practice development time should be allocated with a recognition of the full range of available options and of where the return on practice development investment truly lies.

CHAPTER 6

LISTENING TO CLIENTS

For professional service firms, no less than for other kinds of business, a primary means of achieving a competitive advantage is to have a better understanding of the wants and needs of clients than does the competition. This deeper understanding, if it is to be obtained, comes from a very straightforward activity: listening to clients.

Listening well to clients means more than informal, opportunistic information gathering during the process of pursuing new client prospects, or "keeping one's eyes open" during current client engagements. Neither can it be restricted to special market research efforts performed as part of a "once-every-three-years" strategic planning activity. Rather, it requires an ongoing systematic attempt to track client preferences, desires, and requirements. The questions "What do our clients want, and how are their needs changing?" must be continuously addressed through a structured program of information gathering, analysis, and action built into the daily operations of the firm.

Few professional firms have such a program. "What clients want" *is* a source of endless debate and speculation in many firms, but few make use of the most obvious means of answering this question: going to the horse's mouth and asking the client. Stated simply, professional service firms don't listen to their clients enough.

This chapter describes some of the various means (and purposes) of

61

listening to clients, and evaluates each of these mechanisms. It should be stated immediately that none of the listening devices described below is meant to be a substitute for any other. On the simple reasoning that knowledge is power, and on the proposition that "you can't know too much about your marketplace," the wise firm will employ as many of these tactics as possible.

WHY LISTEN TO CLIENTS?

Listening—soliciting clients' evaluation of current services and getting them to describe their unfilled needs—has two interrelated purposes: (a) improving the competitiveness of current services and (b) identifying opportunities to develop new services.

By inviting evaluations of current services, firms create the opportunity to improve. As the Japanese manufacturers say, a "defect is a treasure." In other words, by eagerly seeking out your "defects" and studying them carefully to identify why and how that performance failure occurred, you get the opportunity to improve. If you avoid feedback from those you serve, you never get the chance to learn how to be a more effective competitor. To study "defects" a manufacturer can examine the product on the shop floor. A professional service firm does not have this option: if there is a flaw in performance, only one person's opinion counts: the client's.

If it is the client's perspective that counts in judging performance on existing services, it is even more important in identifying the need for new services. The professional may form an opinion of the market's need for an additional service, or speculate on how the market's needs are changing. But these conclusions are useless until the client has been heard from. Accordingly, no professional firm can engage in strategic thinking, or decide which of two forms of investment is worthier, until it has received client input. Obviously, the firm that has a program of continuously soliciting, analyzing, and acting upon such input will be better positioned to capitalize on strategic opportunities than the firm that gets such input on an opportunistic, irregular basis.

THE VARIOUS MEANS OF LISTENING TO CLIENTS

There are, of course, numerous means of listening to clients, including many not listed here. However, we shall examine those listening activities that I have observed (or helped to install) in my client base of professional service firms. These include:

1. User groups
2. Reverse seminars
3. Attending client industry meetings
4. Market research
5. Senior partner visits
6. Engagement team debriefings
7. Systematic client feedback

USER GROUPS

The concept of user groups, familiar in industries such as computer software, is, I have learned, equally applicable and valuable in the professional service arena.

A workable structure for a professional firm user group is as follows. A small (five to seven participants) group of respected clients is asked whether it would be prepared to attend periodic meetings (two or three times a year) to discuss the firm's service offerings in a particular area.

Such meetings are often held after a good dinner in a private room at a fine restaurant. After dinner, the firm presents its plans for developing its practice in the specified area, including the development of new services, enhancement of existing services, and other strategic changes it is considering. The clients are then invited to critique the plans, to say whether the proposed investments make sense from their point of view, and whether or not there are other things that the firm should be considering to enhance its practice.

The theory of the user group is straightforward: There can be no better judge of how the firm can improve the competitiveness of its practice than the clients who will, after all, be the ultimate arbiters.

My experience with user groups in professional practice is that they work best when they are formed for a particular service (or well-defined practice area), rather than for the firm as a whole. I have learned that clients readily consent to participate (after all, the firm is trying to find out how to be more valuable to them, and it is in their interest to be of assistance). More often than not, I have seen clients be both candidly critical and constructive in their comments. They readily point out which proposed changes "do nothing for them," and which needs they have that are going unmet. In effect, a well-functioning user group does strategic planning for the firm.

REVERSE SEMINARS

If a seminar is where the professional firm invites a group of clients together and talks to them, then a reverse seminar is where the firm invites the client executive to come and talk to the members of the firm.

A typical request would go something like this:

Dear Client, We are very interested in you and your business. Unfortunately, only a few of us get the chance to visit with you in the course of our work for you. Accordingly, would you be prepared to come to our offices (or a nearby location) after business hours for a drink or two, and then give us a brief talk about what is going on in your world? Perhaps you might be prepared to answer a question or two from our people. We do hope you will accept, as we are keen to learn even more about you, your company, and your industry.

The benefits of this practice are many. First, most clients would be flattered to be asked to speak, and would take the invitation as what it is meant to be: a sincere indication that the firm cares about its clients and wants to learn more about them. To this extent, the reverse seminar is a powerful client relationship management mechanism. Second, reverse seminars add to the knowledge base of the firm. In most firms, the individual professionals are skilled in their technical specialty, be it law, accounting, actuarial science, public relations, or whatever. However, to be a skillful advisor requires that the professionals understand not only their specialty but also the business environment in which their clients operate. Yet in few professions is any formal provision made for people to acquire general business knowledge as they progress in their careers. The reverse seminar, particularly if done on a regular basis (some of my clients hold one every two weeks, with different clients) provides the mechanism to expose the staff of the firm (juniors and seniors alike) to the thinking of business people.

A third benefit of reverse seminars is, of course, the chance to identify future business development opportunities, particularly if the audience contains not only professionals from the practice area currently working with the firm, but those in other disciplines.

These seminars must be treated carefully. If the clients come to perceive that they are being invited not to be listened to, but to be sold something, they are unlikely to participate. My experience informs me that this is not too difficult to police, and is as much a matter of style and timing as anything else. If the client expresses a need in the presentation, he or she can be *asked* if a further meeting to discuss this issue is desired. Most clients who express a need would be willing to listen to a proposal about solving that need.

ATTENDING CLIENT INDUSTRY MEETINGS

A valuable opportunity to listen to clients talk about their challenges, interests and needs is to go where they go to discuss such subjects, that is, to their industry or trade meetings. My clients report to me that the value of attending such meetings is greatly enhanced if the professional attends *with* a respected client, so that an instantaneous evaluation through the client's eyes of materials and ideas presented from the speakers' podium can be obtained. (" Do you agree with what that speaker said? Do you think you'll have to deal with that? What does this really mean for you?"). Such conversations can only enhance the professional's own evaluation and interpretation of subjects covered at such meetings.

Naturally, the value of attending the client industry meeting is greatly enhanced if the professional attending has an obligation to circulate within the firm a written summary of the intelligence gathered.

MARKET RESEARCH

In most industries, formal (often third-party) market research is a primary means of listening to the market. In the professional service world, it continues to play an important role, but often has a slightly different purpose.

Almost by definition, professional service firms do not serve a mass market. Each of their projects, engagements, or "matters" is customized to specific client needs. Accordingly, that form of market research which provides aggregated results of what large numbers of clients "think" about various issues tends not to be as directly helpful as it may be in other situations. This is not to say that there is no role for market research, but that the more disaggregated methodologies (such as focus groups) may be more applicable for professional environments. Focus groups work well, I have learned, particularly if the clients participating consent to be videotaped. A tape of clients expressing their needs, concerns, and challenges has a much greater impact on professionals than numbers on a page, no matter how statistically valid.

SENIOR PARTNER VISITS TO KEY CLIENTS

A major, and common, form of listening to clients is a more or less formal program of visits to key clients by senior partners of the firm (or, if the firm is not a partnership, then by office or practice managers or "executive committee" members). Frequently these "visits" are conducted not in the client's offices, but over dinner.

The virtues of this practice include not only quality assurance ("How are our people serving you? Are you getting all you need from them?"), but also the opportunity to converse on the longer term issues that it might be difficult for the engagement team to do. Frequently, the professional firm's senior partners or managers can, because of their position, arrange meetings "higher up" in the client organization than can the engagement team leader, thus gaining exposure to a broader and deeper view of the client's challenges, concerns, and needs.

ENGAGEMENT TEAM DEBRIEFINGS

At the best professional service firms, it is routine practice to require that, at the end of each and every client project, the engagement leader will sit down with the client to obtain the client's feedback on what went well, what less well, and how the engagement might have been improved. These discussions might cover not only the technical quality (and success) of the project, but also how the professional firm's interface with the client might be improved.

These conversations, if conducted with candor, are often the source not only of good ideas for improvement that can be deployed on subsequent engagements, but (I have heard repeatedly from my clients) often highlight additional unresolved issues (perhaps not formally within the scope of the current engagement) that represent immediate new business for the professional firm.

The power of these debriefings is such that some of my clients impose a firmwide requirement on their professional staff to file a debriefing report so that ideas for improvement obtained from their clients are formally captured and become part of the intellectual capital of the firm. Such a requirement ensures that the debriefing meetings are indeed held on a routine basis, and that there is a mechanism for capturing and disseminating the feedback obtained.

SYSTEMATIC CLIENT FEEDBACK

As valuable as engagement debriefings can be, another form of client feedback can be even more powerful: a system whereby the firm adopts a mandatory policy of sending a questionnaire to clients at the end of each engagement, inviting the client to evaluate the firm. (For a specific sample of such a questionnaire, see Chapter 8, A Service Quality Program.)

Although common in the general consumer service world, such feedback questionnaires are as yet uncommon among professional firms. They are frequently resisted on the grounds that they are "unprofessional," and represent a poor substitute for person-to-person means of getting feedback such as engagement debriefings.

Recognizing that one device is not a substitute for the other, but rather a complement, we must ask what a questionnaire will accomplish if engagement debriefings are already being performed. The answer is that the questionnaire comes to the client from the firm, not the individual, and may solicit comments that the client might not be willing to express face-to-face. Second, the questionnaire is an *institutional* mechanism, and helps accomplish the goal of firmwide quality assurance, as well as providing a means for the firm to systematically track its quality performance, watching for trends (and hence opportunities for improvement that might not be highlighted with a series of engagement debriefings). Finally, the questionnaire itself, the act of asking for feedback, signals to clients a willingness to listen and respond.

CONCLUSION

The mechanisms described here are not new. Individual examples of each tactic can be found in many separate firms. In all good firms, individual practitioners are actively listening to their personal clients. What may be missing in these firms, however, is a mechanism to *assemble* each of these data points, these specific pieces of client intelligence, and transform them into useful information that the firm can use to improve its performance and plan its strategies.

It is this need not only to *get* client feedback, but to *use* it, that constitutes the challenge to professional firms today. A firm that put together a full program using most, if not all, of the elements described above would indeed have a competitive advantage.

CHAPTER 7

QUALITY WORK DOESN'T MEAN QUALITY SERVICE

Consider the following scenario: You have had your car repaired at a new local garage. A week or two later, your neighbor, curious about whether she should also use this new garage, asks, "Did they fix the car?" "I think so," you reply. "It seems to be running smoothly, so I guess they did a good job." Then your neighbor asks an interesting second question: "Did you get good service?" What does this second question mean? Surely, fixing the car is the service, isn't it? Well, yes and no. Fixing the car is part of it, and an important part it is, but by itself it doesn't constitute good service.

Your neighbor is asking about a whole range of other activities that influence your satisfaction with the service providers. Were they accessible? Was it easy to make an appointment? Did they deal with the matter expeditiously? Did they take the time to explain to you (in language appropriate to your level of understanding) what they had found, what, precisely, they did, and why?

When you first approached them, did they ask intelligent questions about symptoms, trying to come up with an informed guess as to the scope of the problem? Or did they just say, "Leave it with us and we'll get back to you," sending you away to worry about how big a problem you had and how much it might end up costing? Did they make you feel as if your car was just one more job to be done, or did they convey the impression that they wanted your business? Did they deal with you with an appropriate mix of respect and friendliness?

If complications arose, did they make strenuous efforts to contact you, inform you of developments, and involve you in the decision as to what to do next? Or did they make all the decisions for you, failing to distinguish between mandatory and precautionary measures and leaving you with a feeling that you might end up paying for work that wasn't truly necessary? Was it easy to settle the bill and understand the charges? Did they provide advice as to how to prevent recurrence of the problem, or to avert other potential problems detected in the course of the repairs?

As these questions show, the practical meaning of good service in car repair extends far beyond technical excellence in servicing the car. It is necessary to service not only the car, but also the customer. Indeed, it may be more important to excel at servicing the customer. Many customers are unable to distinguish between outstanding technical work and the simply competent: In choosing garages, they may pay more attention to the quality of service received than the quality of work performed—which, of course, is not the same thing. And even if the customers *are* sufficiently sophisticated to distinguish between outstanding and competent work, their technical needs may call for only the competent: They know that any number of providers can fix the car, and, rather than seek out the most highly qualified (and probably most highly priced) technician in town, these intelligent consumers will appraise providers along a number of dimensions, including responsiveness, attitude, and other nontechnical "service" criteria.

The lessons from this example extend far beyond the car-repair industry. They apply to all service industries, and most significantly to the professions. Firms that provide legal counsel, tax advice, investment banking services, advertising services, and consulting services all share with our garage mechanic the need to service the client as well as the car. The questions posed above could all be equally well asked of a professional service provider, and they provide a useful guide to the client's *perception* of the quality of the professional service. I, the client, may *think* my provider did a good technical job at dealing with the professional matter, but as with the car repair, I am not an expert. However, with the unfolding of time I will learn more, as the car does or does not continue to run well, as my legal contracts do or do not result in problems, as my tax arrangements do or do not result in financial benefit, as my merger attempts are successful, and so on.

But even time may not allow me to judge unequivocally whether my professional service provider rendered truly superior advice: A large number of contingencies can cloud my ability to assess the work performed. Even with the most brilliant legal mind on my side, I may lose the case; even the most superior consulting talent available may not prevent me from making what turned out to be a false strategic move. How, then, am I to appraise my service provider?

Whether logical or illogical, sensible or not, even the most sophisticated client will, in such an environment, come to focus more heavily on the quality of service than on the quality of work. Because of the ambiguity that surrounds technical excellence (and the difficulty the client has in appraising it), the personal relationship between the client and the provider takes on great significance in all of the professions.

Just as with my garage mechanic, when I find a professional service provider whom I trust, in whom I can have confidence, and who provides me with peace of mind and reassurance, I will tend to remain with that provider. Indeed, on most technical or professional matters outside my own area of expertise, I am as much shopping for trust, confidence, peace of mind, and reassurance as I am for "cold" technical expertise. As all clients do, I consider style, manner, and, above all, *attitude* in choosing professional service providers.

It is important to note that while goods are consumed, services are *experienced*. The professional service provider is (or should be) as much in the business of managing the client's *experience* with respect to professional services as in the business of executing technical tasks.

Much of the previous discussion can be summarized by what I have come to call "The First Law of Service," expressed as a formula:

SATISFACTION *equals* PERCEPTION *minus* EXPECTATION

If the client *perceives* service at a certain level but expected something more (or different), then he or she will be dissatisfied.

The significance of this seemingly simple formula is contained in the observation that neither perception nor expectation necessarily reflects reality. Both are experiential, psychological states of mind. Accordingly, the central challenge to service organizations is to manage not only the substance of what they do for clients but also to manage clients' expectations and perceptions. Consider the restaurant chain that consistently overestimates the time it will take for a table to become free. They lose some customers, but those who remain are seated before they expected: a pleasant surprise and a good beginning to the service encounter. Trivial? Perhaps, but a pleased client is easier to keep pleased than one who is in a state of annoyance and impatience because he was led to believe that service would begin earlier than it did.

My late colleague Daryl Wyckoff told the story of checking out of a hotel in San Francisco and commenting to the clerk on the beauty of the view from his room window. The next time he stayed there, he was greeted, "Welcome, Professor Wyckoff. We have assigned you the room with the view that you liked so much." A powerful service experience, and one that is relatively simple to arrange, given the organization's desire to please.

The most important of perceptions and expectations is not restricted to consumer services such as these. It is possible (indeed, all too common in the professional service sector) that the professional does substantively superior work but that this is not perceived by the client. Or, in another case, the professional may invest significant amounts of time and effort in dealing with unforeseen contingencies but, because the client did not expect the contingencies, he or she is irritated by the extra delay and expense rather than thankful for the abilities of the professional.

This isn't solely a matter of unsophisticated clients being unable to appreciate what is truly being done for them. In case after case, I have heard stories (and observed examples) of professionals so completely oriented to their own values (e.g., pride in technical craftsmanship) that the clients' true needs are placed second to the professional's desire to create a monument to his or her technical ability. "We could do great work," I have heard frequently, "if the client did not keep getting in the way." Architects run the risk of falling in love with their artistic designs, lawyers with the elegance of their briefs, consultants with the sophistication of their analyses, all to the exclusion of consideration of what the client needs and expects or of how the client perceives the provider's efforts.

The need to be "client centered" is a constant theme of modern management writings, and it is the professional service sector that is in most urgent need of hearing this message. Because of the proclivity of professionals to become more fascinated with the intellectual challenge of their craft than with being responsive to clients, all too often clients are mocked for their lack of professional knowledge, despised because of their demands, and resented because they control the purse strings and hence the autonomy of the professional.

There is an old saw in the medical profession that the three most important keys to success are availability, affability, and ability—in that order. The same profound insight can be equally well applied to other professions. In all professions, clients gripe that "they do great work, but you can never get hold of them. They don't return my phone calls!" Another common complaint is "I wish they would keep me informed of progress. This may be just another engagement to them, but to me it's critical. I want to know what's going on."

This last statement is particularly telling. People and organizations turn to professional service providers for matters of significant uncertainty, importance, and risk. It is this atmosphere of risk and importance that makes them prepared to pay the traditionally high fees of the professional service sector. Whether it is health, legal concerns, finances, office accommodations, internal organization, or advertising, clients of professional service firms are almost by definition in a state of anxiety and nervousness: They need to be confident that they are in good hands. The slogan of one rapidly growing professional service firm I have studied is "People don't care how much you know until they know how much you care"—a cute phrase but an important one. Clients of professional service firms want to know that they are not being lost in the shuffle. They want to know that their matter is receiving the attention it deserves. The professional service firm that is adept at projecting a *caring* image, and that backs the image up with a substantive reality, will do well in the marketplace.

The importance to clients of how they are treated is not restricted to unsophisticated buyers. Consider again our car-repair example. To the mechanically unsophisticated, good service may mean clean facilities, a pleasant receptionist, understandable explanations, fast turnaround, and convenient access. To the automobile buff who performs minor repairs himself, good service will mean the opportunity to be involved with decisions, to discuss with the mechanics the intricacies of the problem, and to walk around the repair shop. The technical neophyte might be intimidated by a dirty-fingered engineer speaking technical language; the initiate might be offended by the unnecessary frills of receptionists, free cups of coffee, and nontechnical descriptions. The point is that both types will be concerned with how they are dealt with—how oriented the organization is to their specific needs and preferred style of interaction. Both will be concerned not only with the content of the transaction—getting the car fixed (or the legal matter handled or the accounts audited)—but also with the *process* by which this is accomplished. Each may wish to be treated in a different manner, but each will want to be treated well.

In many professions, the importance of understanding that different clients want to be treated differently is becoming accentuated. Corporations are becoming more sophisticated purchasers of professional services, often with in-house capabilities to handle selected matters. While in the past a lawyer dealt directly with a senior executive, outside counsel now often have to work through in-house counsel. The in-house lawyer is in effect the client and will expect to be dealt with in a different manner than a general manager. Similarly, in investment banking, consulting, and architecture, chief financial officers, planning departments, and facility-planning committees are, respectively, beginning to act as knowledgeable clients. In all cases, the message is the same: The nature of the client has changed, and hence the process of interaction must change. Precise definitions of "good service" must evolve. The professional can no longer assume that the client will place trust, confidence, and respect in him or her.

Power, in all professions, is moving from the professional to the client. The professional firm must increasingly demonstrate a willingness to be cooperative, responsive, and adaptable in order to win the confidence of today's client.

What, in concrete terms, can be done? For many firms, a wide range of seemingly trivial but practically powerful actions are possible. One lawyer in a large firm relates the following anecdote: "One of our competitors [in real estate transactions] makes it a common practice to get a copy of the deal into the hands of their client within twenty-four hours of the closing of the deal. We think we write better contracts with more protection for our clients, but there is no denying that their clients are impressed. We are told that they have a better reputation for quality of service than we do." A fine example of the gap between perceptions and reality: If my friend's firm wants to keep its clients, perhaps it could do a better job of managing the expectations of its clients—clearly explaining how long it will take to produce a copy of the deal and why it is in the client's interest to wait the extra few days. The key is anticipating the client's perceptions and reactions and explicitly dealing with them in advance. The prescription is clear: Discuss at the earliest possible point all potential roadblocks, detours, and contingencies that may arise, and make it clear how your firm will handle them.

There is a danger that in a vigorous attempt to win new clients, excessive promises may be made, creating expectations that cannot be fulfilled. One professional I know describes the syndrome this way: "The most depressing day in the office is the day after we have won a new client. We all look at each other and say, 'How on earth are we going to deliver all we promised for the budget we agreed to?' "

Client expectations can also be managed by vigorous efforts at keeping the client informed as to developments, progress, and discretionary decisions. One professional I spoke with describes his techniques as follows: "Whenever I reach a decision point, I call the client, lay out the alternatives, make a recommendation, then ask for his opinion and instructions. Ninety-nine percent of the time, he tells me to do what I was going to do anyway. But it makes him feel good to be consulted, and he is taking direct responsibility for specific expenditures and time—consuming activities. He is never surprised by what I got up to on his behalf, and he is constantly informed as to what I'm doing for him. If I don't have a decision for him to make, I call him anyway just to let him know what the status is. And every conversation ends with two sentences: I ask if there's anything else he wants me to do, and I tell him when I'll next call him." This may not be an appropriate strategy in all cases: Some clients may interpret constant telephone calls as harassment rather than good service. But it is the preferences of the client, not of the professional, that should determine the manner in which the professional behaves. The professional must discover each client's style preferences and work to communicate the appropriate attitude. The individual quoted above is concerned that he be perceived as responsive: His telephone calls are but a way to symbolize that.

Steven Brill, publisher of *The American Lawyer*, tells how pleasantly surprised he was on receiving a letter acknowledging payment of a legal bill and thanking him for his business: an attitude conveyed through a simple, trivial action. The business world is filled with creative examples of this. For example, the hotel room that places a paper strip across the toilet bowl to symbolize that the bathroom has been sanitized—a reassuring touch. Another example: The car-repair shop that hands back the burned-out part that was replaced. Useless, but comforting to know that the part was indeed in need of replacement. Or consider the financial services company that sends a client a clipping from some obscure financial journal about his or her business: The clipping may or may not be useful, but the gesture tells the client that the company cares. Such trivial actions create the *experience* of client satisfaction.

Examples in the professional service sector *can* be found: The firm that consistently follows up client meetings with brief memoranda summarizing the discussion and points agreed to, with a request to the client to call if any misinterpretation has taken place. The firm that routinely explains *in advance* the format of its complex bills so that the client knows what to expect when it arrives. The firm that ensures that all referrals from clients are followed up with a thank-you note, whether or not any new business resulted. The firm that makes the effort to find out the client's real deadlines, and works hard to meet them. The firm that *demonstrates* its trustworthiness by advising clients on how to avoid fees by doing some things themselves, or that demonstrates its integrity, either by admitting areas of weakness and recommending other professionals or by refusing work when it knows it is too busy. Such actions are not matters to be dealt with only by systems and procedures, although these can help. Fundamentally, they are the result of an appropriate firmwide *attitude* toward clients—an attitude that must be created by the senior professionals of the firm through exemplary personal behavior and role modeling.

Many professional service firms have procedures and mechanisms to assure the quality of the work they produce: review committees, senior-partner oversight, documentation of working papers. However, relatively few have given much attention to improving the quality of *service*. Many firms seek to avoid the increasing price-sensitivity of clients by trumpeting the eternal battle cry of the professional: "We must compete on the superior quality of our work, not on price." An entirely proper sentiment, but one that can easily be misunderstood and misdirected. Improving the quality of work can be costly and hard to demonstrate. Improving the quality of service can be as cheap as instilling more responsive attitudes in professional staff, and it tends to be infinitely more visible to clients.

In a service business, and particularly in the professions, the words of the old song remain true: "It ain't what you do, it's the way that you do it: That's what gets results."

CHAPTER 8

A SERVICE QUALITY PROGRAM

The importance of client service is well understood by most professionals and most professional firms. Most, if not all, firms acknowledge the critical distinction between technical quality (how good is the work?) and service quality (what kind of experience does the client have with the firm?). Similarly, virtually all firms acknowledge the importance of service quality in determining client satisfaction. They have preached it, internally and externally, for years. It is contained in most firms' mission statements and strategy documents.

Yet consistent, outstanding performance in this area is scarce. In a large-scale study I supervised for a major international professional service firm, corporate purchasers of a broad range of professional services (including audit, actuarial, consulting, legal, and marketing communications services) were asked, among other things, to rate their experience with professional firms on two key dimensions.

First, we asked them to evaluate their satisfaction with the technical quality of the work done for them. Satisfaction levels were consistently high. Clients, it seems, do not have too much difficulty in finding technically competent people to help them.

We then asked about the clients' level of satisfaction with the way they were dealt with by the professionals involved during the course of the engagement, transaction, matter, or deal. Satisfaction levels were low, and complaints numerous.

That this should not be surprising can be tested against your own experience as a purchaser of professional services. Think back to your own use of outside professionals (you've probably used one or more of the following professionals recently: a lawyer, a doctor, an accountant, an actuary, a consultant, an interior designer, a public relations counselor). Did the professionals you dealt with:

- Make it their business to understand what was special and unique about you and your company?
- Listen carefully to what you had to say and what you wanted, rather than substitute their own judgment for yours on what needed to be done and how it should be done?
- Give good explanations of what they were doing and why?
- Let you know in advance what they were going to do?
- Help you understand what was going on and help you reach your own conclusion, rather than tell you their conclusion?
- Keep you sufficiently informed on progress?
- Document their work activities well?
- Avoid confusing jargon?
- Make sure they were accessible and available when you needed them?
- Notify you promptly of changes in scope, and seek your approval?
- Keep their promises on deadlines?
- Involve you at major points in the engagement?
- Make you feel as if you were important to them?
- Show an interest in you beyond the specifics of their tasks?
- Make an attempt to be helpful to you beyond the specifics of their project?

My own experiences (and those of the clients I have surveyed) suggest that it is extraordinarily rare to find a professional who is *consistently* good at these things, and even rarer to find a whole firm that can be relied upon to act in this fashion.

Few of us have trouble citing real examples, not caricatures, of adverse behaviors that we encounter routinely in our dealings with the *other* professionals we use. We have no problem reporting what we hate about having to deal with "those guys."

As it turns out, accountants, consultants, and public relations people complain about the same things when talking about lawyers or actuaries that lawyers and actuaries complain about when referring to accountants, consultants, and public relations people. What "we" hate about having to deal with "those guys" is a very good predictor of what our clients hate about having to deal with us.

What this reveals is that what clients seek from their professionals has nothing to do with "being nice to the client," "shmoozing," "stroking," or "hand holding". Rather, what we are talking about is finding ways to make client assignments substantively *more valuable* to clients by changing the way professionals interact with their clients during the project. Client service is not a "frill": How a professional deals with us is an essential determinant of our judgment of value received.

Unfortunately, it has been my experience in discussing this topic with thousands of professionals that large numbers of them believe that client service *is* about "shmoozing," "stroking," and "hand holding." Many professionals appear to associate client service with activities such as having lunch, taking the client to cultural or sports events, and so on. With such a view, it is not surprising that client service is held in low esteem by many professionals, and results in a low level of performance in this area.

The importance of good relationship management (in the sense intended here) is borne out by another question in the study referred to above, in which we asked corporate executives about referrals. Only 10 percent of all referrals were found to be cases where technical considerations or "results" were given as the reason for the referral. Fully 90 percent of all the reasons given for referrals were related to the relationship issues discussed above.

Most clients say that if they could find a provider who *reliably* behaved in the ways described above, they would be

a. More likely to return to that provider
b. More willing to refer that provider
c. Less fee-sensitive about that provider's services

There is a paradox here. Service quality is widely acknowledged to be important, yet the typical firm does not perform well in this area. What is the explanation?

The answer is that few firms have any systematic *program* for ensuring and improving the experience the client has with the firm. In most firms, client service is a matter for speeches at annual meetings, and the occasional training program.

It cannot be stressed enough that achieving excellence in client service is *not* an "educational" issue (i.e., enlightening staff and training them). Almost all client service training programs, taken by themselves, fail to be implemented in the press of daily business. Most firm personnel, if asked, could easily describe most of the activities that would represent good service. We must ask why they don't already do these things.

Look again at the list of behaviors described above. Do any of those items take great skill to perform? Are any of them intellectually challenging? I think the answer is no.

But there are so many items! The bad news about achieving excellence in client service is that it is made up of hundreds of little, trivial actions, not a few grand gestures. It means rethinking every communication and interaction with clients, no matter how mundane. It takes an attention to detail, an *attitude*, that is essential if individuals are to find the self-discipline to handle all of their client-contact activities with empathy.

HOW TO MAKE IT HAPPEN

What many firms have yet to learn is that the issue of improving client service is overwhelmingly a *managerial* one. They, and their professionals, know what good service is, but how do they make it *happen*? What does management have to do to provide the context within which firm personnel will actually execute and implement what they already know they should do?

Achieving excellence in client service is similar to people's desire to give up smoking and lose weight. They know and want the goal, they believe it is worth the effort, they know what to do—but, like all human beings, they are very bad at incurring short-term discomfort to achieve a long-term goal. People are terrific at postponing diets. Do they feel guilty that they're not doing what they know they should? You betcha! Are they likely to change? Not unless they're forced to!

Sticking to a diet requires a well-thought-out program, a system. It doesn't work to preach the benefits: I already accept the goal. It doesn't work to just give me more tips: I already know what works. What I need is a program to help me find the discipline that I seem unable to find in myself.

Guilt, alone, I have learned, doesn't change people. But the right degree of embarrassment does. Tell me I have to show up at a weight clinic every week in front of the same people and have my weight announced to all and sundry, and I might find a little more self-discipline during the week.

If firms are to achieve excellence in client service quality, a *system* must be designed—an inescapable, mandatory diet. Not one that the firm leaves to each individual's best intentions. That's like saying "Make your New Year's resolution and we'll get you on the scales on December 31. See you then!" That's not going to work.

What is required is a monitoring system that, like a diet, is often uncomfortable, will require disciplined changes in daily life-style, and that will *force* practitioners to live up to goals they have already agreed to.

A full program to differentiate the firm through client service requires action on five fronts (in this order):

1. Measurements
2. Management
3. Tips and tools
4. Training
5. Rewards

We shall discuss each element of the program in turn.

MEASURES

As a way of measuring client satisfaction, many firms have, particularly in recent years, instituted various means of obtaining feedback from clients, including such approaches as engagement team debriefings, occasional managing partner visits, and so on. (See Chapter 6, Listening to Clients.) However, sensible as these are, I have learned that they are no substitute for a mailed questionnaire to each and every client at the end of every single client project.

A mailed questionnaire, such as that shown in Figure 8–1, when used as a supplement (not a substitute) for other means of obtaining feedback, has the virtue that it is *systematic*. Its importance is that it not only obtains the feedback but, more importantly, it introduces an *accountability* for client satisfaction into the firm's management systems. By measuring client satisfaction on *every* assignment, and doing so in a way that can be monitored, it *commits* the members of the firm to inescapable implementation of good service.

The test of a feedback system is thus not whether or not it *measures* successfully, but whether or not it induces changes in behavior. There is a contrast between feedback as a market research tool and feedback as a management tool. For the former, periodic, selective face-to-face methods are adequate. For the latter, a program of mandatory questionnaires is necessary.

Face-to-face feedback devices (engagement team debriefings, senior partner visits, third party market research, etc.) *may* generate better information and *may* be more welcomed by the client, but they do not provide a "conscience" mechanism that forces all firm members to feel personally accountable at all times for executing those actions that lead to client satisfaction.

Many partners, on meeting this system for the first time, say "If we ask about these things, don't we run the risk that we'll make the client aware of something he's unhappy with that he wouldn't have bothered about if we hadn't asked?" (This question comes up frequently.)

It should be reasonably clear that it is in the firm's interest for the client to surface concerns if he or she has them. Only if the client tells the firm where he or she is less than completely satisfied can we respond. Suppose the client is unhappy about something minor, and further suppose it's due to a misunderstanding. Are we ahead of the game or behind the game if we get him or her to tell the firm about it? Obviously, we're ahead!

The system must be designed to make it *easy* for the client to surface concerns—hence the virtues of a detailed specific questionnaire and also the virtue of the mailed questionnaire. (Evidence shows overwhelmingly that more candid comments are made in mailed questionnaires than in face-to-face debriefings.)

The act of asking can *never* hurt the firm—except if we fail to respond and deal with the client's concern. Thus the whole program

FIGURE 8–1

CLIENT FEEDBACK QUESTIONNAIRE

For each of the following statements about our firm, please indicate whether you: Strongly disagree (1); somewhat disagree (2); neither agree nor disagree (3); somewhat agree (4); strongly agree (5)

You are thorough in your approach to your work	NA	1	2	3	4	5
You show creativity in your proposed solutions	NA	1	2	3	4	5
You are helpful in redefining our view of our situation	NA	1	2	3	4	5
You are helpful in diagnosing the causes of our problem areas	NA	1	2	3	4	5
Your people are accessible	NA	1	2	3	4	5
You keep your promises on deadlines	NA	1	2	3	4	5
You document your work activities well	NA	1	2	3	4	5
Your communications are free of jargon	NA	1	2	3	4	5
You offer fast turnaround when requested	NA	1	2	3	4	5
You listen well to what we have to say	NA	1	2	3	4	5
You relate well to our people	NA	1	2	3	4	5
You keep me sufficiently informed on progress	NA	1	2	3	4	5
You let us know in advance what you're going to do	NA	1	2	3	4	5
You notify us promptly of changes in scope, and seek our approval	NA	1	2	3	4	5
You give good explanations of what you've done and why	NA	1	2	3	4	5

(continued on next page)

FIGURE 8–1 (cont.)

You don't wait for me to initiate everything: you anticipate	NA	1	2	3	4	5
You don't jump to conclusions too quickly	NA	1	2	3	4	5
You involve us at major points in the engagement	NA	1	2	3	4	5
You have a good understanding of our business	NA	1	2	3	4	5
You make it your business to understand our company	NA	1	2	3	4	5
You are up to date on what's going on in our world	NA	1	2	3	4	5
You make us feel as if we're important to you	NA	1	2	3	4	5
You are an easy firm to do business with	NA	1	2	3	4	5
You deal with problems in our relationship openly and quickly	NA	1	2	3	4	5
You keep us informed on technical issues affecting our business	NA	1	2	3	4	5
You show an interest in us beyond the specifics of your tasks	NA	1	2	3	4	5
You have been helpful to me beyond the specifics of your projects	NA	1	2	3	4	5
You have made our people more effective at what they do	NA	1	2	3	4	5
My own understanding of your area has improved from working with you	NA	1	2	3	4	5
Overall, I would rate your service very highly	NA	1	2	3	4	5

Thank you for your assistance. Please feel free to add any additional comments.

turns on this issue: Are we or are we not prepared to meet and be accountable for these standards? If we are, we should ask. If we are not, then clearly we should not even consider such a feedback system. It should also be noted that the act of asking can be a good service action in its own right ("Hey, these guys care"), but the act of asking by itself does not necessarily produce higher client satisfaction—it merely creates a productive "let's wait and see" attitude in the client's mind. What happens after the feedback is provided is the test of the system.

MANAGEMENT'S ROLE

Asking for client feedback and not having the procedures to deal systematically with the responses is obviously a disaster. Consequently, there should be no such thing as a stand-alone client feedback program. Either it is an integral part of a total quality program, or it shouldn't be done at all.

Since the point of the system is to create a conscience mechanism, how the responses are dealt with when they are returned is as critical as asking for the feedback. This should be obvious, but I've seen more than one example of a poorly designed follow-through system.

Obviously, each partner and member of the engagement team receives a copy of their client's response. The managing partner should examine each response and discuss the individual replies with the engagement partner (or engagement team). This is time consuming, but is there a higher-value use of a managing partner's time? The partners should agree on which of the following responses the client should receive:

a. A letter saying thank you for your flattering comments
b. A visit from the engagement partner to clarify areas where the client is less than fully satisfied
c. A visit from the managing partner

More follow-up is needed to make the system work. The responses should be tabulated and, every six or twelve months, the managing partner should discuss the aggregate results with all the partners (and other staff), *explicitly* comparing group averages between different parts of the practice.

This is necessary because of the need to implement an accountability system that will have a high probability of creating changes in behavior. To create the "right" degree of embarrassment, it is necessary to discuss publicly how different practices are doing, how different offices are doing, how responses vary between different types of engagements.

The results for an individual partner should *not* be discussed in public—that's too much embarrassment—but group averages work fine. Individual partners must get "embarrassed" in *private*. Once the group averages are public, the head of the practice area visits the individual partner in his or her office and closes the door, saying "Only you and I know these figures, but here's how your personal aggregate scores (i.e., all clients you're responsible for) compare to our group's average. How can we help?"

Administering the Questionnaire

Who should send out the questionnaire? My experience with these systems (over forty firms worldwide with a variety of professions) suggests the following procedure. After the engagement partner has forewarned the client (in person) that it is coming, and explained why the firm is doing it, the questionnaire should be sent out over the firm name (with the firm or office managing partner's name attached), not the name of the individual engagement partner. This signals to the client *the firm's* commitment to quality, in addition to the individual partner's.

For similar reasons, the return address should be to the firm—either the office or firm managing partner. Experience shows that this promotes candor, reinforces the firm's image and, perhaps most importantly, introduces a conscience mechanism into the loop, so that each client service team realizes that their performance in this area *will* be monitored.

Experience shows that response rates to questionnaires of this kind are very high (75 percent plus, plus). If a client does not respond, a letter asking again for the feedback, reminding the client of the firm's commitment, is appropriate. If there is still no response, well, that's the client's privilege.

Experience also shows overwhelmingly that clients appreciate the opportunity to give feedback and respond positively to the system. Adverse reactions ("This is tacky, like a hotel chain") *do* occur but at a rate of less than 1 percent.

Who in the client organization should get the questionnaire? There is no reason not to send out multiple questionnaires. Indeed, most firms find that there is rarely one client on an engagement. Accordingly, the rule should be that at least one must go out, but after that, the engagement partner and managing partner (or practice leader) will decide how many questionnaires are appropriate for each engagement.

There is little, if any, downside to asking multiple people, but it cannot be solely the engagement partner's decision—bitter experience has shown that if allowed to, some people will game the system and only send it to friendly client personnel and avoid unfriendly client executives, which defeats the point of the system. It sounds paternal, but this *is* an accountability system—given a chance, we'll all find ways to cheat on our diets unless we'll be embarrassed if caught cheating.

Questionnaire Design

Some partners look at Figure 8–1 and say "That's too much to ask, there are too many questions." This is a cop-out. Experience worldwide has shown that from the client's point of view, a scaled (1 to 5) questionnaire with twenty-five questions does not take too long to fill out, and the specificity of the questions both communicates a sincere desire to probe *and* allows the client to express mild reservations in some areas while expressing high satisfaction in others.

Some Cautions

Some of my clients have designed the questionnaire so that the client feedback system becomes an opportunity to sell more work. There is grave danger here. It is absolutely true that client feedback systems, if properly applied, do create additional opportunities to sell. However, the feedback form *must not* be used simultaneously for selling.

For the feedback system to work, either in the clients' eyes as a sincere desire to meet quality standards, or in partners' eyes as a serious attempt to create excellence in service behavior, the quality feedback and the selling tasks *must* be separated.

A quality questionnaire that asks "What else would you like to buy from the firm?" will be treated skeptically by clients and will divert partners' emphasis away from the key task, which is to earn the next engagement by raising the value of *this* one. Selling is, of course, valuable, but it works most effectively when it convincingly *follows* a demonstration of a commitment to service and feedback; it must not be a substitute for it.

Many firms have learned that if the enthusiasm of the professionals for this program is to be achieved, then management must be seen to be doing its part. For example, there is often a need for expenditure by the firm to ensure that support systems are in place to sustain a client service effort. A common prime example is the need to spend money on telephones and receptionists to ensure that the phone system is client friendly. These expenditures are *mandatory* to prove to firm staff that management is committing itself, not only them, to this strategy.

TIPS AND TOOLS

Having discussed *measures* and *management*, we now turn to the third element of a service quality program: the development and dissemination of specific, concrete ideas, to be shared among the professionals, for enhancing value to clients during their assignments.

This can be done formally or informally. I will describe a more formal method, but the goal is the same in either case: to document and share the best ideas available, so that each professional has a source of help in finding ways to enhance his or her value in conducting the client project.

A good idea that has had much success is to form a small team within each discipline (or service area). Their task is to develop a proprietary client-service methodology: that is, to come up with value-enhancing action ideas that are appropriate to the specific discipline.

This methodology should include activities that will ensure that the way the firm deals with clients during a client assignment is demonstrably more valuable to the client than the competition's approach. In essence, the firm should be creating a differentiation in the marketplace: "We're different because of the way we *deal* with you."

This can be initiated through a detailed exploration of every stage of a client assignment, identifying *every* opportunity the firm has to enhance value in the client's experience. It should include, inter alia, methods for making written communications (including reports) more useful to the client, ways to involve the client more in the process, ways to make meetings more valuable to the client, and devices for keeping client informed.

In some firms where there is, more or less, a common pattern for many client assignments, the teams construct a flowchart of the unfolding of a client assignment, identifying each detailed step where the firm has the opportunity to influence the client's experience with the firm. They examine the flow-chart of client's experience in order to identify all "moments of truth." For each moment of truth, they try to figure out what should happen: what the methodology for handling this stage of an engagement should be.

Having identified each step, team members interview experienced firm personnel to get their best ideas on how to manage the client's experience (hot tips). They accumulate and disseminate the best practices of these top service providers, and integrate these client management practices into written operating methodologies.

The team also generates ideas by reviewing the client feedback forms for common client concerns, and may interview clients as well as leading discussions in their own departments.

The end product of the team's labors is often a workbook, containing both good ideas and a methodology for client service teams to plan their individual client assignments. Examples of the typical hot tips are shown in Table 8–1.

TRAINING

In many firms, there may be a need for training programs in client-contact skills. These should include training in classic client situations such as "How do you tell a client he is wrong?" and "What do you do if the client doesn't like your ideas?" Accumulated wisdom in the firm on these and other client contact situations should be built into training programs so the firm disseminates its best expertise quickly.

Training programs divide into knowledge transfer ("here are the elements of good service") and skill building ("we're going to give you practice at dealing with this client situation"). The former can be delivered as soon as the methodology described above is developed.

TABLE 8–1

Tactics to Enhance Client Value

Dictate and transcribe summary of all meetings and significant phone conversations and send copy to client same or next day.

Involve client in process through: brainstorming sessions; give client tasks to perform.

Give client options and let client choose.

Explain clearly and document what is going to happen; make sure process is understood in advance. If appropriate, develop printed booklet laying this out.

Make meetings more valuable:
   Establish specific agenda and goals prior to meeting
   Send info, reports in advance—save meeting time for discussion, not presentation
   Find out attendees in advance, research them
   Always establish next steps for both sides
   Call afterwards to confirm that goals were met

Make reports more valuable:

   Get client to instruct the firm on format, presentation

   Provide summary so client can use it internally, without modification

   Have all reports read by nonproject person prior to delivery to ensure readability, comprehension

   Provide all charts, tables, summaries on overheads for internal client use

   Write progress summaries in a fashion that client can use internally without modification

Help client use what is delivered:
   Assist client in dealing with others in client organization
   Empower client with reasoning steps
   Advise on tactics/politics of how results should be shared inside client organization

TABLE 8–1 (cont.)

Be accessible and available:

Home phone numbers

Anticipatory calling when we're going to be unavailable

Ensure that secretaries know where we are and when we'll be back

Ensure that secretaries know names of all clients; and names of all team members on the account

Work at getting clients comfortable with "junior" personnel, so they can be available when we're not

---

Skill-building programs will require the identification of classic client situations, the development of role-play scripts, and the design of materials. In some firms, these include a critique of current programs on "how to handle a meeting," "presentation skills," and the like (assuming the firm has these).

It should be stressed that training in face-to-face client skills is a key area: These tend to be taken for granted, but *can* be taught—it's not just a matter of "well, this is my personality and style and I can't change it." Skill-building topics included in some firms' programs include:

- Learning to persuade, not assert
- Helping clients understand what you're doing and saying and why
- Empowering clients with reasons, not just conclusions
- Running meetings in ways that add more value to clients
- Reporting to clients in ways they find more valuable
- Coaching clients to use what we deliver
- Facilitating client's ability to act on what we deliver

REWARDS

The final step in a full-service quality program is ensuring that those who excel in this area (as revealed by client satisfaction scores) are rewarded, and those who do not are penalized in some way. Without this step people quickly develop the attitude that: "This service quality stuff is all very well, but it's not what the firm really values."

It would clearly be a mistake to use the client satisfaction scores in the partner compensation scheme in the first year of keeping score—first everyone has to be given a chance to shape up, everyone has to get comfortable that the data is real and valid. However, this must happen sooner or later. It is inevitable that once scorekeeping has begun, the results will influence compensation—and so they should. Is there anything more "professional" to reward partners for than client satisfaction?

GETTING STARTED ON A FEEDBACK PROGRAM

For any firm without a client feedback program, the first step must be a controlled pilot program. This is necessary to test some of the claims made in this chapter, such as:

- Clients are very willing to participate in such a program, and, if asked, will complete a questionnaire.
- You find out things that trouble your clients that you didn't know about, and hence it's worth asking.
- Clients do care about most of the items on the questionnaire in Figure 8–1.
- They'll tell you which questions you should include, i.e., which aspects of client service they care about.

All these propositions (indeed most of this chapter) can be tested for your firm by doing a pilot study (perhaps of one subdiscipline).

Once you have decided to launch a service quality program, the next step is to invite comments and suggestions from partners on what the questions should be, how they should be phrased, and so on.

You should choose a date six months hence (or so) for the first questionnaires to go out, thereby giving everyone a fair chance to get ready and know in advance what they're going to be held accountable for. And right at the beginning, you should determine when the first partners' meeting will be held to review the first round of results and the first step of group aggregates.

OTHER USES FOR FEEDBACK QUESTIONNAIRES

Once the firm has established the principle of using client feedback questionnaires, it will soon be discovered that there is no need to wait for the end of the engagement to share the feedback form with the clients. Indeed there is great power in using it at the following times:

> Mid-engagement, to track "how well we're doing"
>
> At the beginning of the engagement, to find out which factors this client really cares about and wants the firm to focus on
>
> In proposals, to prove, through the existence of the system, that we are different from our competitors

CONCLUSION

For those who consider all of this to be a dramatic change and strenuous effort, I invite you to examine Figure 8–1 one more time, asking yourself the following questions:

a. When *you* are the client, do you care about these issues?

b. What is your experience in finding providers who excel at this behavior?

c. Do any of these questions represent an "unreasonable" client expectation—when you're the client?

d. How confident do you feel that your firm would outperform the competition on these questions?

e. How valuable would it be if your firm were to earn top scores on this stuff consistently?

f. Can you think of another way to ensure consistent execution of these things?

Yes, the diet is tough. But the health it produces will ensure a long and prosperous professional life.

CHAPTER 9

MARKETING TO EXISTING CLIENTS

Most professional firms say that their existing clients represent the most probable (and often the most profitable) source of new business. However, when one examines their behavior, one finds that while they have well-established and organized programs for "new client" business development, there is little, if any, organized effort to obtain new business from existing clients. Similarly, most firms' expenditures for business-getting (either out-of-pocket expenses or in allocation of people's time), are overwhelmingly spent trying to get new clients, with only a small fraction of the total devoted to winning new business from existing clients.

Simply put, firms say they believe one thing, but appear to be doing another. What's going on here?

WHY EXISTING CLIENTS ARE GOOD PROSPECTS

The best place to begin our exploration of this apparent paradox is to examine the reasons why existing clients are said to represent the "best" source of new business. The possible explanations are many.

First and foremost, it is most firms' experience that time spent marketing to existing clients is more likely to result in new business: *Existing clients represent higher-probability prospects.*

This is so because the ability to win the client's trust and confidence

97

is a dominant influence in the sales process of professional services. Often, this single criterion is the deciding factor in competitive situations. Accordingly, where the firm is already working for the client, it has a head start on the single most important purchasing influence, resulting in a higher probability of success. Other aspects of the sales process, such as discovering the real (often unstated) client concerns and needs are far easier to do in an existing client setting. A third factor which increases the probability of winning new business in existing client situations is the basic fact that such new-business opportunities are usually noncompetitive: If the firm uncovers a new need in the course of its current work, it can often win permission to proceed with the new work without going through a competitive proposal process.

A second attraction in targeting existing clients is that, in most situations, marketing costs to win a given volume of new business are lower. The firm does not have to spend as much (unbilled) time researching the client and its industry, since this will already have been done to win the existing account. There will be less need to conduct a wide variety of activities that are a major part of the new prospect sales process: awareness building, qualifying activities, comfort building or investigatory interviews, competitive proposals and presentations, and so on.

A third advantage in targeting existing clients is that "follow-on" engagements from *existing clients* often are more profitable than first-time engagements from *new* clients. There is less risk of "write-offs" of time spent getting up to speed on the client or the client's industry. There is less risk of false starts or misspecification of the project dimensions, which also lead to written-off time. Being noncompetitive, the existing client situation usually implies less pressure on fees, and a greater ability to charge full rates: The client has already been exposed to the firm and its ability to deliver value for money. In new-client situations, where the firm and its capabilities are unknown, prospects will always be more skeptical and fee-sensitive.

A final factor contributing to greater potential profitability with existing clients is that there is a higher probability that the firm can work with them, over time, to integrate more juniors into the delivery of services to the client, by building up the client's acceptance of, and comfort with, the juniors. In contrast, a new client may not be fully comfortable with this new provider, and will often insist on extensive senior-professional involvement. Thus new client opportunities may be less leveraged than is possible with existing clients, and the higher profitability that comes with greater leverage is more difficult to achieve.

A fourth reason to give priority to existing clients is that if firms are to grow their capabilities, and strengthen their position in the marketplace, then they must conscientiously pay attention to the types of work they bring in. They must seek new types of work that give the firm the opportunity to stretch and build its skills. By very definition, the firm does not have an established track record of performing this work, and it is work that is hard to market to a new prospect. However, once existing clients have developed an appropriate level of trust and confidence in their providers, they are more likely to "give them the chance" to work on more challenging matters. It is in the existing client base that firms are most likely to find the opportunity to conduct the type of work that not only contributes to this year's bottom line, but adds to its capability to earn more (and higher) fees in the future: to make a contribution to the firm's intellectual capital, and not just exploit its existing capabilities.

THE IMPORTANCE OF WINNING NEW CLIENTS

If existing clients offer such attractions, why is that so many professional firms devote the vast bulk of their nonbillable marketing time (and budget) to the pursuit of new clients?

Part of the answer, of course, is that a steady flow of new clients is important to any professional firm. New clients are needed to "reseed the gene pool," by providing new environments for the professionals to work in, and thus build skills. New clients provide a "freshness," a "reinvigoration" that can be motivating to professionals who might have become overly familiar with existing client situations. There exists somewhat of a link between the volume and variety of new clients, and the motivation, morale, dynamism, and enthusiasm of the professional staff.

If firms are active in nurturing existing client relations, existing clients can and do become "saturated," creating the need for new clients. Even before this state is achieved some firms are more comfortable pursuing new clients for fear that if they target existing clients too vigorously, they may be perceived by existing clients as too "leechlike," putting the firm's need for additional revenues ahead of the client's interests.

Many firms give great priority to getting new clients on the grounds that new clients are worth more to the firm than the value of the initial engagement, because they offer the potential for additional future revenues. This simple insight leads to an important conclusion about the relationship between new client marketing efforts and marketing to existing clients. The weaker (or more neglectful) a firm is at developing new business from existing client relationships, the lower the value (and hence the "return on marketing investment") of getting new clients. The better the firm is at marketing to existing clients, the higher will be the value of its new client marketing activities.

The issue then is not whether firms should pursue one or the other, but rather, what the appropriate balance should be in expending the marketing effort and budget. As noted above, my research suggests that the balance today is excessively tilted toward new clients and away from organized attention to generating new business from existing clients. We must now try to understand why this is so.

WHY IS THERE A RELATIVE NEGLECT OF EXISTING CLIENTS?

I have learned from numerous conversations on this topic with consultants, lawyers, accountants, actuaries, and other professionals that primary among all the reasons for the relative overemphasis on new clients is the simple fact that pursuing and getting a new client is more fun. New clients provide the "thrill of the chase" in a way that nurturing existing relationships does not. Pursuing a new client proposal opportunity usually has the characteristics of a well-defined, finite project with relatively clear tasks and specific deadlines. Nurturing an existing relationship often has few inherent deadlines, little obvious structure, and more ambiguous tasks. Consequently, it is reported to me, it is a less "satisfying" activity: It doesn't provide the same "rush of adrenaline."

If this is indeed a basic human proclivity ("We always give more love and attention to those we're trying to seduce than those we're married to"), then it is unfortunate that firm management practices reinforce rather than try to counteract this natural bias. In most firms, I have learned, there is a tendency to overreward the bringing in of new clients, and underreward bringing in new business from existing clients. As one consultant expressed it to me, "When a new client is brought in, rockets go off, bells sound, your name gets in the firm newsletter and you can bank on a good bonus. If you bring in an equivalent amount of business from existing clients, the management yawns and says 'at last he's doing his job' ."

In similar spirit, obtaining new business from existing clients is often taken for granted: "If we do good work, they'll give us the new business, so we don't need to spend nonbillable time on it." A related attitude is: "If it's an existing client, everything we do is, or should be, billable. Our marketing takes place on billable time." As might be expected, this posture frequently leads to the result that good marketing activities don't get done.

Accounting practices at some firms compound this problem. If all time spent on existing clients must be accounted for, then things done in the name of pursuing more business from existing clients often show up in the accounts as extra costs (and hence lower profitability) on the existing engagement. As a consequence, the desirable marketing activities are not done.

There is something strange in such environments. In the pursuit of a new prospect, often in competition with other firms, firms appear willing to spend hundreds of nonbillable hours pursuing opportunities that have lower probability, happily "giving away" time to bring in new revenue. But they don't or won't invest an equivalent (or smaller) amount of nonbillable time to bring in an equivalent volume of new business from existing clients. Existing clients are charged for what is readily given away to prospects.

Further explaining why firms tend to overallocate time to new prospects, and underinvest in existing client marketing, is the fact that the types of marketing activities necessary to get the two types of new business are fundamentally different. As we shall see below, the pursuit of new business from existing clients requires an "intimate" involvement with the client and his or her business: It requires getting "close" to the client, and developing a high level of interpersonal trust. By contrast, the activities that make up a campaign to pursue new prospects are less "high-touch," less intimate, more detached: Doing research on the prospect (rather than dealing with him or her), writing proposals, giving seminars, making structured presentations. For better or for worse, I have learned that many professionals are more comfortable pursuing new clients.

Another key explanation, I have found, is that at many firms, marketing is reactive—that is, responding to an external impetus such as an RFP (request for proposal). Accordingly, available marketing time is quickly filled with activities initiated by these external stimuli. Since existing client opportunities must be actively sought out, and brought to the surface often before the client is aware of the need, a reactive posture inevitably results in underexploitation of existing client opportunities.

HOW TO MAKE IT HAPPEN

It is clear that there are strong forces biasing individuals and firms away from the targeting of existing clients. Many, if not most, professional firms could benefit substantially from a studious look at how they are allocating their nonbillable marketing time between new and existing clients, and deciding whether they could benefit from an explicit program of targeting existing clients more than they do at present. It is equally clear that if such a program is to be implemented, firm management must take some concrete steps to make it happen. Fortunately, once a firm has resolved to go in this direction, the management process necessary to make it happen is relatively easy to describe and to implement.

The process begins with the identification of the key client prospects in the existing client base. As with all aspects of marketing, the fundamental rule is to focus and target one's efforts on the best opportunities. Accordingly, it is not wise to launch a program of marketing to all existing clients, but only to those carefully selected prospects where the firm concludes that (a) there are additional client needs that the firm can serve, and (b) the relationship is good enough to raise the probability that a marketing effort will pay off.

This review should be conducted by the head of the firm (or office) with the senior professional responsible for each client relationship. From this review process should come a ranking and/or prioritization of the best opportunities.

Next, it is necessary to establish a budget for each target account, including both out-of-pocket expenses and, more importantly, the allocated amount of time that should be spent on this opportunity, given the likelihood of generating this business and, of course, its attractiveness.

This budgeting should be done on an equivalency principle: First, figure out how much non-billable marketing time the firm spends to obtain a given volume of revenue. For example, the firm may discover that, on average, 100 person hours are spent to obtain a $200,000 engagement. If there are prospects of obtaining a $200,000 engagement from an existing client, then the firm should be prepared to establish a marketing budget for the existing client that approximates this amount, usually being a little less because marketing to existing clients should be more cost effective. As an illustration, the firm might conclude that the situation warrants fifty to seventy hours in nonbillable marketing time for the designated existing client.

Because of the accounting problem described above (confusion between chargeable activities for the current engagement and nonchargeable time to get the next engagement), it is wise to establish this "Marketing to Client X" budget as a separate, formal "charge number" in the firm's accounts. Now there is a budget and the firm should assign responsibility for that budget to the senior professional on the engagement. That individual is now responsible for two budgets—running the current engagement for quality and profitability and using the marketing allocation to maximum effectiveness.

An advantage of this approach is that it provides a vehicle for each member of the client service team to get involved with the business development effort. Junior members of the team can (subject to the approval of the team leader) charge time to the marketing budget when they engage in activities directly targeted at "developing the account." Without such accounts, it is often difficult to get junior staff members, subject to personal billability targets, to engage in these "nonbillable" tasks. Since there is only a finite, predesignated amount in the marketing budget, there is little chance that excessive, unproductive nonbillable activities will result.

The potential role of junior members of the engagement team in the marketing effort needs to be stressed. They often have more frequent and direct client contact (especially in the research and interview stages of the project) than more senior professionals and are in a better position to pick up the signals and clues that the client organization has additional needs. One major consulting firm makes it a regular practice to hold meetings of the client service team every two weeks, not to discuss the current engagement, but to ask each team member, from the most junior to the most senior, "What have you learned about what is going on in the client organization since last we met two weeks ago?" Naturally, this practice forces each team member to keep his or her eyes and ears open and to operate continuously with two agendas: performing the current engagement and finding the next.

Once the budget has been agreed upon, firm management should require of those senior professionals who are responsible for the "target accounts" that they formally develop a written marketing plan for obtaining the target client's additional business. As with all marketing, a written, specific plan (with target dates) provides the structure and discipline to ensure that the desired activities are actually carried out. Once the plan has been developed by the account team it should be reviewed and approved by the head of the firm (or office), and become a concrete commitment against which subsequent activity can be reviewed and appraised. While this may sound excessively bureaucratic, I have learned that only in this way can the firm ensure that execution follows. As we have noted above, there is an inherent bias against this sort of activity, and the (hopefully) continued arrival of RFPs will continually work to distract senior professionals from execution of the existing client marketing plans.

DESIGNING THE CLIENT-SPECIFIC MARKETING CAMPAIGN

If a client service team has (as a rough approximation) fifty to seventy-five hours to spend trying to get more business from an organization via an executive with whom they already work and have access to, what should they do with this time to maximize the chances that additional revenues will be obtained?

Successful marketing to existing clients, I have learned, has three basic stages, none of which may be omitted. They are: (a) making the client predisposed to use the firm again; (b) increasing the firm's capabilities to serve the client; and (c) finding and pursuing the next engagement.

MAKING THE CLIENT PREDISPOSED TO USE THE FIRM AGAIN

The first element, making the client disposed to use the firm again, is probably the most critical stage of the process. If the firm is to win new business from an existing client, then that client must not only be "satisfied" with the firm's services, but "superpleased." The pursuit of new business thus requires that time and energy be expended on the current engagement, in order to lay the groundwork for the subsequent "selling" effort.

The activities involved here are those that most professionals would acknowledge as good client relations on any engagement, but which most professionals would also acknowledge are often neglected or not fully performed. They include going the extra mile on the current engagement, increasing the amount of client contact, building both the business and the personal relationship. Some specific tactics for this stage are shown in Table 9–1. None of these tactics are new: What may be new is providing the budget, the incentive, and the specific plan to ensure that these activities actually take place. There is a profound difference between acknowledging the wisdom of the tactics listed in Table 9–1, and having an organized plan of action to ensure their execution.

One or two of the activities listed in Table 9–1 deserve some elaboration. "Volunteering to attend client's internal meetings" is a particularly powerful tactic. As an illustration, suppose that a client service team learns that its client is holding a national meeting of, say, all of its branch managers, on a topic that is not covered by the team's current engagement. The team leader could approach the client and say "Would you like me (or one of my partners) to attend the meeting, free of charge, to be a resource to you?" Many, if not most, clients would accept such an offer, and the firm is then in the position to accomplish two important marketing tasks: first, attend a client meeting where the client's problems, issues and needs are being discussed, and second, have the opportunity to demonstrate expertise and be helpful on a new issue. In terms of getting new business, there is perhaps no other tactic that has as great a return on time invested.

The list of tactics in Table 9–1 include building both the business relationship and the personal relationship. There is no better way to build a relationship than to find some way to be helpful or useful to the other person. To get a favor (the next engagement) one must first give a favor (do something for the client, free of charge, that demonstrates both caring and a commitment). It should be stressed that, in terms of impact, building the business relationship takes precedence over the personal relationship. Making a friend of the client is helpful,

TABLE 9–1

Making the Client Disposed to Use the Firm Again

1. Going the extra mile on the current engagement
   Use new business budget to fund extra analysis
   Use budget to improve turnaround time, service
   Improve quality of presentation
   More documentation, explanations, accessibility

2. Increasing the amount of client contact
   Telephone regularly
   Visit at every opportunity
   Schedule business mettings near mealtime
   Invite to firm offices
   Introduce one's partners
   Get firm leaders involved

3. Building the business relationship
   Help client with contacts
   Put on special seminars for client's staff
   Volunteer to attend client's internal meetings
   Offer free day of counseling on nonproject matters
   Send client useful articles
   If possible, refer business to client

4. Building the personal relationship
   Social activities
   Remember personal, family anniversaries
   Obtain scarce tickets
   Provide home telephone number
   Offer use of firm's facilities

but only as a supplement to, not a substitute for, a strong business relationship.

INCREASING THE FIRM'S CAPABILITIES

The second stage of marketing to existing clients is the investment of time in increasing the firm's capabilities to serve the client. The goal here is to do those things that persuade the client that the firm's knowledge and talent not only can be but are customized to the specific client situation. As in all marketing, new business from existing clients must be earned, by being seen to work for it. As Table 9–2 suggests, some of the nonbillable marketing budget should be dedicated to encouraging and performing the familiar tasks of increasing the firm's knowledge of the client's industry, business, organization, and the client himself or herself.

These activities are not just symbolic ways of pleasing the client and demonstrating interest. If done thoroughly and well, in a planned, systematic fashion (i.e., as part of a structured marketing plan), they

TABLE 9–2

Increasing the Firm's Capabilities to Serve this Client

---

1. Increasing knowledge of client's industry
   Study industry magazine/newsletters thoroughly
   Attend industry meetings with *client*
   Conduct proprietary studies

2. Increasing knowledge of client's business
   Read all client's brochures, annual reports, other public documents
   Ask to see strategic plan
   Volunteer to critique internal studies
   Conduct reverse seminar

3. Increasing knowledge of client's organization
   Ask for organization chart
   Ask who client deals with most
   Ask about the client's boss
   Ask about power structure
   Arrange to meet other executives
   Spend time with client's juniors

4. Increasing knowledge of client
   Find out precisely how client is evaluated inside his or her company
   Find out what he or she is unhappy with

---

will serve to uncover new client needs, reveal areas where the client is dissatisfied with the current state of affairs (a critical condition for him or her to commit to a new project), and also provide the documentation and evidence to persuade the client to proceed in new areas. In essence, the firm is "preparing the proposal" as it simultaneously improves its capability to be of value to the client.

FINDING AND PURSUING THE NEXT ENGAGEMENT

The third and final category for which the nonbillable marketing budget can be used is the explicit process of selling the client on the new project. As should be clear, this task has not been neglected in the first two stages, which have included the traditional sales tasks of building trust and confidence, discovering client needs, and demonstrating specialized capabilities. If done well, the third stage often requires little time.

If they have not already been done, activities in this stage involve creating opportunities to demonstrate initiative and competence (rather than waiting for them to arise). It requires a planned program of digging out intelligence on new needs, assembling this evidence, and crafting opportunities to make the client aware of the new need. Table 9–3 lists some of the tactics that may be employed.

CONCLUSION

It should be clear that few existing client opportunities would warrant the application of all of the tactics described in Tables 9–1 through 9–3. Rather, the tables should be seen as "menus" from which the best selected set of tactics can be chosen which (a) fit what has been deemed to be the appropriate level of effort in each specific case (i.e., what the budget is); and (b) are most likely to be effective in the specific client situation. In all cases, however, some time must be spent on each of the stages. As a matter of effectiveness, one cannot skip stages one and two entirely and hope to be productive with marketing efforts solely from category three.

What should also be clear is that the time spent designing and executing a targeted marketing campaign for a specific client along the lines described above would indeed be more likely to result in new work than the same amount of time spent trying to generate new leads and convert those leads into new clients. As we have seen, both need

TABLE 9–3

Finding and Pursuing the Next Engagement

---

1. Creating opportunities to demonstrate initiative and competence
   Volunteer services of one's partners
   Arrange meetings with one's partners

2. Digging out new intelligence on new needs
   Use entire projects team to gather info.
   Get invited to their meetings
   Arrange to meet other executives
   Spend time with client staff at all levels

3. Assembling evidence of new need
   Conduct additional analysis
   If possible, conduct additional interviews
   Conduct special studies

4. Creating awareness of new need
   Bring problem areas to client's attention early
   (Find ways to worry client)
   Document evidence of problems
   Compare client company's statistics to others
   Share results of work done for other clients

5. Finding sponsor/friend/coach in client organization
   Figure out who wants change

6. Asking for the new engagement *at the right time*
   "Point out" opportunities early and often, with no "hard sell"
   Concrete proposal only when confident it will be accepted

---

to be done, but firms should not forego the ripe opportunities available in the existing client base.

A final, mandatory step in capturing these opportunities is to modify the reward systems of the firm so that each line professional perceives that time spent on this activity is valued by the firm at least as much as pursuing new clients. Rewards mean not just financial compensation, but celebration, status, strokes, and hoopla. If firms wish to capitalize on the new business opportunities available to them in their existing client base, they must ensure that their management practices and behavior actively encourage and reward this activity. As we have noted, there is no, or little, argument in professional circles about the desirability of the activities described above. There is, however, significant room for firms to move in creating the environment in which these activities will actually take place. If professional firms' management want the substantial benefits that flow from developing existing client relationships, they can have them. But they won't occur automatically: They must be explicitly managed.

CHAPTER 10

HOW CLIENTS CHOOSE

The single most important talent in selling professional services is the ability to understand the purchasing process (not the sales process) from the clients' perspective. The better a professional can learn to think like a client, the easier it will be to do and say the correct things to get hired.

Fortunately, this is not difficult. Most professionals have themselves been through the process of retaining other professionals: lawyers retain accountants, actuaries hire consultants, and public relations counselors, like the rest of us, need tax advice. All professionals can deepen their understanding of what's really going on in the purchase process by drawing upon their own experiences as a client.

Professionals traditionally view their practice development task as divided into two stages, marketing (generating the lead) and selling (converting a lead into a sale). From the buyer's perspective, these two stages are experienced as qualification and selection.

First, I, the client, try to reduce the large number of possible firms and professionals that might be considered down to the set of those I judge to be qualified. In this qualification stage, I consider such facts as "Who have you worked for?" "What are your capabilities?" "What depth of personnel do you have?" "How good are your references?"

Except in the most unusual of situations, where the problem is so

111

complex and high risk that there is only one viable candidate, even the most thorough due diligence (examination of available facts, references, interviewing of candidates, etc.) usually ends with more than one firm or individual that is technically qualified to handle my problem. Most typically, after exhausting my abilities as a client to make technical distinctions, I am still left with a choice of reputable firms with good references, all eminently capable of solving my problem.

This leads to an important conclusion: Unless their skills are truly unique, unmatched by any competitor, professionals are never hired because of their technical capabilities. Excellent capabilities are essential to get you into the final set to be considered, but it is other things that get you hired.

Once I have decided which firms I will consider in the final set, my focus of enquiry shifts significantly. I am no longer asking "Can you do it?" but rather "Do I want to work with you?" I am no longer interested in the institutional characteristics of your firm, but am now trying to form a judgment about you. By the fact that you are sitting here talking to me, you can assume that you have successfully marketed your firm: now the time has come to sell yourself.

WHAT IT FEELS LIKE TO BE A BUYER

Buying professional services is rarely a comfortable experience. Table 10–1 lists some of the unpleasant emotions that are frequently felt.

For one thing, I feel that I'm taking a *personal risk*. By hiring anyone, I am putting my affairs, or my company's affairs, in the hands of someone else and have to give up some degree of control. This is my area of responsibility, and even though intellectually I may know I need outside expertise, emotionally it is not comfortable to put my affairs in the hands of others. Even if the matter is relatively routine, I will need convincing (beyond protestations of good intentions) that my problems will receive prompt and serious attention.

I'm feeling *insecure*. Since I find it hard to detect which of you is the genius, and who is just good, I'm going to have to commit myself without feeling totally confident about my decision. What is more, I don't yet know if I've got a simple problem or a complex one; that's why I need you, the specialist, to help me. But, I'm not sure I can trust you to be honest about that: It's in your interest to convince me it's

TABLE 10–1

What It Feels Like to Be a Buyer

---

1. I'm feeling *insecure*. I'm not sure I know how to detect which of the finalists is the genius, and which is just good. I've exhausted my abilities to make technical distinction.

2. I'm feeling *threatened*. This is my area of responsibility, and even though intellectually I know I need outside expertise, emotionally it's not comfortable to put my affairs in the hands of others.

3. I'm taking a *personal risk*. By putting my affairs in the hands of someone else, I risk losing control.

4. I'm *impatient*. I didn't call in someone at the first sign of symptoms (or opportunity). I've been thinking about this for a while.

5. I'm *worried*. By the very fact of suggesting improvements or changes, these people are going to be implying that I haven't been doing it right up till now. Are these people going to be on my side?

6. I'm *exposed*. Whoever I hire, I'm going to have to reveal some proprietary secrets, not all of which are flattering. I will have to undress.

7. I'm feeling *ignorant*, and don't like the feeling. I don't know if I've got a simple problem or a complex one. I'm not sure I can trust them to be honest about that: it's in their interest to convince me it's complex.

8. I'm *skeptical*. I've been burned before by these kinds of people. You get a lot of promises: How do I know whose promise I should buy?

9. I'm *concerned* that they either can't or won't take the time to understand what makes my situation special. They'll try to sell me what they've got rather than what I need.

10. I'm *suspicious*. Will they be those typical professionals who are hard to get hold of, who are patronizing, who leave you out of the loop, who befuddle you with jargon, who don't explain what they're doing or why, who . . . , who . . . , who . . . ? In short, will these people deal with me in the way I want to be dealt with?

---

complex. You professionals are always making mountains out of molehills. Nothing is ever easy.

I'm *skeptical*. I've been burned before by these kinds of people. I get a lot of promises: How do I know whose promise I should buy? I'm *concerned* that you either can't or won't take the time to understand what makes my situation special. Will you be one of those typical professionals who are hard to get hold of, who are patronizing, who leave you out of the loop, who befuddle you with jargon, who don't explain what they're doing or why, who . . . In short, will you deal with me in the way I want to be dealt with?

To a degree, I am also *exposed*. Whoever I hire, I'm going to have to reveal some proprietary secrets, not all of which are flattering. I'm also a little *threatened*. You will be working on things for which I am responsible (marketing consultants are hired by the VP of marketing, lawyers by the general counsel, actuaries by the benefits manager). By the very fact of suggesting improvements or changes, there is the risk that you will uncover things that I haven't been doing right up till now. Are you going to be my ally or my enemy?

What all this reveals is that, among the set of qualified candidates, I am looking for the one I can *trust*. The act of hiring a professional is, by very definition, an *act of faith*. I must, inevitably, believe a promise. In selecting a professional, I am not just buying a service, I am entering into a relationship. Your selling task is to earn my trust and confidence—with an emphasis on the word "earn."

WHAT A BUYER LOOKS FOR

How am I to determine with which candidate I want to have a relationship? Certainly the answer is not contained in the promises you make. Talk is cheap. Someone who told me "Trust me, we'll show a special interest in you," is not likely to win my confidence simply by that assertion.

Inevitably, even if I view myself as a sophisticated buyer, I am forced to rely on *clues* obtained through the interview process in order to guess at what kind of person you are. My impressions and perceptions are created by small actions that are meaningful for their symbolism, for what they reveal. How you behave during the interview (or proposal process) will be taken as a proxy for how you will deal with me after I retain you. Unlike the process of qualification, which is predominantly rational, logical, and based on facts, the selection stage is mostly intuitive, personal, and based on impressions.

The first thing that will catch my attention is your preparation. There is little so off-putting as someone who begins the meeting by asking me some basic facts about my company or situation that she could have found out in advance. It not only reveals laziness, but makes me feel like one more "cold call." You don't have a special interest in me, you're on a fishing expedition, trying to drum up some revenues. On the other hand, someone who can say "I noticed from your annual report that you recently opened a new plant. What has that meant for your department?" has caught my attention. It may not have been intellectually challenging to read my annual report, but it shows that you do your homework. It tells me something about you.

The point can be taken further, for preparation is your opportunity to demonstrate initiative. Why not contact my industry association and get some comparison of my company's public data compared to that of my competitors? It will help you ask me more substantive questions, and will demonstrate your willingness to *earn* my business. If you want to bring along some printed material, I will be a lot less impressed by your preprinted brochure than something that has clearly been put together for me. At least that shows a little thought and consideration.

Professionals who are overeager to impress, and thereby spend the whole meeting talking about their accomplishments, what their firm has done, and why they are qualified to help me come across as insensitive to me, my company, and my situation. It sounds like what it is: a standard spiel, reflecting no special interest in me. I do not want to hear about you and your firm, I want to talk about me and my situation. The only way to influence me is to find out what I want, and show me how to get it. I hate to be sold, but I may be willing to buy, if you can show me that I and my company have some problems to solve or some opportunities to capture.

Getting me to acknowledge that there is an opportunity or a problem won't necessarily be easy, because I'm suspicious of your motives. First you must make me feel comfortable. Perhaps ask me what's going well. Give me some *new* information. Tell me what my competitors are up to. Tell me what you've been doing for other companies like mine. Find a way to be helpful to me. You've got to give a favor to get a favor—

there's no better way to win my trust than to be helpful to me right from the beginning. Someone who brings me new ideas and suggestions, without pressuring me, comes across as someone who is really trying to help, and isn't here just to ratchet up their own billable hours. If I'm your prospect, treat me as if I were already a client.

Give me an education. Tell me about alternate ways the common problems of my industry might be dealt with. Help me understand the advantages and disadvantages of some of the things I have been reading about. Ask me how I am doing things now, and use that as an opportunity to help me understand some options I may have for doing things differently. Tell me something I didn't know. If I walk away from the meeting saying "That was interesting, I hadn't thought of that," you've won. I may or may not hire you today, but I'll certainly want to talk to you again. Don't be afraid to float high-risk ideas early ("just an idea"). Demonstrate your creativity.

I discount all your *assertions* about your expertise until you give me some evidence to back them up. For example, don't tell me about your experience in my industry (or on a particular topic). Rather, illustrate it by asking questions that reveal your knowledge of key industry terminology, facts and figures, or latest events. That way, I'll draw my own conclusions (which I'm going to do anyway) about how well you understand my business and my issues.

While I want you to know my industry, don't patronize me by trying to tell me what's going on in my business. Instead of saying "Here's the three most important things happening in your industry," say "Our experience suggests that these are the three most important things. Do you agree?" If I agree with you, fine. If I disagree, we can have a conversation. To avoid coming across as arrogant, patronizing, and pompous (common experiences with you professionals), turn your assertions into questions. By doing so, you convert possible signs of assertiveness into evidence that you'll respect my opinions, involve me in the thinking process, and be sensitive to the need for a congenial relationship. Your manner of speech, how you choose to phrase your sentences, tells me something about how you deal with clients. Make our meeting a conversation. Don't talk all the time, and similarly don't grill me.

Show a sympathetic understanding of my role in my company. Understand who I report to, how I'm measured, what my budgets are. By asking me about these things, I'll believe you are treating me as a person, not just a purchasing agent. This doesn't mean I want you to wine and dine me or try to win my business by becoming my friend. It does mean that I want you to be sensitive to the fact that your prospective client (me) is a person, not a corporate entity.

Don't start telling me how you can solve my problems until I have acknowledged that there's a problem or an opportunity here. Simply asserting to me that I have problems or opportunities isn't enough. If you say it, I can and will doubt you. If I say it, it's true. The key talent in good selling is being good at getting me, the client, to reveal my problems, needs, wants, and concerns. If I'm talking, telling you about my company and my needs, you're ahead: if you're talking you're losing. Professionals talk too much. Ask good questions and listen.

As you try to get me talking about my problems, demonstrate your sensitivity. I do not respond well to someone who asks me right up front "What are your problems?" That's too assertive and you haven't yet earned the right to an answer. Similarly, don't ask "What's not going well?" I'm not going to answer that. But I might answer "What don't you have time for?" I can answer that without feeling uncomfortable.

While I am unlikely to tell you my problems, I may be willing to acknowledge problems you already know about. For example, ask me why we do things the way we do, why we haven't tried certain options. Instead of asking "What problems do you have with that way of doing things?" say "Some of our other clients who do things the way you do have had to contend with the following issues as a result. What have you done to deal with those consequences?" That question gives you an opportunity to show you are familiar with my type of situation, and it doesn't confront or challenge me.

If I do begin to show interest in a given issue, your next task is to convince me (or get me to convince myself) that the issue is big enough to bother with. Remember, I don't *like* working with professionals, and only do so when I have to. So I'll only proceed if I'm convinced the benefit is big enough and certain enough (two separate issues) to justify the expense, discomfort and disruption of using you. Before I want to hear how you'll solve my problem, you need to get me to agree that it's worth solving.

Your most productive tactic here is to ask me "How valuable would it be if . . . ?" and complete that sentence by describing some future state of affairs that you can get me to. Help me picture in my mind the benefits I will receive by reaching that state of affairs. If you get me excited about the possible benefits (not by asserting them, but by getting me to admit that they would be desirable), I will then want to know more about how you can get me there. If I don't acknowledge the benefit, nothing else you say will be of any interest to me.

If I'm still with you, interested in (maybe) proceeding, I may ask you how you would go about handling my affairs. Don't rush to give me a singular, concrete answer as to "your firm's approach." It may be one I'm not interested in. For example, maybe I want the "permanent fix"—that version of the assignment that deals with the issue once and for all. Or perhaps I might want the "quick fix"—that version that shows results as soon as possible. Perhaps I will be more interested in proceeding so as to incur the minimum disruption to my ongoing operations, or concerned about the extent of involvement and effort required by me and my people.

The key here is to give me options, help me understand their advantages and disadvantages, and let me choose. If you tell me "your firm's approach," it strikes me as standardized. By educating me as to alternate ways to proceed, I get value from the education. By letting me choose, I am also left with the sense that you're the type of professional who will respect my judgment and involve me.

Recognize that it's unlikely that I'm going to say "yes" or "no" in front of you. I'm going to consult before I make a decision. So don't pressure me. Don't try any "closing techniques" on me. Give me reasons and reasoning I can use when I consult with my superiors and colleagues. Instead of reaching for a sale every meeting, make your objective one of making progress in our relationship. Maybe I'll agree to meet one of your specialist partners, or consent to provide additional information to you, or provide access to one of my other executives. Perhaps I'll participate in one of your seminars or agree to an additional, more focused meeting. Any one of these should be taken as a success. If you try to rush me, I'll take it as a sign that you are more interested in making a sale than in helping me.

I may ask you to submit a proposal, but never forget that since my ultimate decision is based on who I trust, the sale will be made in the face-to face time we spend together. The vast majority of professional projects are awarded at the preproposal stage: the formal proposal and/or presentation merely confirm (or destroy) a decision already made. If you can't afford to spend time, in contact, up-front, don't bother writing the proposal.

Here's what I want if I ask you to make a presentation. Sit down, distribute your materials in advance, and let's go through them together. Don't lower the lights, put up your slides, stand up, and walk me through your canned speech. It makes me feel I am being lectured to. If I want to ask about something, don't say "we'll get to that." It makes me feel that you're inflexible.

If I interrupt you, deal with my question. I want to see how you handle yourself when I ask a question, not judge how practiced you are at your standard spiel. Most of you rehearse your presentations, but rehearse the wrong things. I'm not looking for how smoothly you can get through your practiced presentation. That's not what influences my decision. Rather, I give great weight to how flustered you get when I ask hard questions. Flunk that test, and I'm not sure you're the one I want to trust. What you should be rehearsing are your responses to my questions.

I want you to prove that you can listen, by picking up on my comments, adapting, in real time, what you say to what I've just said. Involve me. Ask what I think. I know someone's listening to me when they show the ability to depart from their prepared scripts and base their subsequent comments on what I've just said. If you don't have the talent to depart from your script when I throw a curve ball (and I'm going to), then why should I believe in your abilities?

When I challenge you with an objection, hear it out, don't interrupt. Don't tell me I shouldn't be concerned about that: I've just told you I am concerned. Acknowledge what I said as a valid concern. I'll let you rephrase and soften it, but make sure you check for my acceptance of your rephrasing. Then give me an answer, and ask me whether I accept your answer. Don't try to "survive the moment" by waffling and moving on. You may get out of an uncomfortable moment, but I'm going to be left with the feeling that you didn't answer my question—and that means I don't trust you. I'll be impressed if you've clearly anticipated me and thought of that objection or concern before—it shows me that you've taken the time to see things from my perspective. So predict my objections and practice your responses as part of your preparation—on such things are sales won or lost.

CONCLUSION

There is an old saying about doctors that they "get fascinated with the disease, but are not interested in the patient." Unfortunately, this attitude (and behavior) is all too prevalent in a wide array of professions. Too many professionals get overly focused on technical matters, and lose sight of the essential relationship nature of professional transactions. This doesn't mean that technical skill is irrelevant—of course, it is critical. But having technical skills is only a *necessary* condition for success, not a sufficient one. Above all else, what I, the client, am looking for, is that rare professional who has both technical skill and a *sincere desire to be helpful*, to work with both me and my problem. The key is empathy—the ability to enter my world and see it through my eyes.

CHAPTER 11

ATTRACTING NEW CLIENTS

The list of possible marketing tactics that a firm can use to attract new clients is an old, familiar one. (See Table 11–1.) It is also a long list, but one to which solid priorities can be assigned. Some simple principles can guide the choice of marketing tactics. The first, and most important, is the "Raspberry Jam Rule"—the wider you spread it, the thinner it gets. The broader the audience you attempt to reach, the weaker is the impact. (The rule was originated by Gerald Weinberg in his book, *The Secrets of Consulting*.[1]) Rather than paying a little attention to a lot of prospects, it is always better to give more attention to a smaller, well-selected audience.

Second, marketing works when it demonstrates, not when it asserts. Marketing tactics that illustrate one's competence (such as speeches, seminars, and articles) are infinitely more powerful than those which assert it (such as brochures, direct mail, and "cold calls" to "let me tell you more about our firm.")

Third, "in person" marketing tactics should be given preference over attempts to communicate with the written word (with one important exception, discussed below).

The main goal of all marketing tactics should be to get away as soon as possible from "broadcasting a general message to a wide audience" and move to a highly individualized face-to-face dialogue be-

TABLE 11–1

Marketing Tactics in Descending Order of Effectiveness

The first team

Seminars (small-scale)
Speeches at client industry meetings
Articles in client-oriented (trade) press
Proprietary research

The Second String

Community/civic activities
Networking with potential referral sources
Newsletters

Clutching at straws tactics

Publicity
Brochures
Seminars (ballroom scale)
Direct mail
Cold calls
Sponsorship of cultural/sports events
Advertising
Video brochures

---

tween prospect and partner. Since the essence of getting hired is getting a specific individual client to talk about his or her problems, the sooner you can commence the dialogue, the better the tactic. Professional services are not a "mass" business—clients are acquired one at a time, and any marketing program must reflect this.

Finally, marketing must be a seduction, not an assault. It must not scream "hire me!" but must gently suggest "Here is some concrete evidence as to why you may want to get to know me better." Marketing is truly about *attracting* clients—doing something that causes *them* to want to take the next step (such as telling you about their problems). Since all clients are skeptical, they need to be given a good reason to expose their problems to you, and need to do so without feeling that, by responding, they are committing themselves to go all the way.

THE FIRST TEAM

The marketing tactics that best meet these tests are small-scale seminars, speeches, articles, and proprietary research. What all four have in common is that they all involve *giving* something to the prospective clients—new facts, new knowledge, new ideas. They pass the test of trying to capture the market's attention by "demonstrating" the firm's usefulness, not just asserting it.

SMALL-SCALE SEMINARS

Seminars top the list of effective tactics, but only if done correctly. Some key guidelines must be followed. Since the goal of marketing is to try to launch individualized dialogues, a seminar must never be more than twenty-five prospective clients. (If you want to reach two hundred people, do it eight times!) To maintain the personalized intimacy, the ratio of prospects to firm members in attendance must never be more than five to one.

As soon as you know which prospects are going to attend, you should instruct your research staff (marketing directors, librarians, junior professionals, etc.) to conduct the most thorough research job possible on each company attending. Don't be hesitant in investing money here. The goal should be to get all there is to know on each company (and possibly even the person attending) that is knowable from the public domain. For example, use computer data bases, call their industry association, get their 10-Ks, call the Wall Street analysts that cover their industry, call their public affairs department to get their product brochures. In short, if it's available, get it! Since partners will be too busy to read large volumes of paper, the research staff should be instructed to prepare an eight-page briefing booklet on what they need to know about that prospective client.

The seating at the seminar will not be random. A specific partner will sit with five specific prospective clients on whom she has received a briefing booklet. Now the partner can begin the conversation with "As soon as we knew you were coming, we tried to do our homework. We noticed that you have had this level of court activity, you have launched three new products, your key ratios seem different from your competitors'. That must be challenging, how are you dealing with the consequences?"

With this opening, something important has been accomplished. By giving direct evidence of having done your homework, you have given the client evidence on which to form some preliminary impressions about you. The prospect will begin to suspect that you are:

- Disciplined and organized
- Thorough and do your homework before meetings
- Enterprising
- Willing to invest in the relationship
- Interested in his business
- Interested in him (or her) and not treating him like a cold call

In short, you're professional in your approach. Already, you have distinguished yourself from the typical professional. And the seminar hasn't yet begun!

When it does begin, the seminar presenter should speak for no more than twenty to thirty minutes, and should then suggest that everyone have small table discussions. Note that the speaker does not say "Any questions?" The goal is to get the conversation away from twenty-five to one "in the mass" conversation toward the five to one "intimate discussion" where people are more likely to open up and join the conversation. Your partner sitting at each table can now say "Was that your issue?" If the prospect says "No, that didn't cover my concern," your person can say "Well, what *is* your concern?" Now we have the client talking about his business—which is the key to all business getting.

The seminar proceeds in this fashion: twenty-minute presentation, twenty-minute small table discussions, then back to the speaker. From the attendee's point of view, such a seminar maximizes the chance that he or she can raise specific issues, and hence is likely to be welcomed by them.

The follow-up to the seminar (the next step in the seduction) should now be comfortable. Your partner can call those who sat at the same table and say: "You and I spent the morning talking about the issues in your business. You said that the seminar didn't cover certain key issues and I've been back to the office and researched them, and I'd like to come by and show you my findings." That sort of follow-up call is comfortable for the professional and usually welcome by the prospective client because the partner will be customizing his or her comments and not wasting his (or her) time.

SPEECHES

The second major opportunity to "give" ideas to prospective clients, in order to demonstrate special competence, is to give speeches at client industry meetings, chambers of commerce, and other forums where prospective clients gather. The goal of an effective speech is *not* to "impress" the whole audience (in case they might ever need your services). That's nice PR, but it doesn't produce much revenue. Your main task in a speech is to make the handful of prospective clients who have need of your services today *want* to contact you afterwards to learn more.

One tactic to make this happen is to offer to hold a small round-table discussion for those who are interested, either later in the day, at a coffee break, or over cocktails. Another is to refuse to hand out copies of your speech at the meeting, but suggest that those who are interested can get copies of it by leaving their business card. A third is to hand out a brief questionnaire and tell the audience that anyone who would like the survey results should attach his or her card and you'd be happy to send them the results. In all of these devices, you are screening out those who are poor prospects (they're not even interested in taking one small step) so you can focus your marketing efforts and time on those few who have expressed interest (the Raspberry Jam Rule).

What all of these tactics have in common is the seduction principle—creating a situation where those who are interested (maybe) can, without commitment or threat, express the beginnings of interest. You make it easy for them to take the next step toward you without the fear that they will be bombarded with a sales pitch.

Don't forget that a speech is inevitably an opportunity to convey not only your content (and your brilliance) but what kind of professional you are. For example, someone who reads his or her speech comes across as insecure and uncertain, and not in command of the subject matter. Never use a script, and never use notes. If at all possible, try for audience participation in the form of questions and answers as early as possible (the goal is not to get through your material, but to create a favorable impression). You want to demonstrate with your speech that you can think on your feet, you can handle unexpected questions, you are interested in listening as well as talking. All these things are characteristics that a client wants in his advisor—use the speech to demonstrate that you have them.

ARTICLES

Although they may fail the tests of being face-to-face and customized, articles in client-oriented trade magazines and newspapers are a powerful means of demonstrating your competence (and having something special to say that distinguishes you from the competition) and hence are very effective in giving prospective clients a reason why they should talk with you. (Articles written for professional and technical journals may bring professional glory, but it is articles in the client-oriented press that bring in the business.)

The power of articles derives from the multiple uses to which they may be put. Apart from the distribution they receive from their initial publication, they may be reprinted and handed out at speeches and seminars, and they can be a powerful substitute for brochures. How much more effective it is when a prospective client makes an enquiry to say "Yes, we've written a few articles on that subject, let me send them to you" than to say "Here's our brochure!" The life of a well-written, reader-friendly article can be many years.

Articles can have a credentializing effect. Since many if not most professionals do not write for the client press, what begins as "an" article on a subject can easily become "the" article. Over time, articles can be accumulated into a bound book which, though less likely to be read from cover to cover, helps to create the image that the firm "wrote the book" on a given area of practice.

Getting ideas for articles is rarely a problem. Most effective articles are 2,000 to 5,000 words of the form "If you have the following issue to address, here are the pros and cons of your major alternatives, here are some things to take into account, and here are some lessons we've learned recently about the best way to proceed." By implication, though never explicitly, the article suggests ". . . and if you'd like to hear more, call me!" There must, of course, be enough substantive content to make the reader want to call.

The power of articles is such that it would be wise to set a target of one article per year per professional. In a medium-to-large firm, this would represent a significant amount of market exposure. The limitation on accomplishing this is not things to write about. Most professionals learn *something* in a year of practice that would be of interest to prospective clients. Rather, the limitation is discipline: the act of writing. To address this barrier, many professional firms make available to their partners free-lance journalist ghostwriters who do the actual writing subject to the partners' dictating and editing.

PROPRIETARY RESEARCH

If the goal of marketing is to demonstrate that you have something to offer that your competitors do not, conducting research on topics of interest to prospective clients is an obvious, if neglected, tool. Though discussed here last, research logically precedes the three main tactics of seminars, articles, and speeches. For each of these to be effective, you need to have special information. If you do have special information facts they cannot get elsewhere, prospects will come to your seminar. If the planned content covers what any competitor could present, they are unlikely to come. (It's usually a good idea to charge for a seminar: It forces you to ensure that you have something special to say, and that there's real value in the content. It also helps you ensure that those who attend are good prospects in that they are willing to pay to discuss the topic.) If you have special information, your articles and speeches will be listened to with interest. (Clients today are bombarded with articles, speeches, and seminars that contain generalities and do not distinguish the author or presenter from any of his or her competent competitors.)

What kind of special information can you collect that your competitors do not have? Obviously, it might be technical or professional, but it can also be general survey research. Imagine, for example, that you have conducted an opinion survey of all the executives in a given industry, and asked them to prioritize the trends they worry about most, list the tactics they make greatest use of, identify which devices they have made use of, and so on. You are now in a position to report that X percent of executives in a given sector have tried Y, Z percent think that these are the most threatening issues, and so on. The information may not be very technical or professional, but you will have created a set of facts that any prospect would like to obtain, since every company would like to know how it compares to others. (Ask yourself how often you have heard clients ask "Who else is doing this?" "What are other companies doing?" "How do we compare to other clients of yours?")

A number of professional firms are very organized in this area, and have used it to great effect. Some, for example, get client industry associations to sponsor (and guide) the research, creating two wonderful benefits: First, a patina of "official research" is created, positioning the firm as a primary source of information for clients; and second, the industry association will sometimes underwrite part or all of the cost of the research. Apart from its support of articles, seminars, and speeches, research can also provide the substance for getting quoted and other public relations, although this is a lesser side benefit.

THE SECOND STRING TACTICS

In stressing the importance of seminars, articles, speeches, and research, I do not mean to imply that other marketing tactics do not work. They all work, to a degree. Rather, the issue is one of effectiveness and return on investment—which tactics should come first. This needs to be stressed as we turn to the tactics of community and civic involvement, networking with potential referral sources (such as bankers, etc.). In many professions these tactics have been the traditional mainstays of business development. Every firm has a major rainmaker who seems to collect business on the golf course, on the opera board, at the cocktail party.

Such activities can be powerful, especially in smaller communities. They have the virtue that they are face-to-face in approach, are not "broadcasting" in nature, and usually are appropriately conducted as a slow courtship. However, I relegate them to the second tier for one simple reason: while the return may be there, the required time investment is high. No one wins new business *quickly* through networking and community activities. The payoff comes after many patient years of getting to know people. Further, my observation of shifts in client buying patterns suggests that "purchasing" professional services is becoming more formal, and fewer deals are done today on the golf course.

The message is simple: if you're doing the articles, speeches, and seminars, by all means get involved in community activities. It's a wonderful add-on, but a poor substitute.

Also in the second-tier category are newsletters. In principle, these should be effective marketing tools, since they represent a form of demonstrating competence, even if they are not face-to-face or customized. However, they lose their effectiveness for a variety of reasons. First, so many firms are using this device, that clients and potential clients tend to receive remarkably similar newsletters with the same information (which probably means that you need to have one, but it won't buy you much by itself). In numerous client panels I have conducted, I have frequently heard clients complain, "Don't just send me your latest firmwide or practice-wide update on latest developments—it's too generic! What I really want [to get] is an interpretation of what it means for my company. "

A similar problem derives from the fact that newsletters are often published on a regular schedule, and this, almost inevitably, leads to a deterioration in quality. A newsletter is put out not because the partners have something new to say, but because it's time to put an issue out. Done well, a newsletter can be powerful. But like a good article, it must have real substance, a point of view, and offer an interpretation of recent events, not just an unprocessed reporting of them.

"CLUTCHING AT STRAWS" TACTICS

When getting organized for marketing, many firms think first about publicity: getting quoted and getting stories on the firm into the business press. For many years, I took it on faith that this must be a powerful tactic, since so many firms spend so much money here. However, over time, I have come to learn that while being quoted and profiled is nice (my mother and my clients' mothers like it), it has rarely proven to be a significant source of new business. It's good for the ego, but it doesn't do that much for the pocketbook. (One of my clients was profiled on the front page of the *Wall Street Journal* and received one phone call as a result.) As always, the message here is not to avoid the press, nor is it to spend nothing on publicity. Simply stated, this is what you do if and only if you have money and time left after doing all of the above.

In a similar vein, I have always been surprised at the emphasis that professional firms have given to brochures. In many firms, it appears that these are viewed as a primary marketing tool. Of course, they are not. They are the glossy equivalent of a business card. You almost certainly need to have one, but it won't do much for you.

Nearly all brochures contain grandiose assertions, and little demonstration of competence. They also frequently break the first rule of selling: "Stress benefits not features," that is, talk about what you can deliver for the client, not the characteristics of your firm. They also break the Raspberry Jam Rule: They list long lists of specialties, trying to impress the reader that they can (and do) do almost anything. Of course, the effect on the reader is quite the opposite: the longer the list of competencies asserted, the more the reader is left with the impression that the firm does not have a special interest in the area of the client's specific problem.

If you are going to use brochures, it might be helpful to keep two guidelines in mind. First, having many practice area brochures is better than having one firmwide brochure. Practice area brochures can be targeted more to the special needs of the reader. Second, the inclusion of specific, real case histories (disguised if necessary) allow you to illustrate what you have done (rather than stress generalities) and stress the benefits obtained for the client.

Also in the "clutching at straws" category are ballroom-scale seminars, where success is measured by the number of people who come to listen to you. These can be worth doing, but only as general public relations. You may raise your "name recognition," and that's not bad, but you won't get much revenue. If you've done all of the above, do this. If not, skip it.

Direct mail is also generally an ineffective tactic, although it can become effective under one condition. First, it depends what you send out. If you send out a firm brochure, or other literature of a solicitation nature, it is unlikely to yield any result. However, if what you send out has a chance of being of value to the recipient (a research study, an article, etc.), then there is a slight chance that it will be read and that you will receive a response. Although it truly is clutching at straws, if you've got the "helpful material" then it is relatively inexpensive (i.e., requiring no partner time) to mail it out.

Do cold calls work? Yes, everything works sometimes. Is it a good investment of partner time to telephone, unsolicited, potential clients? Almost certainly not. Some large firms have added this to their marketing mix, and report that if a meeting can be arranged, and if research on the prospect is done prior to the meeting, then a customized, face-to-face conversation can take place. However, I see little evidence that this tactic should precede any of those higher on the list.

Should you sponsor cultural/social events or PBS programs? Should you advertise? Sure, if you've got money to spend. Are these things better than articles, seminars, and speeches? Heck, no.

Finally, what about the latest idea, video brochures? I've seen a couple of effective ones. What made them effective was that they presented case histories, including client interviews (with an implicit testimonial), telling the story of a difficult case and how the firm tackled the issue, dealt with the client, and brought about a wonderful result. They were dramatic, fun to watch, full of detail, and showed how the partners and client worked together. They left the viewer feeling "If they can do that for that client, maybe they can do that for me!"

Unfortunately, I've also seen deathly boring video brochures telling the viewer about our fine firm, showing the dots on the map where we have offices (including all the foreign countries where we have correspondent relationships) and listing the two hundred services we provide. How many times does it need to be said? Boasting doesn't sell.

CONCLUSION

What is eternally fascinating to me is that when I poll partners in individual firms as to which of the tactics they think really work, their order of priorities is rarely much different from that presented here. However, when I ask where the marketing resources are actually going, I find an abundance of "clutching at straws" tactics and a significant underinvestment in "first" team tactics. The issue, as I see it, is for firms to begin implementing what they say they believe.

Another challenge is presented by the fact that many firms are employing the right tactics, but in a disorganized way—a seminar for this audience, a speech to that target group, an article aimed at a third part of the market. This is clearly inefficient and ineffective. No one tactic, no matter how well executed, will work alone.

The seduction or courtship that marketing should be requires a planned, organized, *sequence* of events, gently drawing the client into an ever deeper interest in you and your firm. Done right, a planned mix of marketing activities aimed at a consistent audience can make you irresistibly attractive, and lead the clients to the right conclusion—that it is with you that they want to have a relationship.

CHAPTER 12

MANAGING THE MARKETING EFFORT

Some time ago, I was conducting a weekend-long workshop with a major professional service firm on the topics of marketing and selling their services. Many subjects were covered, including strategic positioning, targeting of key prospects, selling skills, client service, and the relative merits of seminars, brochures, and newsletters.

Toward the end of this two-day workshop, one of the participants stood up and said, "This has all been very interesting, but you have just confirmed what we all already knew about this subject. Why don't you ask us why we haven't been doing it?"

This challenge sparked a spirited discussion that led to a litany of managerial, operational, and personal reasons that had impeded these professionals from executing past marketing initiatives. Indeed, they did already know what they should and could be doing, but had not implemented what they knew.

This same pattern has been repeated time and again within professional firms. Past attempts at organizing marketing efforts simply have not delivered results, in spite of a good understanding of "what works." From these experiences, I have learned that, for many professional firms, the "marketing problem" is frequently not really about marketing. Rather, it is a managerial problem: how to ensure that "things happen."

THE PROBLEM

The central issue, I have learned, is that, in most firms, billable time is carefully monitored, but marketing time is considered "extra." Marketing activities represent an *investment*, requiring nonbillable time to be spent with uncertain, long-term results, and few firms are well organized to manage their investment activities. Billable time has a high profile and receives close attention; nonbillable time is a disorganized jumble of sometimes productive, often times nonproductive activities that no one understands (or cares to tackle).

Some firms attempt to "manage" their marketing by rewarding marketing *successes* ("We reward results; effort is rewarded in heaven"). This, I have learned, is insufficient. Many professionals, especially those unsure of their abilities in marketing, view investments in marketing, even where there is a reward for success, as a more risky way to spend their time than the more certain path of staying highly billable. Rewarding results only is no way to encourage marketing novices to participate.

There is also the problem of recognizing teamwork. If marketing success is rewarded, who then gets the credit for organizing a seminar, writing an article, giving a speech? Each of these may have played an important role in landing new assignments, but it can be very difficult to attribute any particular new piece of business to any one of these activities. As a consequence, there may be many volunteers to participate in a concrete, specific proposal, where the efforts and result are highly visible, but a reluctance to accept responsibility for the background efforts (such as conducting proprietary research) that generate the opportunities to propose.

An additional problem in many firms' approach to rewarding results is that success in winning new clients is often rewarded more (or at least achieves higher visibility and is celebrated more) than winning new business from existing clients. Professionals often "know" that their existing clients represent the best source of new business, but are lured by the reward systems of the firm to devote their energies to trying to win "origination credits" by landing new clients.

The result of all of this is that many marketing activities go neglected, unmanaged, or uncoordinated. Each professional decides whether or not to participate, and which activities to engage in. The result is a somewhat random allocation of the firm's marketing investment. Certain high-visibility activities often receive excess investment, while others, frequently crucial to the firm's success, are neglected.

MANAGING THE EFFORT

The solution to the problem is for firms to learn how to manage their marketing *efforts*, not just results. In doing so, all senior professionals need to be involved. There is a common misconception that marketing and selling are specialized skills possessed by a limited number of professionals ("natural rainmakers"). This view ignores the fact that, to develop its practice, a firm needs to invest in a wide range of activities, each of which requires a different set of skills and behaviors. For example, most firms should invest some of their nonbillable marketing time in:

- Writing articles
- Spending time with executives of existing clients, to understand their business better and to win follow-on assignments
- Conducting publishable proprietary research
- Organizing and delivering seminars
- Giving speeches
- Gathering market intelligence on new needs by, for example, attending client industry conferences
- Community involvement and networking

None of these activities requires "rainmaking skill" (whatever that is). Each requires a very different skill. Participating in a winning proposal is often where the glory is in many firms, but it should be seen for what it is: the culmination of a marketing process, not the end-all and be-all of marketing. A professional who cannot "sell" may nevertheless be perfect to write an article that, when published in a client magazine, gains the firm significant attention. Someone else may be perfectly suited to developing and organizing a seminar that another person would better at delivering.

The central point is that practice development is inherently a *team* activity. No one person is likely to have all the skills (let alone the time) to perform *all* of the steps necessary to develop the practice. Rather, firms need individuals to cover all the bases: existing clients as well as new, generating leads as well as pursuing them, back-room preparation as well as public presentation.

A first step is to adopt a policy that each and every partner is expected to contribute in some way to the marketing effort. Specifically, I recommend setting a minimum time allocation for each and every partner to invest in practice development. Knowing that all of one's peers will be investing roughly the same amount of time can be very motivating in ensuring diligent execution of marketing tasks. Partners are not told *which* activities to do. To a large extent, they are free to play to individual strengths. But everyone must do something.

In most firms, this could and should involve senior nonpartner staff, who are a vastly underused resource in business development. There is a clear merit in starting to build practice development skills early in a professional's career. While they may not be ready to participate in, say, giving speeches, they can be well used in other activities such as article writing, preparation of seminars, researching client needs, and the like.

For example, a perfect place to get junior professionals (and other marketing novices) involved is with existing clients. Frequently, firms attempting to obtain greater involvement in practice development find that there is less resistance to (and more enthusiasm for) learning the best ways to maintain good client relations than there is to learning "how to sell." Yet the skills are the same. Professionals who are good at client counseling are the same ones who excel at selling. Both areas require the same set of skills: understanding the client's business, listening, asking the right questions, persuading, and following through.

If firms wish to get more people involved in practice development, they should reward marketing experimentation and not just successful experiments. Anyone learning a new skill will suffer early failures and temporary setbacks. To encourage perseverance, firms should concentrate as much on praise and recognition for the quality of effort as they do for immediate results. In doing so, they help breed the activity that builds skills and hence leads to future success. Managing efforts rather than results means that marketing cannot be "managed by the numbers." A structured, highly personal and interpersonal program must be devised.

THE POWER OF THE SMALL TEAM

To manage a marketing program successfully, firms should organize teams of professionals who, together, design and execute *their own* marketing action plan. The benefits of small-group teamwork are many.

The existence of many small teams (rather than a few large ones) both permits and encourages a high degree of focus in marketing activities. Individuals are allowed (if not required) to pick the team that interests them most: one focused on a target industry, perhaps, or a particular specialty. By becoming a member of a specific team, with specific colleagues, focused on a specific target client group (new or existing), they avoid the isolation of being left alone to do something in marketing (often without guidance), and also escape from being one among a large horde all jointly responsible for a huge (and ill-defined) marketing task. The structuring of teams with a specialized marketing focus (not just generalist groupings) will improve the chance that marketing time will be used productively.

By pooling their available nonbillable practice development time, a team can create an investment budget that is of sufficient scale to be allocated sensibly across the range of marketing activities required in their specific segment. (Obviously, the marketing plans of different teams will include different activities, depending on the need of their market). A well-orchestrated campaign is now possible. This approach avoids the (common) syndrome where, as an example, a professional may not find it in his or her best individual interest to try to put on a seminar, but will willingly accept this role as a contribution to a team effort.

Teams that have developed a joint plan and allocated responsibilities among themselves tend to keep each other honest: the planned activities have a higher probability of being executed if there is an obligation to one's peers (and not just to firm management). In addition, small teams provide an excellent vehicle for coaching, mentoring, and the transfer of skills. They provide a route for marketing novices to work together with experienced rainmakers, without being a burden on the latter. They provide the supportive framework for individuals with little or no marketing experience to begin to participate.

Small teams also allow a degree of team spirit and competitiveness between teams that, if managed well, can be energizing without destroying collaboration and firm feeling. For example, simply publishing and discussing the level of activity of each team (not just team results) on a regular basis (say, quarterly) can cause an extra degree of added motivation to follow through on commitments. If each team is asked to report on its activities at regular partner meetings, teams will act as consciences to each other.

In designing teams, care must be taken to join together partners who truly have a shared interest in a common market segment or practice specialty. For this reason, it is best to allow people to decide for themselves which team to join. For teams to work, the members have to be interdependent on each other to achieve their personal goals: they must be *real* teams. When team assignments are handed out by others, too often they end up being teams in name only, with members perceiving no practical business purpose for being on the same team.

Team assignments do not have to be, and should not be permanent. Group thinking can become stale and inertia can set in. If this happens, firms should shake up teams by creating new ones—task forces of partners who don't normally work together.

How the teams are managed is important. Each team should be required to develop a concrete plan of action, showing specific steps to be accomplished by each individual. These plans are then reviewed with a managing partner or practice leader, who accepts only strong commitments to action. Too often the marketing plan is a wish list of goals (e.g. "raise awareness of the practice"), instead of what it should be: a listing of concrete actions that can be monitored to see if they were executed or not.

Team plans should show a specific time budget for the designated actions. This is necessary to ensure that the plans are reasonable. Two tests must apply. First, each proposed action needs to have sufficient time budgeted to do it well. This seems trivial, but I have observed many marketing plans with a list of actions that clearly could not be fulfilled in the time available. Naturally enough, the team failed to complete the actions, became dispirited, and abandoned the whole effort. As is always true of management, the job of the managing partner or practice leader is to ensure that stretching but attainable goals are set.

The second "time test" is to look at the total budgeted time for the team, and compare it to the total available marketing time. Clearly, it would not be wise to schedule, in advance, all of the team's marketing time, since that would not allow for unforeseen proposal opportunities, new existing client requests or any of a host of other required marketing activities that cannot be predicted. I have learned that, as a rule of thumb, it is wise to schedule approximately two thirds of the available marketing time for planned marketing activities, saving one third for unforeseen opportunities. While situations differ, I believe it is wise to plan for three months at a time. This will require a review of progress (and a possible reshuffling of priorities) four times a year—frequent enough to make the oversight real, but long enough to execute most planned activities.

The managing partner or practice leader exercising the oversight function for the team can also critique the plan according to the allocation of investment time given to various categories of marketing activity. Has the team got the balance right between investing in new and existing clients? Between generating opportunities and saving enough time to do an effective selling job when they do have a lead? Should the team focus on fewer targets and devote more time to each, or vice versa? If action plans are developed and discussed in advance, significant influence (if not control) can be exercised over where the firm's marketing investments are going.

The system should be built on "contracts for action" to secure strong commitments, ones that can be monitored and that professionals will follow through on. Negotiating these contracts with the team will force tough choices among competing marketing priorities, and will focus attention on those few activities that will actually get done. Team leaders must make sure that each part of the marketing plan is assigned to a specific individual. What is everybody's responsibility is truly nobody's. So, team members should be asked to specify what their individual action responsibility is in their personal contract of action, and how their activities will fit with the team plan.

Through negotiation of these contracts, firm leadership can gain a better understanding of the personal goals, strengths, and direction of each professional. Over time, firm management (and team leaders) can better align the individual's actions and interests with others who can be valuable to him or her, and find better ways to provide support.

Partners (and teams) should aim for small improvements and build from success. Business development is a new experience for many professionals, and a painful stretch for some. It is also an activity full of rejection and disappointments. Getting beyond these setbacks is difficult for many professionals. One-on-one supportive coaching is needed, a critical role for each team leader. If people are to learn new skills, it is *not* enough to set goals and monitor them.

Team and individual results should be monitored through face-to-face methods, with a practice manager outside the team reviewing plans, activities, and results. Memoranda and statistical reports are too easy to "file and forget," and don't tell the whole story of what was done, what succeeded, and what did not. It is therefore necessary to use peer group meetings and one-on-one sessions to act as a conscience, review results, and set new goals. Only in this way can team motivation be maintained, by demonstrating that "the firm" notices, cares, and appreciates what is being done.

CONCLUSION

If marketing is an investment activity, it should be managed as such. My experience suggests that most firms' marketing problem is not that they spend too little time marketing, but that, because of the lack of organization, much of the time they do spend is wasted. With large numbers of partners, each making independent decisions on how much time to invest, where to invest it, and how to invest it, an unproductive jumble of activities results.

The small-team approach suggested here is very simple to implement. It requires only that a firm organize small teams, require each team to submit of a concrete plan of action specifying what will be done by each team member, and then monitor progress against that plan. As simple as this is, many firms fail to achieve even this level of organization. If they choose to follow this approach, they will be able to:

a. Plan their investments, ensuring that effort is going in the appropriate areas
b. Encourage broader participation in the marketing effort
c. Monitor that planned activities really do take place
d. Allow each professional to play to individual strengths

The steps are simple, and the payback significant.

PART THREE

PEOPLE MATTERS

CHAPTER 13

HOW'S YOUR ASSET?

At the end of my first full year as a management consultant, at the age of 39, I decided to take stock. How healthy was my career? I quickly discovered a disturbing paradox. My income statement was fantastic, but my balance sheet was deteriorating so badly I was in danger of ruining my career, of going out of business.

Just before starting my consulting career I had published a few articles which had caught the attention of my target clientele, and I also had the advantage of having been a faculty member at the Harvard Business School for the previous six and a half years. The consequence was that I was incredibly busy. What is more, I had to do no practice development (otherwise known as marketing and selling), because the phone constantly rang with requests for me to do work in the area in which I had built my (budding) reputation.

I was not only very busy ("highly chargeable"), but, because I was being hired to do things that I already had a reputation for, I had relatively few problems with fee levels (I had a "high realization percentage"). I made a lot of money, more than I had hoped for. All seemed to be going very well.

But was my business (and/or my career) truly healthy? I remembered my business-school training, which taught me that to judge the health of a business you had to look at the balance sheet as well as the income statement. What made up my balance sheet? I could think of two groups of assets for a professional. (We'll ignore for the moment my liabilities, particularly the personal ones.)

The first group of assets on which my career was based was my inventory of knowledge and skills. Professionals get paid for their time, but that's not what we sell. We sell knowledge and skill. The second (potential) asset was my client relationships. Much to my surprise, I discovered that both had deteriorated badly.

The problem with my knowledge and skill was that I hadn't learned anything new. By definition, the unsolicited phone calls requesting my services had been for things that I was already known for. Even though each client project was customized (to a degree), I found myself doing basically very similar work for a variety of clients. I had not added to my abilities. What was even more shocking (and depressing) was the realization that not only had I not grown my asset, but its value on the market was going down—rapidly. Left untended, knowledge and skill, like all assets, depreciate in value—surprisingly quickly.

When I first started out, the ideas contained in my articles (on which I had launched my business) were relatively new to the market, and I could therefore command a premium fee to consult or speak about them. However, with each passing month (and, I could foresee, each passing year) the price the market would pay for those ideas (and the related skills and knowledge) would decline. There were probably more potential clients out there to whom I could keep selling the "same old stuff," but if I kept this up, my skills eventually would be out of date and worthless.

Already the danger signs were there. Friends among my client base told me that people were saying "Oh, yeah, we've had Maister in and heard his stuff. What else has he got?" Even with ongoing clients (and I had a few) they clearly didn't value as highly what I was doing the second or third time I did it for them as they did the first time. The value of my asset was definitely going down.

There was also a strange problem with the second group of assets, my client relationships and reputation. If I had published a personal brochure (or resume) about my consulting career to date, it would have looked very impressive. I had worked for a large number of very prestigious clients. It felt like my client and contact list represented a real asset. But was there any real value there?

It quickly became clear that my client relations would have a high value if and only if the next time the client had a problem in my field of interest, I had a high probability of getting the job. That would have been worth something. But the truth was, that wasn't the case. I realized that having done "one thing" (or a limited set of things) for a wide variety of clients meant that I really hadn't developed relationships that promoted the chances of me getting their next (interesting) assignment.

I realized that the value of my client relationships was not to be measured by the number of clients, nor by their prestige, but by how *deep* the relationship was. I would have been better off, I realized, if I had worked for fewer clients, but done a variety of things for them so that they would have had a chance to see the range of my skills, and had had the chance to work with me enough to learn to know me and trust me when new things came up.

As I worked to address these problems in subsequent years, more harsh realities about professional life became evident. Unfortunately, I discovered that it was harder to generate asset-building work than to sell what I was already known for, already had methodologies for, already had written articles about, already had references for. If I took the line of least resistance in my practice development activities (i.e., sold what it was easiest to sell), chances were that I would milk my asset, not build it.

Second, I learned that doing asset-building work was often more stressful, and sometimes less fun, than doing what I was already good at. Doing the type of work that was easiest and most comfortable was not necessarily what was best for my career: in fact, it rarely was. I realized that, in professional life, if you're comfortable, you're heading for trouble.

In sum, I learned that unless I actively worked at it, my career prospects would inevitably decline, even when (or perhaps especially when) I was making lots of money. Having a good current year financially was clearly a necessary condition for my success, but it was far from being a sufficient condition. Keeping my career moving forward, even staying level, was going to take conscious effort.

There were two pieces of good news in all this. First, I discovered that, if I was prepared to work at it, then there did not have to be a trade-off between my balance sheet and my income statement. If I could be diligent and clever enough in my practice development, then I could be as busy on asset-building work as I had been on asset-milking activities. Furthermore, if I did it right, I could deserve and earn higher fees for learning, growing types of projects than I was able to earn for the stuff I knew how to do years before. My current charge-ability and realization did not have to suffer; I just had to learn to manage my flow of work and be sure to build new skills—continually and forever.

The second piece of good news was that it was possible to get hired for assignments for which I had no methodology, no references, and little, if any, experience. The secret turned out to be that while new clients were unlikely to hire me for such things, an existing client who had, during the current assignment, had a chance to see me in action and learned to trust me, might, if I played my cards right, give me a chance. I learned that investing my practice development time with existing clients rather than new clients was more likely, by far, to help me grow my asset. The second (or third) assignment from an existing client (assuming the projects were different) was definitely more likely to deepen my knowledge, broaden my skills, and make an asset out of my client relationship than another "first" assignment for one more new client.

That's what I learned in my first year. Since then, I have learned that these experiences were not just the problems of the early stages of a career. In fact, the more "successful" I got in later years, the greater was the temptation to exploit existing skills and relationships and the harder I had to work to make sure that I didn't just cruise, letting my balance sheet slip away unexamined.

After having observed thousands of partner-level professionals in a wide variety of professions in numerous countries, I conclude that the lessons (summarized in Table 13–1) still apply, not only to me, but to every professional, at any stage in his or her career.

MOVING TOWARD A SOLUTION: THE PERSONAL STRATEGIC PLAN

To grow your asset well requires a plan, one designed to make your asset increasingly more valuable on the marketplace. You have to find ways to (continue to) develop the knowledge and skills that *your* target clients value. In essence, we all need a personal strategic plan for our careers.

TABLE 13-1

The Lessons

LESSON ONE
What you know now and are able to do now, what your current success is built on, will unavoidably depreciate in value unless you actively work on learning new things and building new skills. Continual professional development is a lifelong requirement, not an option. There may have been a time when once you got good at something, maybe "made partner," you could live off that for the rest of your career. If those times ever existed, they're gone now. The minute you start thinking you know how things work, you're dead.

LESSON TWO
The health of your career is not dependent so much on the volume of business you do, but the type of work you do (whether or not it helps you learn, grow, and develop), and who you do it for (whether or not you are increasingly earning the trust of some key clients). In any profession, the pattern of assignments you work on *is* the professional development process—you just have to learn how to manage it.

LESSON THREE
No matter how busy you are, you still owe it to yourself and to your career to get involved with and take charge of your own practice development activities (marketing and selling). If you let others in your firm generate the business you work on, you are putting your career development in other people's hands—a risky move at best. If you rely on business flowing to you unsolicited, then, with high probability, it is going to be "asset milking" rather than "asset building." What marketing and selling are about is truly practice development: influencing the qualitative nature of what you work on, so that you use your work experiences to continue to build your career.

LESSON FOUR
Since asset building is about managing your affairs for the long-term health of your career, you'd better take charge of it yourself. Don't wait for your firm to establish formal policies to reflect concern about the balance sheet as well as the income statement. It probably should, but whether it does or not, it is in your own interest to get started yourself.

LESSON FIVE
Alas, you cannot automatically assume that what your firm "asks you to do" will always be the right thing to build your asset. For example, if you are already experienced in a certain area, chances are that others in the firm will turn to you every time an issue comes up in that area. If you don't take charge, others will exploit your asset. You've got to be a good corporate citizen, but you've also got to learn to balance that with what makes sense for your own development.

LESSON SIX
Among the worst mistakes a professional can make is underinvesting in marketing to existing clients. Existing clients are not only more likely to give you new business, but the business they'll give you (if you work to earn it) is likely to promote the value both of your skill asset and your client relationships asset.

What can you do to promote your learning, apart from being exposed to a variety of experiences? Traditionally, most people acquire their skills and knowledge by opportunistic insights, not structured learning (the phrase is from Donald Schon). However, you can rely too much on "random" experience as a teacher. To learn well, you have to set out to learn some specific *something*.

Unfortunately, this requires focus. Like most professionals, I enjoy variety in my work life. I have wide interests and enjoy learning new things about lots of subjects. Yet I have learned, from my own career and from watching those thousands of other professionals, that if you want to create a truly valuable asset, then you have to focus your attentions on building a highly specific set of knowledge and skills.

This is true not only because focus means that individual pieces of learning are more likely to be cumulative and hence speeds up the value creation process, but also because (with ever increasing intensity in each profession) clients demonstrably value specialization. If we want our asset to be valuable on the marketplace, we have to consider what our clients define as value.

With every passing year, I have relearned the importance clients give to specialization in "their kind of business" (i.e., specialization either by industry or by "type of client" such as family-owned businesses, government agencies, entrepreneurial companies, Fortune 500 companies, or international organizations). Meeting a client need *not* mean working only in one industry, 100 percent of the time. It *does* mean being sufficiently well informed and experienced to stay current on industry developments, converse with the client about industry-specific issues, being able to offer your professional counsel in a way that does not require the client to do any "mental translation" of generalities or terminology into his or her specific situation.

For example, I have learned that the (seemingly "low-level") tasks of diligently reading my clients' industry trade magazines, newsletters, trade association materials, every single month without fail, has made me a better professional in their eyes. It has made me, in their judgment, substantively more valuable to them. Sometimes reading these materials (or attending their trade association meetings) doesn't feel like a "professional development" activity, but I have to remind myself that, in the clients' eyes, my asset is not defined as just my technical skill. For them, my asset is valuable if I have technical skill *and* the ability to apply it in a customized way to their situation.

Choosing an industry (or "type of client") focus is a problem for many professionals who worry about overspecializing. When I began, I too wanted to work with more than one industry (or, in my case, profession), and faced a common problem. How did I get to the ultimate goal of both *breadth* (the variety of clients that I find fun and fulfilling) and *depth* (the detailed knowledge of industry specifics that clients value?)

By observation of others and from my own experience, I conclude that the correct approach is depth first and then breadth. By first focusing on clients in a specific industry, you will more quickly build knowledge and skills they value, will more quickly be exposed to a variety of (asset-building) types of assignments, and will more quickly build client relationships. Only after having done this is it wise to begin branching out. If one took the opposite route, breadth first, one would be accumulating lots of little pieces of knowledge in a wide area, and establishing numerous minor client relationships: not the best strategy for fast skill building.

It is important, I have learned, to make a distinction between knowledge and skill. Knowledge is relatively easy to accumulate quickly, but it also depreciates quickly. Skills are hard to win, but keep their value a little longer. Further, I have learned that it is important to distinguish between technical skills and counseling skills.

Growing one's professional, technical skill is, of course, a minimum requirement for keeping one's career alive. However, it has been a fascinating lesson to observe lawyers, accountants, consultants, and other professionals and to note that it really is only a very special few that have been able to build their careers on technical skill alone. These few are the gurus, the rocket scientists, the brain surgeons of their professional specialty, who have somehow persuaded the market that they are closer to the frontier of their discipline than their competition.

For the vast bulk of the remaining professionals I know (including myself), technical skill alone is rarely enough. To be a valuable professional in the eyes of clients, I have learned (sometimes through bitter experience), takes a variety of interpersonal skills that I lump together under the title of counseling skills.

Professionals are more valuable to clients if they not only solve their clients' problems and "tell" them what they should do, but help the client understand more. This includes helping the client look at the issue in a fresh, more revealing way, and helping the client see what the options are and what are their relative advantages and disadvantages. This activity sounds simple, but I have learned that it truly is a skill, and like all skills, it takes practice. By observation, I can report that some professionals are terrific at this, and others (probably the majority, including myself) could do with some improvement. What can not be in doubt is that effectiveness in this area is something that clients value highly, and hence builds one's asset and one's career prospects.

Other skills fall into this category of counseling ability. Most professionals find themselves working with more than one executive in a client's firm. Accordingly, the client will receive greater value from any ability the professional has to deal with groups, help the client organization arrive at consensus where none existed before, reconcile and handle diplomatically conflicts of views among client personnel, and so on. Again, what I have learned is that these skills are called upon, not infrequently, but in the regular activities of most professionals' work.

HOW TO SPEED UP YOUR ASSET BUILDING

With these thoughts in mind, I worked hard over the years to manage the mix of my business, and, I think, succeeded. I was lucky enough to be given the chance to work on a variety of interesting, challenging new types of assignments. A while ago, I gave myself a test.

"OK, David," I said to the face in the mirror, "What do you know now, or what can you do now, that you didn't know or couldn't do one year ago? In what way are you a better professional than you were one year ago?"

I watched my face turn red. "I know I've learned something," I replied, "but I'm not sure I can tell you what it is." "Why not?" I quizzed myself.

"The problem, you see, is this. I've had lots of interesting experiences, but I'm not sure I've figured out what they taught me. I've had my share of successes, but I've never paused to reflect on why that particular assignment went well—I was always too busy dashing on to the next assignment. And, unfortunately, I've had my share of failures—client assignments that didn't work out as planned. And there I was even more eager to dash on to the next piece of work, and not look back on what went wrong. And even if I did look back, I have to confess that it was more normal for me to think about what the client people did wrong ('Those darn clients!') than what I could have done better."

Since I was talking to myself, I indulged myself in an old joke. "The trouble is that some people have five years' experience, and other people have one year's experience five times." The difference, of course, is in the ability to learn. Experience *is* the best teacher, but you have to do the homework.

I realized that if I was going to build my knowledge and skills, it was not enough to have a wide variety of experiences: I had to work at learning from them. I stole the following quote from somewhere, but now cannot remember where. I'd love to give appropriate credit, because it sums up very well what personal asset building is all about:

> What we are is determined by what we experience, which is determined by what we do, which is determined by what we learn, which is determined by how we interpret events.

The lesson of this (inspirational?) quote is that, just like my experience of looking at myself in the mirror, the essence of personal growth lies in taking the time to look back at what you've been doing and working at extracting the lessons from it.

There are four kinds of "debriefing" that I have found valuable in promoting learning:

a. By oneself
b. With the team (assuming that others, including juniors, worked on the assignment)
c. With the client
d. With one's peers

First, debriefing alone. I find that if I force myself to examine my work experiences, taking the time at the end of a project to ask myself "What went well, and why? What didn't go so well, and why not," I almost always come up with something that will help me get better next time. For myself, I find that if I take notes (i.e., keep a written personal journal) I am more likely to remember and apply the lessons next time.

Debriefing with the team has the same goal, and the same questions. However, debriefing with the client adds an entirely new perspective. By asking the client to review the assignment with me, and tell me, in retrospect, what "we" (the client *and* I) could have done better, what we might do "if" there were a next time, I have found that I get a great deal of assistance in growing my asset, particularly in those areas of working with client personnel that are so important to clients but so easy to neglect in the hurly-burly of "getting the project done."

There are immense benefits to be gained by asking your clients for feedback on your performance on a regular, systematic basis. I have learned that if you ask, clients will be honest with you about what you could improve. Often the things they say you already were aware of, but the act of asking forces you to confront (and deal with) your weak areas. Many firms have organized efforts in this area, including mailed questionnaires. Whether or not your firm adopts this approach, my experience suggests that it is in individual professionals' self-interest to arrange their own client feedback program just for themselves. Not only does this activity help build skills, but the act of asking for feedback is a powerful tool in cementing client relationships.

By taking every opportunity to discuss your work with peers, you create the chance that you will derive value when they ask "Why did you do it this way? What would have happened if you did that?"

Other devices can help skill building. Many of the key interpersonal skills all professionals need fall into the category of what I call "The Cabin Attendant Test." The airlines teach their cabin attendants how to deal with a rowdy drunk at 35,000 feet. They even coach them in prepared scripts on precisely what to say to accomplish the desired soothing effect. However, knowing what to say is easy; having the skill to actually "pull it off" in real time is an entirely different story.

So it is with some counseling skills. How, for example, do you tell a client he or she is wrong, without being rude, confrontative, or challenging? Doing it well takes skill, not knowledge, and a professional without that skill will not have great career prospects. The answer, of course, comes from practice. But it must be practice in a situation where you can afford to fail, afford to watch yourself, try different approaches and learn. That means rehearsals and role plays. Some of us can develop these skills rapidly by repeated experience in front of real clients. For most of us, a little off-line practice would work wonders, particularly if there's a video camera around!

It's also a good idea to get on as many joint projects with professionals from other disciplines as possible. We learn and develop from our work experiences, and if you get a chance to be on the same assignment as a top professional from some other area, you're going to learn. And learn in a way that no amount of reading or "off-line" conversations with that professional will ever provide. Figure out who has something to teach you, and find a way (even if it means cross-selling their services to your client) to work with that person.

CONCLUSION

Whether you are twenty-five or fifty-five, you will always need to worry about where your career is going from today. As you think about your career, here are some questions to ponder:

In what way are you personally more valuable on the marketplace than last year?

What are your plans to make yourself more valuable on the marketplace than in the past?

What specific new skills do you plan to acquire or enhance in the next year?

What's your personal strategic plan for your career over, say, the next three years?

What can you do to make yourself (even more) special on the market in the near future?

What, precisely, is it that you want to be famous for?

CHAPTER 14

HOW TO BUILD HUMAN CAPITAL

Managers in professional firms spend a lot of time worrying about marketing and selling their firms' services. But few give much thought to developing the "product" that the firm is trying to induce its clients to buy: the knowledge and skill of its staff.

Attempts at quick fixes in this area abound: If we need to enter a new market, bring in a lateral hire. If we need to add to partners' skills in a particular service area, send them to continuing education courses. If we need to train junior staff to handle certain matters better, schedule a Saturday seminar or prepare a manual.

Each of these devices has its role. But they are frosting on what needs to be a more substantial cake: To add to the firm's human capital—the collective judgment, knowledge, experience, and ability of its members—there must be an *ongoing, continual* effort at all levels.

Precise definitions of "professional skill" are hard to come by. The true added value of professionals lies less in what they *know* than in what they can *do*: interview clients effectively, win their trust and confidence, diagnose their needs, and make the myriad judgmental decisions as to how each matter should be handled. While professional *knowledge* can be codified and easily shared, professional *skills* can only be developed through practice.

155

Like all skillful arts, a professional craft is learned through apprenticeship. Clearly, it is in the firm's interest to ensure that this apprenticeship process works effectively and speedily. By developing the skills of its junior members, the firm adds to the only resource it has to sell: professional judgment and talent. So why, in many of the professional firms that I have studied, is this process ignored?

WORK ASSIGNMENTS

Consider, for example, the work assignment system. Most firms would acknowledge that the kind of assignments junior members receive; the various cases, industries, and clients they encounter; and the mix of the senior people they work with largely determine the kind of professionals they become. Skills, after all, are developed through experience, and assignments define the experience.

Nevertheless, many firms take an unstructured, even haphazard, approach to staffing projects. There may be an assignment committee, but in the day-to-day press of events, it is often circumscribed. Junior staff are assigned to whichever project appears most pressing—or to the senior partner who screams the loudest. While periodic conferences may be held about the need for longer-term professional development, in practice, work assignments are made according to short-term criteria.

There *are* merits to this free-for-all approach: To survive in such a system—to "get developed"—young professionals must demonstrate initiative. They must be able to differentiate projects that are routine from those worth working on, and to lobby effectively to get desirable assignments. They must be good at inspiring the confidence of useful, powerful partners—and adept at avoiding others. They must know when to "invest" time working on pedestrian matters in order to get a chance to work on more important matters. In short, juniors must learn how to sell themselves inside the firm and make busy partners want to take the time to share their expertise. This takes drive, charisma, political skills, and judgment—the very qualities a senior professional uses in dealing with clients.

In such a Darwinian system, only the fit survive. Good, promising young professionals are more frequently chosen for worthwhile projects by top professionals: These juniors spiral upward to ever increasing glory. "Weak," unpromising, quiescent professionals tend to be sucked into pedestrian work with few learning opportunities: They spiral downward. Such, at least, is the theory and, in many firms, the practice.

This system seems most common in those firms that, because of high junior-to-senior ratios and limited growth plans, expect a reasonably high turnover rate among junior people. For these firms, significant investment in training juniors may be wasted if a high proportion of them are expected to leave. Investments of partner time in coaching, mentoring, and training are made only on a very selective basis, once the "stars" have been identified and separated from the "dogs."

But not all firms can afford such an unforgiving and potentially wasteful system. For most, the goal must be to develop as many young professionals as possible: Only in this way can the firm accumulate and maintain the skills it hopes to market. Increasingly, therefore, firms are asking staff committees and/or departmental chairpersons to plan assignments more carefully—to trade off among the conflicting pressures of professional development; client demands for quality, cost effectiveness, and speed; and the preferences of the firm's members.

Actively managed work assignment systems are not easy to implement: Unless composed of powerful individuals, a committee may find it hard to enforce the discipline of routing staffing requests through the proper channels. Moreover, short-run pressures often force the sacrifice of this longer-term goal. To make such a system work, there must be firmwide recognition of the need for it and broad-based commitment to its success. As in so much of professional service firm management, developing this commitment is the responsibility of the firm's leaders.

COACHING

Work assignments are, of course, only part of the story. A junior professional may have received a rich and varied set of experiences, but this alone will not guarantee that he or she will learn the right skills. The difference is in the ability to derive the correct lessons. What is needed to turn exposure into usable knowledge and skill is good coaching—*guided* experience.

One senior professional puts it this way: "If I want to help my people acquire the skills I have, I must get them involved in planning the work, understanding how their task fits in, and interpreting the discoveries made as the project unfolds. There is no use in their sitting in on client meetings unless I am prepared to discuss with them why I handled myself as I did. They could too easily not realize the context-specific factors that affect my decisions. I'm not trying to train them to *do*, I'm trying to train them to *think* as I do."

Being a good coach or mentor is not easy. It takes a genuine interest in helping juniors improve, not just in appraising their performance. The coach has to ensure that assignments provide stretching but realizable challenges, and that feedback on what was done right and what needs work is detailed and prompt.

The professional quoted above takes his coaching responsibilities seriously. Yet all too often one hears young professionals complain about a lack of attention and specific, helpful advice from the partners they work for. In turn, partners too frequently view these requests as unreasonable, or at least as less pressing and less important than the other (very real) demands on their time.

Clearly, coaching is a time-intensive investment in the long-run health of the firm. Frequently, however, the firm's organization, structure, method of performance appraisal, and culture discourage mentoring. Other responsibilities—business getting and servicing of clients—are usually more visible and have quicker "paybacks" to the individual. For example, most partner-compensation systems reward short-term business getting and billable hours more than the time spent working with junior staff.

The professions, no less than industrial companies, find it all too easy to sacrifice the long-term profitability—building actions in the name of short-term pressures. Accordingly, coaching is not recognized and rewarded, and it tends to fall to those who find it personally fulfilling or who value the future benefits to the firm more than their own short-term self-interest.

Coaching *can* yield short-run payoffs. In the fee-sensitive world of the professions, firms can ill afford write-offs of professional time resulting from poorly trained juniors taking too long to accomplish tasks that a more skilled professional could do in a fraction of the time. Clients are as prepared as ever to pay the high fees of the superior professional. What they are less willing to do is subsidize inefficient training of junior staff. The days when juniors could be trained by bringing them along to client meetings as "bag carriers" (and billing their time to the client) are gone. It's still an excellent coaching device (accompanied by appropriate debriefing), but firms must view it as their own investment in training.

Attention to coaching is no longer an option at many firms, it is mandatory. In a rapidly growing firm, the need is obvious. But even in a firm that anticipates slow growth and high turnover, training is important: The firm must maintain its attractiveness to potential associates so they will join in spite of diminished partnership prospects. One of the best ways to accomplish this is by providing superior training, which makes it worth having been at the firm even if one doesn't make partner.

TEACHING PARTNERS

The need to develop skills does not cease on becoming a partner. Senior partners should continue to coach junior partners. The results of failure to pass on senior-partner skills can be seen at many second-generation firms where client getting was the responsibility of the founders of the firm and junior partners were charged with doing the work that the rainmakers brought in. With the rainmakers' departure, the partnership is left without skills essential to the success of the enterprise, and the younger (and now senior) partners are forced to develop the missing skills on their own, without the guidance of good coaches.

At other firms, a failure to develop human capital has resulted in a situation in which all of a firm's expertise in a given area or for a certain class of clients is in the head of a single partner (or a small group). A departure (for whatever reason) leaves the firm with little, if any, capability to serve the given markets.

ADDING TO THE KNOWLEDGE BASE

I have focused to this point on skills already possessed by the firm. However, even more important in building human capital is *adding* to the firm's skill and knowledge. A firm should be constantly seeking to increase its understanding of client industries, to improve service, and to add to technical capabilities. As obvious as this need is, it is frequently neglected.

In a variety of contexts, I have asked members of professional service firms to write down what they have learned from their activities over the past year that has made them better at what they do—to identify something they learned about serving clients, managing projects, or approaching certain matters in a new way. In many cases, this has proven a difficult exercise. The professionals seem to have been too busy rushing from project to project to stop and reflect on their experiences. They say that they *feel* they have learned something, but they cannot either identify or communicate what it is. This doesn't mean they haven't learned it—but it does mean the experience has not been converted into knowledge that can be shared.

One mechanism for sharing knowledge is provided by a prominent consulting firm: Every Monday morning all professional staff, senior and junior, attend a one-hour meeting. At each session one staff member presents a case his team has worked on and describes how they handled it, what new approaches were attempted, how they dealt with client problems, and so on. In brief, the staffer reports on what was learned on a recent matter. Discussion follows, with junior and senior colleagues providing critical feedback and examining whether the activities described offer anything useful to others in the firm. Each person (or team) has to take a turn at making a presentation. Since everyone knows this is coming up, each is forced to reflect continually on his or her experiences; thus, each is more likely to succeed in converting the knowledge available from his experiences into a shared resource.

In addition, such meetings provide an opportunity for the senior partners, through the questions they ask, to communicate the diagnostic process that is a large part of their professional skill. ("Did you try . . . ?" "How did the client respond to . . . ?" What would have happened if . . . ?) Specific client or industry knowledge can be rapidly communicated to others who may find it useful. And the firm ensures that everyone knows who is working on what.

In small, close-knit firms, sharing of experience and knowledge takes place informally, over drinks and in the corridors, and everyone knows whom to call for assistance. In larger (particularly departmentalized or multioffice) firms, leveraging the collective skills of the members is more complicated. For this reason, some firms have created client-industry committees that cut across functional or disciplinary boundaries. One barrier to this kind of effort, however, is created by many of the common systems of rewarding and appraising professional performance. Most rely strongly on individual (or departmental) performance and thus discourage efforts on the firm's behalf. And even if such efforts are taken into account in compensation, they don't afford the same status as client work does.

A departmental structure can both help and hinder knowledge sharing and skill building. Placing professionals working in similar areas closer together forces them to interact. But it also reduces interaction with professionals in different areas. For this reason, rather than organizing departments around functional professional disciplines, some firms are reorganizing to create groupings where the opportunities and need for sharing knowledge or getting new knowledge are greatest: small-business-client groupings, for example, or industry-based departments. Short of this, other firms are starting interdisciplinary (or interoffice) committees to encourage communication between otherwise isolated professionals.

MANAGING THE PROJECT MIX

Perhaps the most important decisions about managing the development of human capital are those made in selecting client engagements. If professional skill and knowledge are developed through experience, then the best way for the professional firm to improve its skill base is to take on projects that not only exploit the firm's existing skills but provide for further development.

This goal is harder to accomplish than it would at first appear. "Frontier-type" projects can be among the least profitable that the firm undertakes. They are among the least leveraged, requiring a high proportion of partner time. In addition, the firm may be forced to write off substantial amounts of time spent gearing up for the new work. In contrast, continuing to practice in familiar areas allows the firm to capitalize on existing knowledge and skills, use its junior time more effectively (and more profitably), and bill all full rates.

Deciding which and how many "investment projects" the firm should undertake should be the task of a firmwide committee. Individual partners may feel an incentive to go after the most profitable work (for which they will receive appropriate kudos and, probably, compensation) at the expense of developing new skills and knowledge. Moreover, the firm's investments in its future should be part of a larger strategic plan. As noted at the beginning of this chapter, the essence of strategic planning for the professional service firm is a clear sense of direction, not only as to which markets to serve and areas of practice to engage in, but in terms of recognizing and developing the skills needed to succeed.

CHAPTER 15

THE MOTIVATION CRISIS

Motivating junior professionals is harder today than it used to be, and it is more important to the success of the professional service firm. In the past, the up-or-out partnership structure of the typical professional service firm provided all the motivating force that was required. Young professionals knew that if they worked hard and well, added continuously to their skills, and kept out of trouble, they had a reasonable chance of reaching for the brass ring: the generous rewards (financial and otherwise) of partnership. Personal attention by partners to motivating juniors was not necessary: the system, combined with the inherent ambition of young professionals, took care of the problem.

A number of changes have occurred which make this "automatic" motivational system cease to function as well as it did. Today's young professional can see that the odds of making partner are lengthening in most firms. Talk of tougher (and changing) partnership standards, prolonged times to partnership and permanent nonpartner positions are common in every profession. Rather than inspiring juniors to even more strenuous efforts to be chosen as one of the select few, the lengthening of the odds has the opposite effect: Juniors are increasingly questioning whether the game is worth the candle.

This attitude is being reinforced by both economic and cultural trends. Given the competitive intensity of today's professional

163

world, the economic and psychological satisfaction of being a partner at many (if not most) professional firms is not as great as once it was. It is not unusual to hear partners make comments (in private conversation) such as "The practice of law [or accounting or medicine or consulting] is just not as much fun anymore. Today's clients are demanding, cynical about the value they receive, and treat you less as a professional and more like an ordinary vendor. The pace, intensity, and workload are greater than ever, and the firm atmosphere is competitive rather than supportive, and certainly less collegial. With all this concern about profitability, it seems like we're being asked to work even harder for what might turn out to be less money."

Similarly, in conversations with mid-level junior staff inside accounting, consulting, law, and other professional firms, I frequently hear things like "The closer I get to the firm's partners, the less attractive their lives seem to be. I'm increasingly questioning whether what they have is what I want. Professional life requires significant sacrifices, for both my spouse and me, and I'm no longer certain that the rewards are there to justify them."

Motivation levels are also affected by the range of options open to young professionals, which is greater today than ever before. It is no longer considered unethical, or even unusual, for young professionals to move between firms to advance their careers: In all professions, the mobility of individuals is on the rise. Satisfying, and frequently less intense, professional careers are also increasingly attainable inside corporations, at salaries that are competitive and sometimes superior to those offered by professional service firms. In addition, in-house professionals are no longer treated as second class citizens in the professions: They continue to accumulate the power, responsibility, and respect that historically was the preserve of the outside professional provider.

Finally, we should note that not only is competition for clients intensifying in the professions, but so is the competition for talented young professionals. The baby-boom generation has passed through its apprenticeship years. Today's twenty-five to thirty-five-year-olds are less numerous than their older siblings, and recruiting, motivating, and holding onto the talented among them is becoming an increasingly challenging task.

THE IMPORTANCE OF MOTIVATION IN PROFESSIONAL WORK

A less than fully motivated work force is a competitive disadvantage for any business organization. For a professional firm, it is a death knell. In few professional firms does the opportunity exist to achieve productivity and quality through the systems, procedures, close supervision, and technology upon which industrial companies have traditionally relied to control work pace and quality of output. For professional work, both productivity and quality are highly correlated with the degree to which the professional worker is engaged and committed to the task at hand.

All professionals must have had the following experience: You are responsible for a piece of work about which you just cannot seem to get excited. It is not that the task is too difficult, too easy, or even inherently uninteresting: just that the spark is not there. Nevertheless, being dutiful, you sit at your desk and try to work at it, being neither productive nor doing your best work.

Then the next morning, for some obscure reason, you begin to see the work in a new light. You approach the work in a new way, and begin to delve into the problem. Gradually, what had appeared as mundane now has an element of interest, which grows into curiosity, into fascination, and ultimately into involvement, effort, and productive, creative work. No amount of procedural work plans, tight supervision or incentive schemes could ever substitute for the inner motivation described here as a means to achieve productivity, quality and, not coincidentally, professional satisfaction in a job well done.

This link between motivation and performance in professional work results in an interesting and important phenomenon: the motivation spiral (see Figure 15–1). The elements of this spiral are as follows: high motivation leads to high productivity and quality, which leads to marketplace success. In turn, this results in economic success for the firm, allowing the firm to be generous with its rewards, including high compensation, good promotion opportunities, and challenging work. This atmosphere of ample reward breeds good morale, which results in high motivation—and the cycle begins anew.

Of course, the spiral effect also works, all too effectively, in reverse. Poor marketplace success means poor economic success which means fewer rewards available to be shared. With lesser rewards, morale,

FIGURE 15–1

The Motivation Spiral

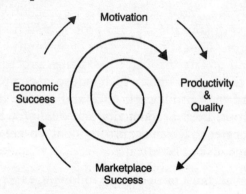

and hence motivation, is low. This, inevitably and inexorably, leads to poor productivity and less than top quality, which reinforces the lack of marketplace success. In professional work environments, success breeds success, and failure sets the scene for more failure. The spiral can begin, up or down, at any point. But once launched, its forces are hard to resist. In consequence, the motivation crisis is a very serious problem for any firm that allows it to take hold.

Addressing the problem of motivation in a professional firm requires an examination of all of the firm's managerial systems and practices, from recruiting, through work assignments, performance appraisal and feedback, promotion, and outplacement. However, the responsibility for achieving high motivation rests not only with those who exercise management functions within the firm: Changing the systems is only a partial solution. Increasingly, it will become the responsibility of every partner to nurture the motivation level of junior staff by developing good supervisory skills.

MOTIVATION AND THE RECRUITING PROCESS

If high motivation inside the professional firm can no longer be assumed, but must be carefully nurtured, how then does one go about this? There is a school of thought that asserts that it is difficult, if not impossible, to motivate anyone who does not have an inner drive, ambition, or energy level. The best that can be done, according to this view, is, first, to avoid demotivating an ambitious individual (a result that many organizations, particularly those that are slow-growing or bureaucratic, seem to achieve all too often); and second, to channel that drive into fruitful, productive efforts. Consequently, a significant component in achieving the highly motivated organization is the recruitment process itself, which, if it is to serve its purpose, must screen as much for drive, energy and ambition as it does for intellectual capabilities and technical skill.

In his Pulitzer prize-winning book *The Soul of a New Machine*,[1] Tracy Kidder describes the "signing on" process used by Tom West, the manager of a team of young computer design engineers, to recruit and select the members of his team. Rather than make unfulfillable promises by, for example, minimizing the scale of the effort required, or by presenting the project as one that would allow for a balanced life-style, Tom West took the opposite approach. He described accurately the high demands that the work would place on people, and presented the project as one that only the "best and the brightest," the truly committed, would be suited for. Not surprisingly, he screened out early those who would not be able to take the pace, and generated an enthusiasm and commitment to success from the very beginning.

In their eagerness to attract the junior professionals needed to staff engagements, I have observed many professional firms compromising the simple principle embedded in the Tom West story: that, to serve the firm's interests, it is more sensible to ensure that potential recruits truly know what they are letting themselves in for. Subtle misrepresentations during the recruiting process (about workloads, variety of work, extent of client contact, the degree of counseling, or any of a number of issues of concern to young professionals) may serve to bring more people (bodies?) on board, but will quickly work against the firm's interests as new recruits discover the realities of the practice: a prime example of how to demotivate.

One lawyer I know describes his firm's recruiting process as follows: "I describe the real life of being a lawyer as best I can. Then I ask them 'Do you really want to be a lawyer?' It's amazing how many hesitate. And if they do, I don't want them. I'd rather take someone with slightly less skill but with fire in their belly than a brilliant but naive student who doesn't understand what it's all about."

Such an approach to recruiting may not produce the raw numbers that many firms think they need (because potentially good candidates are 'scared off'), but this is a less serious error than the opposite result:

bringing people on board who are not temperamentally suited to today's practice realities. Furthermore, a professional firm should always have slightly more work than it can handle with its current staff putting in a normal work week. Professionals flourish with a full workplate in an atmosphere of challenge. Expressions of discontent, complaints about the firm, and poor morale never surface more frequently than when there is not enough work to keep everyone occupied. I have observed more firms get into trouble by attempting to hire too many people than by hiring too few.

THE PROFESSIONAL PSYCHE

Are professionals different from other types of workers? Do they need to be managed (and motivated) in special ways? While it is difficult to support the assertion that all professionals are different from all other workers, my work has led me to suspect that, when it comes to motivating forces, the average professional *is* different from the average worker in other environments: a difference based, I suspect, not on such things as educational levels, but on the psyche of those who choose professional careers.

The typical professional is apt to describe him or herself in the following way: "I am the type of person who gets bored easily. I hate doing repetitive sorts of work, and always like to seek out new challenges. Once I know I can do something, it tends not to satisfy me anymore." This is, of course, a somewhat self-flattering description. In my experience, however, it is an accurate one. Professionals, certainly the best among them, are constantly driven to seek out the new, the unfamiliar, the challenging. The key word here is driven.

People who feel the (neurotic?) need to constantly and repeatedly test their skills against unfamiliar problems with an uncertain probability of success are frequently insecure, with a low sense of self-worth (never expressed in public), in constant need of external tests of their merits to prove (to themselves) that they have still "got it."

Many professionals, I would assert, are prime examples of what is now termed "The Impostor Syndrome"—successful people who live in constant dread that someone will, one day, tap them on the shoulder and say "We've found you out. You've been faking it all these years."

Because of this, professionals tend to exhibit some clearly defined behavioral characteristics. They require continual challenge and personal growth to retain their interest, and are impatient when they do not receive it. They constantly ask themselves, and their superiors, "Am I still on track?" Because of their insecurity, and the ambiguity that surrounds the definition of "good work" in professional contexts, they need quick, repeated feedback on their performance to validate their efforts. They tend to be "scoreboard-oriented": eager for visible, well-defined measures of success that can reassure them (see Table 15–1). They like to have unambiguous goals to shoot at. From their need to achieve self-respect by receiving the respect of others, it follows that professionals value both autonomy in their work and involvement in policy decisions, whether on engagements or firm-management matters. As much as these "rewards" are valued in their own right, they are valued more as signs that the organization trusts and respects them.

MOTIVATION AND SUPERVISORY STYLE

From these observations flow some simple rules for maintaining motivation among professionals. You must provide clear goals; give prompt feedback and reward performance quickly; treat them like

TABLE 15–1

Motivational "Maintainers"

---

1 Provide clear goals
2 Give prompt feedback
3 Reward performance quickly
4 Treat them like winners
5 Involve in decision making
6 Seek their opinions often
7 Provide autonomy in work
8 Hold accountable for results
9 Tolerate impatience
10 Provide varied work opportunities
11 Keep them aware of upcoming challenging goals

Source: C. Bell, "How to Create a High Performance Training Unit," *Training*, October 1980, pp. 49–52

winners, involving them in decision-making and seeking their opinion often; give them autonomy in their work, but hold them strictly accountable for results; be tolerant of their impatience, and provide variety in their work experiences, always keeping the next challenging goal out front.

As straightforward as these principles may seem, they are frequently missing in many professional work environments I have encountered. Unfortunately, the demotivating forces of ambiguous goals, lack of variety, an absence of feedback, and postponed rewards are all too present in professional firms.

The best method I have seen of preserving a high level of motivation in a professional work group is the maintenance of a constant challenge to individuals composed of two key statements: "Yeah, you're good . . . But how good are you?" Both parts of this challenge are essential to its effectiveness. The first, "Yeah, you're good," is necessary to speak to the typical professional's delicate ego ("Treat them like winners"). The second part, "But how good are you?" is necessary to keep the air of challenge needed to engage the professional's determination to succeed ("Always keep the next goal out front").

A good example of the successful application of this management approach is also given in *The Soul of a New Machine*. A young professional suddenly had a flash of brilliance about how to solve a particularly difficult problem that had appeared intractable. He rushed in to his supervisor, saying "I've solved it, I can have it finished in two months!" (a short time in the world of computer design). Instead of saying "Terrific, well done. I'll certainly remember you at bonus time," the supervisor merely said, "Oh, come on!" whereupon the young professional said "Well, maybe six weeks"—thus committing himself (an important point) to a self-imposed goal.

Given the importance of eternal challenge in a professional's life, there is nothing so motivating as a statement like "Bet you can't do this." One does not motivate a professional by being the "good guy" and lessening the pressure: rather one does it by helping that individual accept the pressure as a challenge to his or her professional pride.

Motivating professionals is somewhat akin to being the coach of an athletic team: Both roles involve trying to bring out the best possible performance in talented individuals. The techniques of doing so are similar in both environments. A good coach is simultaneously the chief cheerleader and chief critic: demanding and supportive (one without the other is insufficient). When the high jumper is attempting to clear a given height, the coach is supportive and helpful. But as soon as that accomplishment is reached, up goes the bar by an inch or two. The next goal, challenging but achievable, is kept out front. (Raising the bar by six or seven inches would clearly be demotivating. The scale of the challenge is clearly important.)

Good coaching requires that close attention be paid to the individual's activities, so that specific, constructive advice can be made about how performance can be improved. While good coaches rarely cosset those in their charge (the best coaches tend to be abrupt, demanding, and frequently SOBs), they clearly demonstrate a commitment to helping their athletes: a commitment that is rewarded with high motivation and high performance.

THE IMPORTANCE OF MEANING

In a survey of research on the management of professionals ("Leadership and the Professional," in *Scientists, Engineers and Organizations*[2]), Morgan McCall notes that successful leaders spend less time worrying about getting their (professional) subordinates to do something and more about supplying their subordinates with a meaningful understanding of what they are doing. This conclusion matches my own observations and experience. As discussed above, a piece of professional work can either strike me as incredibly stimulating, inspiring the energy and attention necessary for creative, productive work, or it can appear meaningless, repetitive, and dull: It all depends on whether or not I can readily see where the challenge in the work lies, and whether or not I feel that this piece of work is a "worthy" application of my talents.

The implication of this is that, perhaps above all else, it is the role of the supervisor of professionals to help create the conditions under which the forces of commitment, creativity, and involvement can be unleashed. The supervisor must help the professional find the meaning in the work to be done. In managing the work of others, in any environment, one can choose to focus either on *what* it is to be done; *how* it is to be done; or *why* it is to be done (its purpose or meaning). In the management of professionals the supervisor should be very clear on the *what* ("provide clear goals"), spend only the bare minimum of time on the *how* ("involve them in decision-making," "provide autonomy") and spend a lot of time on the *why* ("provide meaning").

This is particularly important for junior professionals. On any given professional project, there is an admixture of diagnosis and creativity together with seemingly picayune but no less important execution tasks: drafting memoranda, crunching numbers, documenting progress, and the like. Here, above all, the manager must help the professional worker place the task in context, see its importance, and accept the task as worthy of professional effort.

Young professionals are no fools: they know that their work will contain a significant proportion of less-than-frontier-level activities. However, it is profoundly demotivating when this work is presented with the attitude, "Yes, I agree it's dull and boring, but it's got to be done and you've been chosen to do it." The good manager can convey the spirit that "There's no task too trivial to be done well: there's just as much opportunity to do good or bad work here as there is anywhere else in the project. It's all important." This is, of course, no more than the truth. But in their own personal distaste for "mundane" work, too many partners I have observed fail to convey this sense of importance.

Rarely have I heard of young professionals becoming demotivated because of too much work; most often (all too often) demotivation results from too much *meaningless* work. And since almost no work done by a professional firm is in fact meaningless (it is all, or should be, valuable to clients), this syndrome represents a failure of management.

MOTIVATION AND PROMOTION

A great deal of the motivation of professionals is accomplished through the interpersonal interactions between the professionals and the partners who lead them. However, as we saw above in our discussion of the role of recruiting, the systems and structure of the firm also play an important role. The work assignment system (how individual projects are staffed) clearly plays a critical role, since it is this system that determines the variety and the challenge of the work to be done by an individual, both major determinants of motivation. In some cases, work assignments can also be used to ameliorate the effects of diminishing promotion prospects.

Such approaches, however, can never completely substitute for career progress, inside or outside the firm, as a motivating force. Professionals, certainly the ones any organization would want to keep, are, almost by definition, ambitious. Any environment where continued career progress is compromised is almost certain to result in lessened motivation. Whatever its other defects, the up-or-out partnership system has the great virtue that it maintains an air of dynamism, of continued progress, of challenge, that plays to the psychological needs of professionals. Further, by removing weaker performers from the organization, the system avoids the (very strong) demotivating effect on good performers of showing tolerance for weaker, less productive people.

In today's environment, this last point takes on a special importance. In a professional organization where the odds of making partner are either lengthening or where the criteria for partnership are shifting (i.e., in most professional organizations), the level of ambiguity felt in the middle and upper ranks of the nonpartner staff rises rapidly. In such an environment it is inevitable that many nonpartners will begin to question their opportunities within the firm, and ask themselves whether or not they should begin to look elsewhere.

If the atmosphere is truly ambiguous, and all nonpartners are kept equally in the dark, it is more than likely that it will be the best young professionals, the most marketable, who will leave to seek greener pastures, leaving behind the less-than-superior individuals. Clearly, to avoid this, professional firms must begin to make distinctions between the best and the competent at an earlier stage, and ensure that those the firm wishes to keep know that they are valued. Only then will it be the weaker performers who will be encouraged to leave. In their attempts to hold on to more nonpartner staff short of partnership, many professional firms are adversely affecting the overall level of challenge and motivation felt in the junior ranks.

Given today's competitive environment, no professional firm can provide continued career progress to every junior professional within the boundaries of the firm. Yet we have seen that commitment to career progress is one of the defining characteristics of the professional. Fortunately, there is a relatively simple way out of this dilemma: outplacement. A firm that is truly committed to (and actively works at) placing its "alumni" (not passed-over partnership candidates) in good positions can respond to the career progress needs of all of its juniors, and thereby create a highly motivational atmosphere. As I observe the professional service sector, more and more firms are discovering the power of outplacement, not as a humanitarian effort, but as one of the key elements of the firm's management system.

CONCLUSION

The appropriate organizational response to the motivation crisis in the professions is not to try to make the atmosphere of the organization less intense. The economics of the practice today do not allow this option. Future success in the professions will flow only to those individuals and firms who are willing to gird their loins and meet the intensity demanded by today's practice. If today's young professionals appear less motivated than in the past, it is not because they cannot be motivated. *Rather, it is because the sources of motivation that existed in the past, and the mechanisms through which they worked, are no longer as forceful or effective as they were.* However, with more attention to personal supervisory skills and a reexamination of the firm's recruiting, work assignment, feedback, and outplacement systems, the professional firm of tomorrow can be as highly motivating (and as satisfying) as the firm of yesteryear.

CHAPTER 16

ON THE IMPORTANCE
OF SCHEDULING

The scheduling of work assignments is the single most important managerial activity in a professional service firm. Whoever makes the work assignment decisions is the person really managing the practice.

Although any single scheduling decision may not have the impact of, say, a major recruiting or marketing choice, the very frequency of scheduling decisions makes having the "right" system a matter of paramount importance. Yet many firms view scheduling as a more or less routine administrative matter. That it is not. It is, above all, a managerial procedure that can powerfully influence the direction and success of the firm.

By allocating the right resources to different assignments, there is the opportunity to influence the *cost* of the work, its *quality*, and the *timeliness* of its delivery. Scheduling has longer-term consequences as well. Over time, the pattern of assignments given to professionals will profoundly influence their *professional development*, their worth to the firm and to clients, their *satisfaction* with the firm, and, as a result, their *motivation* and *productivity*. Viewed as a connected set of decisions, assignments will also play a large role in the *dissemination of expertise* throughout the firm, acting as a primary vehicle for converting the experience and knowledge of individuals into the experience and knowledge of the firm as a whole.

Scheduling decisions require a delicate balancing act among goals that often conflict—profitability versus quality service, short-term versus long-term benefits to the organization, putting the needs of one client before another, the morale and development of one staff member before another.

WHAT MAKES A "GOOD" SCHEDULING SYSTEM?

PROFITABILITY CONSIDERATIONS

Since, in the short run, staff expenses are fixed, some firms are lured into acting as if a good assignment system is one that results in high overall utilization of staff resources. Indeed, in many firms, this is the dominant consideration in scheduling. The system is driven by the "Gotcha!" approach—when a new matter is brought in, we look to see who is not yet fully chargeable and say "Gotcha! You're assigned." In such firms, scheduling is predominantly an administrative activity, designed to ensure that everyone is kept busy. In fact, high utilization should be a major (and probably *the* major) objective for any scheduling system. However, it is far from the whole story.

CLIENT SERVICE

Scheduling decisions clearly affect the level of client satisfaction to a significant degree. One senior staff member may be particularly expert in a field required by two competing projects. The decision to assign that individual to one project or the other will regrettably, but inevitably, affect the quality of service delivered to each client. Deciding which client will receive the services of the "office superstar" is a profoundly strategic decision.

Such necessary trade-offs between clients go beyond technical skills. One staff member may be particularly well suited to a particular client because of a match in "style." Although equally competent, another staff member may not be appreciated as much by that client. Perhaps the second person works best with small businesses and that client is a large firm; the problem is not one of the individual's deficiencies, but merely very real client preferences. Choosing the right team to match the "personality" of the client will be a major influence on the project's success, and is an issue of profound strategic importance. Wise use of assignment decisions can profoundly influence the chances of earning follow-on business and strong referrals.

SKILL BUILDING

As well as profitability and client service, the needs of professional development must also be met. In a professional firm, skills are developed on assignments, through exposure to new challenges and new responsibilities. The assignment system thus influences (and may even determine) the amount of skill building that takes place in any given period.

The issue is not only one of the *amount* of skill-building, but its nature. The pattern of assignments will determine how functional or industry skills are built up. If the same individual is always assigned to the same functional topic, the firm builds a functional expert. If it wishes, it can manage the pattern of assignments to build an industry expert. Or it can not manage the process at all, and develop generalists.

In making these decisions, the firm must balance the interests of the firm with those of the individuals. Above a certain level, there may be no benefit to the firm in an experienced staff member performing yet one more assignment on the same industry. He or she may be well down the learning curve, and the firm's interests might be better served by having someone else assigned to the project in order to build breadth in the firm's expertise. Yet the system also must be responsive to individual staff member's needs for development. In most professional firms, the prospect for advancement is a prime motivating force among junior personnel. Accordingly, the scheduling system must provide individuals with the opportunity to gain the experiences and develop the skills required.

Considerations of development imply not only that individuals are assigned to the relevant mix of industries, functional areas, and types of tasks, but also that they are exposed to a variety of senior staff members. This is important for two reasons. First, senior staff members differ in their capabilities and their willingness to share knowledge, skills, and expertise. A junior who always has worked with the same senior staff member is less likely to be exposed to the range of talents and knowledge that are expected to be developed. Unless he or she is exceptionally well rounded and particularly capable of helping juniors, no single senior can fulfill all of the needs in the development of an individual.

There is another reason that juniors should be assigned to work with a variety of senior staff members. In most firms, promotion decisions are based on the judgments of senior staff who have worked with the individual concerned. The more senior staff members that have worked with a given junior, the more likely it is that good decisions will result from the promotion process.

MOTIVATION AND MORALE

Finally, we must add another evaluative criterion to profitability, service, and development. This is the criterion of staff satisfaction and morale. While the personal fulfillment of the work force is important in any enterprise, it is particularly crucial to the professional service firm. Professional firms compete not only for their services, but also in the highly competitive market for superior professionals. Professionals are strongly motivated by their opportunities for development not only in organizational terms ("Will I get promoted?") but also in professional terms. They seek challenge; they seek self-improvement. Furthermore, they have their own interests. Their personal preferences for specific assignments are a valid "input" to the scheduling system.

On a more mundane but no less real level, staff satisfaction with assignment decisions is determined not only by the professional content of the work but also by such practical matters as: location ("I've been out of town on my last three jobs; I deserve one at home"), urgency ("Every one of my projects has been a crisis situation; I *know* not all of our jobs are like that"), colleagues ("Don't give me Ted or Julie again; they're very competent, but we just don't click"), and a host of other personal matters.

The last of these mentioned is particularly important. Most professional projects, and the productivity of the effort put into them, will be significantly affected by how well the team works together. The explicit criterion of building successful working teams is included in many firms' assignments procedures. Even without this factor, however, professional firms must take *some* account of the staff's personal preferences in assignment decisions.

SCHEDULING RELATES TO OTHER SYSTEMS

If the importance of wise management of scheduling decisions needs further demonstration, it is worthwhile to examine scheduling in the context of the firm's other human resource management systems. The linkages are shown in Figure 16–1.

The link between scheduling (work assignments) and recruiting is strong. It is a common experience in all professions that potential recruits carefully investigate how their work pattern will be determined. "How soon will I have to choose a specialty?" "Will I get a chance to work with a variety of individuals, in a variety of industries, in a variety of functional areas?" "How much freedom will I have to choose the work I prefer?" These are common recruiting interview questions.

Since a large part of the long-term success of any professional service firm is determined by its ability to attract and retain superior professionals, the role of the assignment system in marketing the firm to young professionals should not be neglected. Apart from this perspective, there is another link between scheduling and recruiting. If the firm's scheduling system requires the individual to take the initiative and lobby to get on good assignments, then there is little point in recruiting those individuals who are seeking direction in their early

FIGURE 16–1

Relationship Between Major Human Resource Systems in the Professional Services Firm

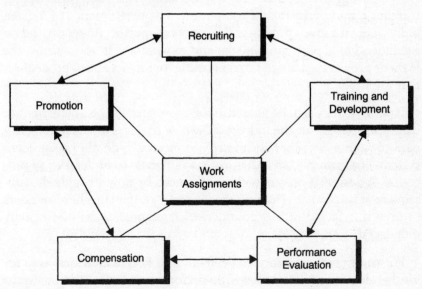

professional years. Conversely, a highly centralized, closely administered scheduling system will strongly influence the personality of the firm and hence the type of people best to recruit. (It is not uncommon for professional firms to place heavy weight in their recruiting on whether or not a given individual "fits in with our way of doing things.")

Many firms have no formal training and development program. Often, the pattern of work assignments *is* the program—no other formal administrative procedure exists to influence the development of human capital. If such a program does exist, it affects the design and function of the scheduling system: The two administrative systems must be matched.

Similarly, the performance appraisal and counseling system that the professional service firm requires must be accommodated to the procedures for work assignments. Where work assignments are centrally administered through a formal department, the discretion of the individual to be assigned may not be great. But if the assignment system allows for more active involvement of individuals, whereby they can or must ask for, choose, or lobby for specific assignments, then career counseling of juniors becomes an important task. They must be guided as to what is useful work, who are useful partners to work for, and what the firm's expectations and criteria are.

There is, of course, a relationship between work assignments, performance, and performance evaluation. The performance of a given individual on a given project will be context-specific. It will depend on the individual's past assignments and experience. In most firms, the team or project leader will be responsible for any feedback procedures that are used.

If performance is to be judged in relativistic terms (i.e., performance demonstrated versus the individual's stage of development), the evaluation system becomes intimately connected with the assignment system. For example, an individual's willingness to undertake an otherwise undesirable project will be influenced by how strongly the subsequent performance is to be judged in context. If no mechanism exists to take this factor into account, work assignments will be heavily influenced.

Forms of compensation for professionals vary widely and are variously related, at different firms, to performance, utilization, value to the firm, experience, profitability of projects and of the firm, and many other factors. Each is significantly affected by the decisions that flow from the assignment system.

The link between assignments and compensation may be explicit, as in a system that ties an individual's compensation to the person's billability or utilization, or it may be implicit, when compensation is influenced by subjective determinants of performances. In either case, the compensation system must be designed around the work assignment system or vice versa. They are not independent.

The pattern of assignments will influence an individual's promotability through the variety of experiences they have provided, the exposure to different partners, and the staff member's subsequent performance. The relationship is two-way. If promotion criteria are such that certain standards must be met (such as demonstrated competence in a variety of areas), the work assignment system must allow for, and perhaps encourage, the relevant experiences.

WHO SHOULD HANDLE ASSIGNMENTS?

In order to understand the problems inherent in the design of scheduling systems, let us imagine that a firm has decided to appoint a scheduling "czar" (or "czarina") to be responsible for all such decisions. What information must be collected in order to make informed judgments?

First, our decision maker would want information about each of the projects: a specific list of the tasks to be performed and, from that, a list of the skills required. This information should indicate when each phase of the project is due and hence what time constraints and flexibility exist. Next, the scheduler would need information on the skill levels and time-phased availability of each of the staff members. If our decision maker really wanted to do the job properly, he or she would consider not only who feasibly could do the work but also how much each individual's time would cost in relation to the likely productivity and quality of that individual's work.

Unfortunately, our service firm scheduler has even more facts to collect, absorb, and take into account. What are the professional needs of the individuals to be scheduled? If these have not been determined, the scheduler needs to review the recent assignments for each of the staff members—what industries they have worked in, what tasks they have performed, what roles and responsibilities they have undertaken in their project teams, what geographical locations they have been sent to, with which partners they have worked.

Apart from the objective development needs of the individuals (as determined by a review committee or the scheduling czar/czarina), the individual's own preferences may or may not be relevant to the decision. Does the individual have a special, personal reason for wanting to work on a particular industry? Does he or she need to work close to home this month? Is there a personal magic between this individual and particular managers or partners? Such considerations may not carry large weight in the assignment process; but if they carry any weight at all, the information must be collected and given to the decision maker.

What of the preferences of managers and partners? Do they prefer to have one professional on their team rather than another? Finally, perhaps our scheduler will want to know if there are client preferences either for individual staff members (for example, on repeat projects for the same client) or for certain categories of staff members ("This is a 'preppy' client, so don't give me Joe. He's smart, but he'll rub them the wrong way"). Also relevant to the decision is the client's relative importance to the firm. If a client or project is a critical one, it should be a higher priority in receiving the firm's best people. Without good judgment in this area, poor trade-offs in client service and client response may result.

We have already created for our scheduling genius a problem of some complexity. (See Figure 16–2.) There is an extensive data bank of facts, judgments, and perceptions concerning the staff members and the projects. In matching the many staff members to the many projects, the scheduler must achieve an "optimum" allocation that is a function of the four major variables of profitability, client satisfaction, staff morale, and professional development.

The scheduling system is, above all, a way to assemble and process large volumes of information and to make *strategic* (not administrative) choices based upon that complex set of facts, judgments, and guesses. Our scheduler needs a procedures to ensure that the four variables are appropriately and consistently weighted, and second, a source of accurate, relevant information—on *real* project skill requirements, *real* capabilities and *real* developmental needs. A scheduling system consists not only of the decision making process itself, but all

FIGURE 16–2

The Structure of the Assignment System

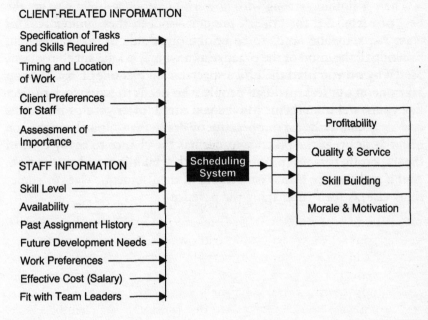

the various organizational devices that are used to communicate information to and from the scheduler.

This analysis clearly leads us to the conclusion that scheduling decisions need to be truly managed. And managed by someone in a position to make sound strategic trade-offs. It is not a task that can be delegated very far from the practice leader (or managing partner or partner-in-charge). Only such people have the knowledge and judgment to take a practice-wide view of scheduling decisions.

For example, it is sometimes necessary for the scheduler to "challenge" the staffing requests of a powerful partner, who has requested many of the best personnel to be assigned to his or her matter. Only a system which had a powerful scheduler (perhaps even the practice leader himself or herself) could force the necessary reflection on the best use of the practice's resources. Wise, strategic allocation of resources among competing uses to accomplish competing strategic goals cannot come from a system that is run by an administrator, nor (as is all too common) from a "political, lobbying, horse-trading" process wherein each senior professional negotiates with the others to get the best resources ("I'll let you have Susan this time, if you'll give me Fred").

There is nothing wrong with powerful partners lobbying to get the best possible staff for "their" projects—indeed they *should* act this way. But someone needs to be on the other side of that discussion, thinking of the good of the practice as a whole, asking such questions as: "Why do you need the office superstar on *this* one? Couldn't you take one of our less qualified people who needs to work on a project like yours and train them? Maybe you could lower your project costs and also build skills for our practice by doing that." It is through such negotiations that the practice leader has the chance to really control the trade-offs between profits, quality, skill building, and motivation. And if the practice leader isn't doing it, then someone else (or something else) is *really* managing the practice.

CHAPTER 17

ON THE MEANING
OF PARTNERSHIP

The defining characteristic of the professional service organization *as
an organizational type* is the expectation of *all* professionals that they
will, with time and personal development, proceed through the ranks
to be considered for some form of ownership or partnership. Professionals want careers, not jobs.

Because of this characteristic, most professional service organizations effectively have an "up or out" system. Even if the firm does not
enforce this policy, the career expectations of individual professionals
will lead them to seek better opportunities elsewhere if their progress
is halted. Reinforcing this system is the tendency of every firm to view
itself as an elite group. Traditionally, the typical professional firm has
acted as if it could afford to take in only the elite as partners; there has
been no room for those who did not excel in the full range of "partner
skills."

Increasingly, firms are beginning to wonder whether this approach
is still appropriate. They wrestle with decisions about partner candidates who may not meet all the criteria for elevation to premier status,
yet represent assets to the firm. They do not want to lose such people,
and are increasingly asking, "How can we keep people without making them partners? Should we consider instituting some new position
or title, such as 'principal,' to handle cases like these?"

185

This issue raises an important question: What is the *meaning* of partnership? What does it symbolize? What are its essential ingredients?

Traditionally, admission to partnership in a professional firm has brought with it a complex bundle of rewards:

• *Equity Participation.* Partners share in the net profits (or losses) of the firm, while nonpartners receive salaries and perhaps bonuses.

• *Tenure.* In most situations, partners cannot be removed except by an extraordinary vote of the partnership.

• *Autonomy.* Whereas juniors must accept the direction or influence of partners (if only because they will be subsequently judged for admission to the partnership by the partners), a partner has, in many firms, a significant degree of autonomy in what and how he or she practices. A partner's work is no longer subject to automatic review by others.

• *Participation in Policy Making.* As an equity participant in the firm, a partner usually has a right to be consulted on major policy decisions of the firm and has a say in how it is to be managed.

• *Income.* While not necessarily a right of partnership, partners usually earn significantly more than nonpartners. For some, the main benefit of being made partner is not autonomy, equity, tenure, or being consulted: It is the simple fact of reaping the financial rewards that they worked so hard for in their apprenticeship years.

• *Internal Status and Recognition.* Apart from all of the foregoing benefits, partnership in the firm is also often eagerly sought because of the internal status and recognition it represents. Professionals, perhaps even more than other types of workers, seek the approbation of their peers: an acknowledgment of their worth. In the culture of most firms, this recognition is embedded in the transition to partnership. To be accepted into the partnership represents an anointing and admission into the ranks of the full professional. To be denied partnership is to be condemned to second-class status.

• *External Status and Recognition.* Professionals seek not only the approbation of peers within the firm, but that of those outside. In the words of one professional, "For myself, I'd accept a nonpartner position within the firm; I understand the internal circumstance. But when my friends and neighbors say, 'What? They haven't made you a partner yet?,' it's very hard to take." In these circumstances it is as much the title of partner as it is the substance that is being sought.

What is significant about this list is that it bundles a large number of separate (or at least separable) rewards into *one* decision. If you are made a partner, you receive, in most firms, all six rewards. If you are turned down, you are denied all six. This strikes me as a somewhat blunt instrument to use in allocating organizational rewards: It is an unforgiving system that does not allow for subtle distinctions to be made. The world is *not* divided into two types of people: partner material and nonpartner material. There are degrees.

These reflections suggest that it might be wise to try to unbundle the six rewards and not embed them all in one "go/no go" decision. It is certainly feasible. There is no reason why equity participation need be synonymous with partnership. Indeed, a number of professional service firms that are incorporated (though operating on partnership principles) spread equity participation to ranks below that of partner equivalent, thus giving a greater number of professionals a stake in the firm's success. Even income levels can be separated from partnership. In some firms a fully productive junior can earn more than a less-than-productive partner, a scheme many other firms could usefully imitate.

Similarly, it is possible to separate tenure from partnership—in *either* direction. Nonpartners can be given security of employment without being made partner, and many large professional firms have partnerships without a guarantee of tenure. Like senior officers at any large corporation, partners can be (gently) asked for their resignation if they cease to perform or meet the firm's standards.

Participation in policy making can also be separate from partnership. At a number of firms there are, in effect, two classes of partner: nominal partners and *real* partners. The latter wield all of the power and make all of the important decisions. They rarely consult the nominal partners, and while there are partnership votes, these tend to be "rubber stamps" of decisions already made by those in power. I am not suggesting that this is the way to run a firm, although it has its merits: The *point* is that there *are* ways to separate membership in the partnership from policy making.

Autonomy, likewise, is a matter of degree. In some firms, partners are truly autonomous, subject only to the constraints of the partnership profit-splitting system. In other firms, junior partners continue to act under the direction of department heads and other more senior partners. The degree of autonomy granted to partners (and expected by them) is a function of the internal *culture* of the firm and the *choices* the firm has made in this regard. It is not preordained.

Finally, status—internal and external. The relative importance of partnership as a sign of *internal* status differs significantly between firms. In firms with a well-developed class consciousness, the difference in status between partner and nonpartner is all important. Partners are royalty and all others are "the common people": A real "us–them" mentality prevails. In such firms, the status value of being a partner is immeasurable.

However, it need not be that way. In other firms, junior nonpartners serve on important committees, take significant responsibility, and, within the internal culture, are treated with as much respect as partners. The difference in status (which still exists) is minimized, and the privileges of rank are suppressed. In such firms, partnership is *not* sought because of status needs. Failing to achieve partnership, or being delayed in achieving it, has its disappointments, but a loss of face in the organization is not one of them. Such firms are more likely to be able to retain desirable professionals short of full partnership.

External status can also be managed. A number of professional service firms have ceased to make any distinctions in the outside world as to the rank of staff members. One I know calls *everyone* an "associate" regardless of tenure, income, internal status, responsibilities, and accomplishments. Internal titles might be used to reflect internal work assignments (manager, department head, executive committee chairman), but to the outside world, all members of the firm have equivalent titles. This is not to say that differences in *external* status do not exist, due to reputation, performance, and the like, but the firm does not go out of its way to accentuate these. External status is a function of the individual's abilities, not his or her place in the hierarchy.

So what does all this mean? It means that professional firms have more options in distributing their rewards—"hard" and "soft"—than many have acknowledged. They have more ways of recognizing individual performance and distinctions between people than the sledgehammer of the partnership decision. By "unbundling" the mixture of rewards represented by partnership, it should, indeed, be possible to retain good people without making them partners.

CHAPTER 18

SURVIVING THE PEOPLE CRISIS

Professional service firms compete in two marketplaces: They compete for clients and they compete for staff. While acknowledging this truism, most professional firms' strategic thinking has nevertheless focused overwhelmingly on the client marketplace alone. Strategy, in most firms, has just been another name for marketing. Human resource issues, such as recruiting, training, and development have been dealt with as matters of administrative detail, not competitive strategy. This, however, is about to change.

In the next decade and beyond, the ability to attract, develop, retain, and deploy staff will be the single biggest determinant of a professional service firm's competitive success.

How do we know this? Simple demographics. Each year since the mid-1960s, the number of new entrants into the work force, in every developed economy, expanded dramatically as the "Baby-Boom" generation reached their twenties. For example, in the United States, the number of people in the twenty-five-to-thirty-four age group rose between 1965 and 1985 from approximately 17 percent of the total population to nearly 23 percent. A similar growth took place in every developed economy.

The increase in numbers was not the only trend favorable to purchasers of professional labor. During this same twenty-year period, in

189

many countries, an ever-increasing percentage of women entered the work force, particularly the professional work force. Further, the "Baby-Boom" group had a higher percentage of university graduates than any previous generation, favoring recruiting organizations that offered professional careers.

In this environment, the relative neglect of strategic thinking about the people marketplace by professional firms may have been appropriate: You don't worry too much about something that is in plentiful supply. However, this environment has begun to change.

In every developed economy, the percentage of the population in the twenty-five-to-thirty-four age group has started to decline from its 1985 peak, and will continue to fall over the next twenty years. In the United States, this group will decline from 23 percent to 17 percent of the total population in the next fifteen years.

The changing *supply* picture must be placed against the background of what is happening to the *demand* for professional workers. Most observers of the world's developed economies have noted a shift to the "knowledge economy." Educated people with a few years of business experience are in increasing demand by businesses of all types, and will have many more options in building their careers than their Baby-Boom elders.

To place the potential impact of this in perspective, consider the following statistic: The "oil shock" of the early 1970s was caused by only a 5 percent shrinkage in worldwide supply. Professional firms are facing a 25 percent shrinkage in their nonpartner labor force. There is going to be a *huge* people shortage, and its effects will be major.

Evidence of the changing supply-demand imbalance was clearly seen in the United States in the late 1980s as entry level salaries escalated rapidly in the accounting, legal, and consulting professions. Its effects have been hidden in the recession of the early 1990s, leading many to believe that there is now an abundance of available people to be hired. However, an examination of the underlying statistics suggests that the effects of the changed supply-demand imbalance will return with full force once the recession is over.

FROM RESOURCE RICH TO RESOURCE CONSTRAINED

To understand the implications of the shift in the supply-demand balance of human resources, imagine you are a manufacturer of products made out of gold, in an environment where gold is relatively cheap and in plentiful supply.

How would you mine for gold in such an environment? You would dig out a mound of earth, stress it out, keep the obvious nuggets and throw the rest away! (The "Up-or-Out" system). When gold is cheap and plentiful, it isn't worth a lot of effort to try to turn medium-grade ore into refined product—it's cheaper and faster just to go dig some more and look for more nuggets. In the Baby-Boom years, turnover at professional firms was high (by design) as many more were hired than were expected to make it through the ranks to become owners or partners, and little emphasis was given to converting medium-grade staff into high performers. In most firms, you made it on your own, or you didn't make it. This was a perfect policy for a resource-rich environment.

When gold is cheap and plentiful, what is your concern about seeking out efficiency improvements in the use of gold? In principle, efficiency is always a good idea, but in practice, firms don't worry very much about the efficient use resources that are cheap and plentiful. In the 1980s few professional firms spent much time and effort looking for new ways to reduce the cost of delivery of their services. As a consequence, few staff members were consistently put to their "highest and best use." Resource allocation decisions (such as staff scheduling processes) were driven by criteria such as the short-term "keep people busy" principle, rather than being driven by issues of productivity, efficiency, and best use of resources.

When gold is cheap and plentiful, how much do you worry about the relative profit margins of the different uses to which you put the gold? Again, product-line profitability is a "nice idea," but the reality is that when the resource is cheap, it's not worth worrying about: Just make whatever you can sell! What about your policy toward growth? In a cheap resource environment, you grow as fast as you can, whatever way you can. If you can sell it, you'll make money at it.

What this discussion shows is that there has been a sound logic to some common managerial policies among professional firms:

- Up-or-out survival of the fittest
- More preaching than execution of coaching
- Opportunistic resource allocation policies
- Lack of attention to seeking ways to reduce delivery cost
- Lack of project-level profitability analyses
- Business development activities that ignore or downplay the profitability of different kinds of work

All of these policies and practices are smart—as long as the environment remains resource rich. But what if it changes? Then the policies firms have used successfully for twenty years might not be so sensible. When resources become relatively scarce and relatively costly, it suddenly *does* make sense to invest in coaching and training in order to extract the maximum value from "medium-grade ore." It suddenly *does* become sensible to worry about the efficient use of resources, and to schedule them carefully, looking for ways to improve productivity (not just production). It *is* now necessary to have a good "job-costing" system so that firm management can track whether resources are being used on the right applications. And growth as a prime strategy is now *no longer* obviously correct. Care must be taken that high-price resources do not get tied up in too much low-value work.

The changing supply-demand balance for human resources clearly affects far more than just recruiting and starting salaries. In fact, these may be the least important aspects of the issue. Many of the entrenched management practices that have proven to be so appropriate for the last twenty years, if preserved, may lead to the firm's downfall over the next twenty years. The key will be the willingness to challenge and reexamine policies that have served the firm well. Will Rogers put it best: "It's not what we don't know that hurts us, it's what we know for sure that ain't so."

WHAT CAN BE DONE?

The changing supply-demand imbalance has three dimensions: *scarcity* (firms might not be able to recruit sufficient numbers of people for their needs), *high cost* (salaries will escalate for all employees), and *retention* (firms will find it harder to hold onto mid-level employees who will be courted not only by traditional professional firm competitors, but by many other businesses).

Of these dimensions, scarcity of entry-level hires is likely to be the least of the problems. Most professions provide attractive *initial* career opportunities relative to other industries. Law school graduates will probably continue to join law firms, accounting graduates to join accounting firms, and business school graduates will continue to find consulting and investment banking attractive first jobs.

The real impact of the people crisis will be felt in absorbing the high costs that will result from competition for educated young workers, and continuing to make the professional-firm career path attractive in an environment when mid-level employees will receive numerous "head-hunting" calls.

To accommodate an environmental shift as large as the one described will take more than tinkering. No single stroke will solve the problem: What will be required is a cohesive strategy built on many avenues of attack. Among these avenues, we can identify three broad approaches that *must* be considered (see also Table 18–1):

a. Find ways to improve the *productivity* of higher-priced resources;
b. Find ways to *reduce need* for costly resources;
c. Investigate the possibilities of *substitution* for costly resources.

PRODUCTIVITY STRATEGIES

Even if firms attract the numbers of people they need (i.e., deal with the scarcity issue), they will continue to face the fact that the bulk of their traditional hires will be at inflated salaries. Accordingly, ways will have to be found to recoup these higher costs by increasing the value of the output produced by the higher-priced resources.

Doing this will be the most significant avenue of attack in dealing with the people crisis. In the competition for scarce, high-priced labor, those firms that can put high-priced people to better (more productive) use than their competitors will be best able to pay higher salaries. Ensuring and raising the productivity of high-priced assets will remain the strategic issue of the coming decade.

WORK MORE HOURS

The most obvious way to obtain more output from any productive resource is to work it harder. A similar thought has occurred to some professional firms who have attempted to extract a "quid pro quo" for higher staff salaries by requiring more billable hours from each of them.

TABLE 18–1

Tactics for Dealing with the People Crisis

PRODUCTIVITY STRATEGIES

Speed up apprecticeship process so that costly resources can handle higher value work

Reward partners explicitly for good coaching

Change engagement staffing so that all are put to "highest and best use"

Use technology to enhance productive capabilities of staff members

Increase expected billable hours from staff

Change pay schemes to reward performance differentials.

REDUCE NEED STRATEGIES

Withdraw from some services and markets that cannot support new salary levels

Drop "up-or-out" system to reduce turnover

Rethink fast growth strategies

Emphasize profitability more, volume of fees less

SUBSTITUTION STRATEGIES

Use more paraprofessionals

Use technology to substitute for labor

Hire "nontraditional" candidates and offset by training

Hire people for "jobs" instead of "careers"

Accommodate part-time, flex-time, "alternate life-style" workers

---

It is less than clear that this is a sustainable, viable strategy for dealing with the people crisis. The increase in billable hours (of the order of 5 to 10 percent) does not offset completely the salary increases, and may work against these firms. The whole point of the escalating salaries seen in the late 1980s (and predicted to return) is that there is a scarcity, and hence a need to be *more* attractive to recruits in a competitive marketplace. Adding to the workload is unlikely to make a firm competitive with others. At best this is a stopgap measure until the other actions discussed below can be implemented.

CHANGE METHODS FOR PERFORMING CLIENT WORK

If a manufacturing company was faced with a doubling of the price of a key machine, it would reexamine the way in which it uses that machine to ensure that it was producing the maximum value of output and was not being wasted in any way. Similarly, a professional firm will need to reexamine whether or not *its* productive resources are truly being put to "highest and best use."

Evidence from my consulting and research suggests that many firms have significant room for improvement here. For understandable reasons—their overriding concern for quality and effectiveness—few professional firms have paid much attention to *efficiency* in their operations. In a majority of professional firms, even the best managed, there is a significant degree of "systemic underdelegation"—work being done by a higher-priced person that could, with more organization and training, be done by someone more junior (and less costly). (See Chapter 4, Solving the Underdelegation Problem.)

In many firms as much as 50 percent of the entire productive capacity of the firm falls into this category. When the price of staff resources escalates, this situation will become intolerable. Firms will need to devise management approaches that will ensure that lower-value work is not being done by higher-priced people except where absolutely necessary.

Ensuring productive use of higher priced staff will require that substantial management attention is paid to the work assignment function (that process which decides who works on what engagements and what part of the work they do). In many firms this aspect of office-level management is relatively neglected, and is dealt with as an administrative function. In a world where, to be productive, every resource must be put to its highest and best use, scheduling becomes a major management topic.

Achieving the goal of more efficient staffing will require firms to invest more in the development of methodologies (so that the more junior people *can* handle higher-valued work and produce higher-value output). In the daily press of business, it is often easier for a senior professional to do a piece of work her- or himself rather than train the junior to handle it. What is more, most firms' measurement systems place great emphasis on personal billable hours: This means that there is little incentive for the senior professional to take the time out to capture and disseminate his or her accumulated wisdom to the juniors. Accordingly, possible methodologies do not get developed.

IMPROVE APPRENTICESHIP PROCESS

Productivity is not just about performing the same tasks at lower costs. It is also about recouping the higher costs of staff by making them more valuable to clients (and hence being able to collect higher fees). In a professional firm there are three main ways to improve the skill-building process. The first has already been discussed: use the work assignment system to expose juniors early to increasingly stretching client work, and ensure that such work is not "hoarded" by those who are overly practiced at performing this work.

The second means of improving skill building is through formal training programs in key areas of knowledge and skill. While these undoubtedly play a role, most firms have learned that formal training serves well for knowledge transfer, but is relatively poor in the more important area of skill building. To speed up the acquisition of critical skills, firms must turn to the third device: better on-the-job coaching and teaching by senior professionals.

This responsibility *is* formally included in the role description of senior professionals at most professional firms, but it is the rare firm today where it has a high priority in the appraisal and reward systems for senior professionals. To achieve the strategic goal of more rapid skill building, firms will have to design reward systems that will convince senior professionals that good performance in this area will be rewarded, and poor performance penalized. (For a method of accomplishing this, see Chapter 4, Solving the Underdelegation Problem.)

Achieving productivity gains will also require a rethinking of compensation systems at lower levels. The majority of professional firms make few, if any, performance differentials in their compensation of junior staff. As the costs of staff escalate, it becomes more important to make distinctions between high-performing and low-performing assets.

VALUE ENHANCEMENT

An additional means by which the high price of staff might be recouped through higher value to clients is "empowering" the individual with the tools, methodologies, experience, and accumulated knowledge of the firm.

A good example of this is provided by those accounting firms that provide low-level staff auditors with laptop computers, which contain in storage the entire audit manual of the firm, together with a quasi "expert" system that allows even the most junior professional to access answers to advanced client questions. In addition, the juniors' computers are compatible with client printers, so that answers to client questions and pro-forma calculations can be produced at the client site.

Another example is provided by the professional service firm that uses a nationwide electronic mail system to allow any professional to access the accumulated wisdom and experience of other firm professionals anywhere in the country.

Value enhancement activities that help junior staff become more valuable to clients need not be "high-tech." At least one major consulting firm has attempted to speed up its knowledge transfer activities by capturing on (many) videotapes the senior staff of the firm explaining in detail how to go about performing the various activities (from client interviewing through data analysis to structuring presentations to maximize client understanding and acceptance) that go toward making a knowledgeable consultant.

Whether low-tech or high-tech, the principle is the same: The more tools that the organization can provide to the staff, the more valuable they can become, and the more likely the organization is to recoup their high cost.

REDUCED NEED STRATEGIES

Even with productivity improvements of the sorts described above, it is likely that most professional firms will end up with a higher cost structure than before. Will clients accept higher fee structures, allowing the firms to sustain their current profitability?

The answer, probably, is that some will and some will not. For critical, frontier-type services (what I have elsewhere described as brains or expertise services), clients will probably continue to be relatively fee-insensitive. However, the majority of professional services are outside this category. For more familiar (or well-defined) issues, clients have a broader choice of potential suppliers, and fee considerations play a greater role in their selection of a professional firm.

As the cost of productive human resources escalates, it will become essential that the uses to which those resources are put be compared, and the lower-value uses be carefully examined for their strategic importance. This will require a serious reexamination of the services professional firms offer, the clients they serve, and the types of business they pursue. Greater selectivity will be the name of the game. Certain services will be dropped (perhaps passed back to the client), and certain types of clients will be judged to be no longer profitable or attractive. For many firms this analysis will require a careful reexamination of how (if at all) profitability is measured at the project or client level.

Not only will these considerations enforce a re-evaluation of which markets and services the firm should be in, but, in addition, firms will have to think more carefully about the relationship between growth and profitability. For the first time in two decades, the growth of professional firms will be constrained by their labor supply. Accordingly, the economics of attracting new business will have to be tested against the economics of staffing that business, including the opportunity costs of tying up staff best deployed elsewhere. Such considerations are rarely included in the "new matters acceptance" policies of today's firm.

If it is to remain vibrant, every professional firm must grow at a rate sufficient to provide challenge and opportunities for advancement to its staff. This has always been so. However, firms will need to ask themselves why they wish to grow at a rate faster than that needed to provide career opportunities.

RETENTION

An important part of any firm's strategy for dealing with the people crisis will be to reduce its need for new hires by doing a better job of retaining its existing staff. If you have paid a lot for a resource, and invested a lot in its training, the last thing you want is for that resource to disappear. Retention will become a major strategic issue.

What will it take to deal with it? As noted above, a great deal more attention will have to be paid to helping individual staff members build their skills. As many studies have shown, morale, motivation, and turnover are affected by nothing so much as the nature of the work given to staff members. Therefore, the productivity issues discussed above are not just a matter of ensuring the effective use of resources: They also speak to the issue of retention. Professionals look for careers, not jobs. As long as their career is progressing, they will stay. When they feel that they are no longer building skills, they will jump.

In addition, it may be necessary to rethink the professions' traditional "up-or-out" philosophy. Letting good people go who are not quite good enough for partnership has always been used as a successful motivating force in the professions. However, it is, by design, a wasteful system, predicated on the assumption there will be an ample supply of new entrants. Clearly, this model of firm structure may not be sustainable in a scarcity situation. (It is interesting that many professional firms are today exploring "alternate partnership models" to address this issue.)

Holding on to good people short of partnership is not an easy task: salary increases alone will not suffice, particularly in an environment where some firms, short of staff, will be constantly looking to "raid" other firms. Ways must be found to help senior nonpartner staff feel valued and not feel the temptation to jump to another firm.

SUBSTITUTION STRATEGIES

PARAPROFESSIONALS

In the search for substitutes for higher-priced workers, most firms will be led to cast a critical eye over their real staffing needs. Does all of their work truly require the services of the highly educated people that make up their traditional work force?

Already, many firms have found that they *can* get significant portions of their work done at a reasonable cost to clients by using paraprofessionals, people who do not have traditional qualifications and can be hired at a lesser cost than the traditional group.

Few professional firms make money on first- and second-year employees: The value of the work assigned to them does not match the salaries they receive. The first year or two are viewed as a training ground for entry level staff, to teach (often by osmosis) the realities of the profession. In the past twenty years, with entry level staff in abundance and comparatively inexpensive, this approach to absorbing new entrants may have been wise. In the future, it may prove to be an expensive indulgence.

Any examination of the tasks performed by entry level personnel reveals that much professional work can indeed be done by paraprofessionals. Of course, executing this strategy will require an investment of time and money to develop the methodologies necessary to make good use of paraprofessionals. It will also require the development of new management structures to oversee the "new" type of employee, and the discovery of ways to train and integrate traditional hires into the practice at a more "advanced" level than heretofore.

For many firms, certain "cultural" issues will arise from this strategy: If there are two *large* groups of staff, one on the professional track and one not, resentments may arise (as they have at some firms). Success with a large-scale paraprofessional strategy requires that the professional "class system" be broken down, and the issue of career paths for paraprofessionals be worked out in advance.

In spite of these difficulties, this strategy is one of the few listed here that has the potential to generate the numbers of staff that many large professional firms require. It has many other potential benefits as well. First, it offers the potential for reducing the "grunt work" component of the early stages of professional careers, thus making firms (and professions) more attractive to scarce potential recruits. Second, it has the potential to lower the cost structure of the firm's delivery of certain services, thus enabling the firm to compete better in a high resource cost environment.

NONTRADITIONAL CANDIDATES

In seeking substitutes for its traditional hires, firms have other sources to turn to apart from paraprofessionals. A major option is to stay with traditional sources of staff, but consider alternatives to traditional hiring criteria. Already the excess of demand over supply for graduates of "elite" schools is leading many firms to cast their hiring net a little wider than in the past.

In the first instance, this often translates into hiring more deeply from traditional schools—that is, recruiting graduates not in, say, the top 25 percent of the class. In addition, many, if not most, law and accounting firms in recent years have begun recruiting programs at schools not traditionally considered to be in the top echelon.

Expanding beyond this, some professional firms (such as accounting and consulting) have begun recruiting graduates from "nontraditional" programs, in the search for "bright" students wherever they may be found. Some accounting firms are targeting math, liberal arts, and science graduates, while at least one major consulting firm has an active program of supplementing its MBA recruiting with hiring programs at major law schools. One can predict with great confidence that this interprofessional competition for bright young people will escalate.

In all of these substitution strategies, firms will need to offset the nontraditional nature of their hires by revised training programs, if the new hires are to be absorbed into the traditional career systems of the professional firm.

However, not all substitutes might require (or expect) to step on to the career ladders of the firms. A major option for professional firms will be to restructure their operations to provide not only "careers" but also "jobs."

Another source of substitutes for traditional professional firm hires will be reentrants to the workplace and experienced people looking for career shifts. As the demographic statistics reveal, there will continue to be an abundance of thirty-five-to-forty-four-year-olds in the workplace, and this may prove to be a useful source of workers for professional firms if these people can be tempted by the types of work traditionally performed by twenty-five-to-thirty-four-year-olds inside the professional firm.

A related substitution tactic would be to accommodate, at any level, those who seek not a career, but a job. Thus, perhaps at any level, some staff could elect to be on the professional, ambitious track (shooting for partnership), while others declare themselves as wishing to stay in a given function or at a given level, perhaps with lesser pay, and fewer demands on them. In essence this is being willing to accommodate the work preferences of a broader variety of people, including part-timers, short-week workers, and others who seek an "alternate work life-style" other than the traditional intense pace that is the hallmark of the professional firm.

TECHNOLOGY SUBSTITUTION

Substitution strategies do not only mean switching from high-priced labor to lower-priced labor. Much professional work is fundamentally made up of knowledge and information processing activities, and hence lends itself readily to the automation of basic processes.

While most firms recognize this, few have fully exploited the opportunities to tap into the power of the microcomputer. In large part, this lag is due to the entrenched practice of charging clients by the hour for work done by professional staff. This circumstance has inhibited the large scale adoption of tools that substitute machines for person-hours.

Yet the opportunities are many. A perfect illustration is provided by one "Big-Six" tax practice, which has set itself the goal of reducing by 50 percent (within three years) the person-hours necessary to produce a tax-return. The exploitation in the legal profession of data-base systems such as Lexis®, together with integrated word-processing activities tied into local area networks, has some distance to go before the full benefits are captured. In many areas of consulting, the software capability to perform relatively standardized analyses has not yet yielded all of the labor savings that are possible, and with the exponential increase of technology, the savings in both time and money continue to grow.

CONCLUSION

Paraprofessionals. Productivity. Rapid skill building. People management skills. Value enhancement. It will immediately be recognized that few of the items listed above are new topics: Most will have been discussed at a majority of firms. Not necessarily acted upon—discussed. What *is* new is the pressure to implement fully the already desirable actions.

One cannot underestimate the difficulty that many professional firms will have in implementing the strategies discussed above. For twenty years, virtually the entire business lifetime of most professional firm leaders, firms could be (and have been) run on the principle that what counted was "getting the business"—if you could get the business, you could get the staff to do the work. The historic abundance of staff has bred a set of attitudes that client-related activities are where it all happens, and that people issues are somehow secondary.

This fundamental philosophy, embedded in the fundamental management practices of the firm (especially its measurement and reward systems) has been validated by two decades of experience, and will be hard to change.

Professional firms, by their very nature, are conservative institutions. Formed from the voluntary collaboration of many powerful and increasingly mobile partners, they can bring about change in the running of their affairs only with broad consensus. By a similar token, the changes that matter are not those made by any central group, but by the collective change of behavior of tens, or hundreds, or thousands of partners beginning to do things differently in the daily conduct of their individual practices.

Take, for example, the simple issue of getting partners to focus on being good coaches of their apprentices; on being good engagement leaders, delegating work as quickly as possible. As noted above, there are few firms that do not "officially" require this of their partners: And there are just as few firms that have any management mechanism of incentive and reward for its performance. In most firms, "business getting" *is* indeed "where it's at," and individual partners do not perceive coaching, training, engagement leadership, skill building, and contributing to retention as high on their priority list; these activities frequently receive more lip service than day-to-day attention.

If a professional firm is to flourish in the new environment, such situations must change. Firms will have to find ways to measure and reward senior professional performance in this area. Successfully implementing such systems is no trivial task. Measuring partner performance in the area of engagement leadership can best be done through some form of regular "upward" reviews by junior staff of their engagement leaders. For understandable reasons, such a management tool is difficult to institute in a partnership. Yet if it is not done, what mechanism will work as well to induce all partners to believe that the firm places an equal weight on performance in this arena as in the client arena? Few firms have solved this dilemma.

Similar challenges face those firms that attempt to wrestle with other countercultural management practices. How many firms will be able to instill the practice of being increasingly selective in new business development to reflect resource scarcity and opportunity costs? How many will be able to make a successful transformation from an "up-or-out" culture to one where staff of varying levels of accomplishment (and status) feel comfortable remaining in the firm?

As may be seen, the firms that will be most successful in adapting to the new environment will be those willing to challenge many of their most cherished notions and most deeply entrenched practices. People *are* the most important asset of a professional service firm. It's time the firms started acting as if they really believed it.

PART FOUR

MANAGEMENT MATTERS

CHAPTER 19

HOW PRACTICE LEADERS
ADD VALUE

What it is that distinguishes the most successful firms (or practices) from ordinary firms in the same market? My experience suggests that it has little to do with creative strategies or unique management systems. Nor is it a matter of IQ or professional talent. The partners I meet in the most successful firms are not consistently smarter or more talented than their counterparts at other firms. What *is* noticeably different at the best firms is a characteristic variously described as energy, drive, enthusiasm, motivation, morale, determination, dedication, and commitment.

While many factors appear to play a role in creating this dynamism, one stands out above all others: the skills and behavior of the practice leader(s). In firm after firm, I have observed marked changes in performance from the same group of partners where the only thing that changed was a new individual appointed to the leadership of a practice. This should not be surprising. A professional practice is like a sports team, filled with talented athletes who will only win if they truly fulfill their potential. Professionals, like athletes, when left to their own devices, don't accomplish as much as they do when they are supported by a good coach.

It is tempting to assume that since the typical professional firm is made up of intelligent, energetic individuals, they can be relied upon to be autonomous, self-starting professionals, with no need to be managed. However, my experience suggests that the best managers really do add a very special value. First, through their actions other people accomplish more, and focus on more important things, than they would if left to their own devices. Second, it is through the skill of the manager that the talents of powerful individuals are shaped into even more powerful teams, learning from and supporting each other.

Professionals lead busy lives with many conflicting demands on their time and attention. In such a world, it is all too easy to be driven by the pressure of events and postpone or neglect activities that may not have to be done today but are essential for the future. All too often, the urgent drives out the important. Examples of "postpon-able" activities that are often neglected due to the pressure of daily business might include those extra touches of client service that build relationships; or the added time it takes to help a more junior profes-sional learn a new approach; or the extra time taken to represent the firm in important meetings of the business community in order to build a presence.

Professionals usually understand the importance of these activities and know what to do to execute them. They *intend* to do them. But they do not always get around to them. After all, each of these actions involves short-term "costs" for a long-term benefit. Left to themselves, professionals, like all human beings, find it all too easy to take care of today, at the risk of underinvesting in tomorrow.

I first experienced the power of a skilled manager of professionals as a young academic, when I lived within a system that had both short-term goals (teach my classes), as well as long-term goals (re-search and publication). I could be relied upon to teach my classes, but even though it was in my own career interest to get the long-term stuff done, somehow I always found ways to postpone it. The school's formal performance appraisal system, conducted annually, was an exercise in paperwork, and never really worked to motivate me (or anyone else I knew.)

Then one day, without notice, a senior colleague dropped by. "Da-vid, we don't have many opportunities to get together," he said, "and I was interested in what you were up to. Why don't you tell me what your research is about?" I stumbled to find an answer. "Well, you might need to get a little more focused," he observed. "Let's chat about it. How can I help?" We discussed my ideas for a while. "What research sites do you plan to visit?" he asked. I had no idea and said I was still working on it. "Perhaps I can help you there," he said. "Why don't you make a list of what you're looking for and I'll review it with you, if you wish."

The conversation continued with the senior colleague gently probing, making suggestions, and making me well aware (without rubbing my nose in it) of what I should be working on. After (only) fifteen or twenty minutes, he said, "Well, I have to leave now, but I'm delighted we had this chance to chat. Perhaps I can drop by again sometime soon. I'll be keen to see what progress you've made."

This individual was very skilled. His tone and questions were gentle and understanding, but I was thoroughly embarrassed that I didn't have good answers to reasonable questions. That fifteen or twenty minute intervention left me motivated and energized, and I was more organized, disciplined, and productive than I had ever been for at least three months afterwards.

The lessons, I hope, are obvious. Before this intervention, I was cruising along, taking care of business, but not really focused or productive, in spite of all the formal incentives and structured performance appraisal systems. Basically, I felt like one more cog in the system. Suddenly, someone was showing a personal interest in me. Someone clearly cared about me and how I was doing. Someone wanted me to succeed, and found a nonformal, nonthreatening way to offer concrete, helpful suggestions. This person let me form my own conclusions about how well I was doing. I wasn't being judged, I was being *coached*.

Since that time, I have repeatedly observed both the need for, and the power of, good coaching. I frequently ask groups of partners to assess the percentage of their capabilities at which they are currently functioning. The answers vary widely, but can be surprisingly low. Partners frequently report that they are diligent and are working hard, but a surprisingly large percentage report that they are not "turned on" and excited by their practice. They are just "grinding it out." This difference between working hard and being excited may be subtle, but it makes a world of difference in leading to marketplace success.

I once interviewed the managing partner of a large office of an international professional service firm. I had been told that, without changing personnel or investing extra funds, he had converted a number of the firm's declining and demoralized branch offices into flourishing practices. I was eager to learn the secret of his success. Would it be strategic planning? Tight cost control? Marketing training for the professional staff?

"The key thing that I do," he told me, "is to call each person into my office and ask a single question: 'What do you want to be famous for?' " He reported that a very high percentage of partners have no answer to the question. "The typical professional," he continued, "is a highly trained, intelligent person, usually ambitious, who wants to feel special and to feel that the firm that he belongs to is special. But it is remarkable how few people are focused. My job as managing partner is to engage, encourage, focus, and channel the partners' energies and ambitions."

My own research with professional service firms of all kinds has confirmed the wisdom of these observations. For firms to function effectively, they must foster an atmosphere of dynamism, of ambition, of aiming to be the best. It is the manager's task to keep the professionals' eyes fixed on this continuous ambition to improve, to grow, to develop.

WHAT GOOD COACHES DO

How do good coaches achieve results? Effective practice leaders recognize that you rarely "turn on" partners (or get them to change) through speeches, vision statements, or inspirational group meetings. They know that the only truly effective way to influence people is one on one, in highly individualized, closed-door counseling. Above all else, they pay attention to the individual. They are close enough to what the individual is doing to be able to offer substantive suggestions. They are always "dropping by" to ask "how's it going?"

Good coaches use many approaches in motivating their people, recognizing that different individuals are "turned on" by different things. What works with one partner may fail with another. Among the many separate and different things that may motivate a given individual are money, external (marketplace) esteem, internal status and recognition, autonomy, appreciation, professional pride, teamwork, an especially challenging assignment, rivalry, or any of a numerous list of "hot buttons." One of the key talents of a good coach is the ability to recognize what motivates each specific individual, and deal with people on their own terms. Good coaches do not theorize about what *should* motivate people—instead, on a case-by-case basis they discover what *does* motivate each person.

A good coach recognizes that coaching is a continuous process and does not "save up" feedback and performance guidance for a once-a-year grand counseling session. Constructive feedback and suggestions are much more likely to be accepted (and hence be effective) if they are offered in small increments. Similarly, if counseling advice is given long before performance is to be assessed, and not when it directly leads to reward, then it is more likely to be seen as a source of help, not as an evaluation. When good coaches give feedback, it should not be just a critique, but should contain concrete action ideas for how to improve. Good coaches tell people not only *what* could be improved, but *how*. They are thus seen by those they coach as a source of creative ideas.

Effective practice leaders go out of their way to celebrate successes and triumphs. They make constant use of approval, visibility, recognition, and appreciation. (Ask your partners how often they hear "well done" or "thank you." Ask them whether they'd like to hear it more often.) However, to be effective, good coaches must also be demanding. When a good athlete successfully jumps over the high bar, what does a good coach do? Two essential things. First, celebrate the accomplishment, and then—raise the bar! ("Come on you can do it!") Coaches must be simultaneously chief cheerleader and chief critic—one without the other is insufficient. Part of the skill of coaching is knowing how high to raise the bar, that is, judging for each individual, separately, what next challenge will be stretching but achievable.

Good coaches know that getting people to change is difficult. People prefer to stick with what they know how to do (and the way they know how to do it) rather than risk exposing themselves by trying to learn something new. To overcome this, good coaches are adept at structuring small pilot projects designed to give the individual (and the group) the experience of an early success. They rarely ask people to make major changes, but instead say "Let's just try this one small thing and see if it will work." Good coaches give people the confidence to try new things, and help them accomplish more than they expected they could.

Good coaches build teams. Since most players will probably be more focused on their own personal performance, it is up to the coach to look out for the overall best interests of the group. The coach must identify opportunities for joint activities. The coach must stay alert for those situations when what is in the best interest of the player is not necessarily in the best interest of the team (e.g., who pursues a specific client, or how a particular matter is to be staffed), and then must negotiate with the individuals involved to do the "right" team thing. This inevitably involves the coach in trading favors. ("Help us out on this one, and I'll do my best to look after you next time.") Good coaches pay significant attention to how the group's resources are being deployed, and whether or not all the bases are being covered.

Good coaches make frequent use of small-group team meetings to discuss "What are we going to do about X?" drawing ideas out of the group. Good coaches are Socratic. They don't present conclusions ("I've thought about this and decided we've got to do X"). Instead, they reason together with their team. If ideas come up that they are uncertain about, they ask "If we did that, how would we handle the following adverse consequences?" Good coaches know that their job is to get people to act differently and to try new things, and that means making people want to do it. This is accomplished, in large part, by leading them to discover the right answers for themselves.

As possible initiatives develop some degree of consensus, they ask for volunteers, or assign roles, to perform activities on behalf of the group. ("Susan, will you be prepared to do that for us? When do you think you can get it done by?") They also make sure that people don't sign up for things they can't get done, because they do not want to set the precedent that action promises to the group can be neglected. Good coaches also work hard at developing joint tasks so that people get the experience of teamwork and joint responsibility.

Perhaps most important of all, good coaches follow up. They monitor the execution of plans ("By the way, Tom, how's that seminar that you agreed to arrange going? Anything I can do to help?") If things are getting off track, they don't wait for the end of the fiscal year to see what was and what wasn't done—they gently intervene while there's still time to get things back on track.

HOW THE PRACTICE LEADER SPENDS TIME

What all this reveals is that practice leaders can be valuable by helping professionals understand and act on their *real* priorities and help them balance their activities between those things that help the individual (and the firm) today and those that will help ensure their tomorrow. Left to their own devices, bright energetic people will look after "today." Practice leaders are needed to be the *guardians of the long-term*. They are valuable when they act as the *conscience* of their colleagues: not necessarily *giving* them new goals, but helping them achieve the goals they have set for themselves. The manager's role is to be the reminder, the coach, the supporter, as individuals struggle to balance today's pressures with longer term accomplishments.

This is not necessarily easy. Of everyone in the firm, it is most likely the manager who is most familiar with and must deal with today's financial results. There is thus a danger that the manager can become the most short-term oriented individual in the office rather than the most long-term oriented.

The best indicator of the orientation of managers is how they spend their time. A manager's time can be divided into five categories:

- Administrative and financial matters
- Doing professional (billable) work
- Personal marketing and selling
- General client relations
- Dealing and talking with senior professionals and staff

Where in this list is the manager's greatest opportunity to "make a difference?"

As pressing as financial and administrative matters can appear, they are not points of high impact from a long-term perspective. Administration is a matter of "hygiene": if done poorly it can hurt the practice, but outstanding administration never promotes the future success of the practice. It must be taken care of, but it does not build for the future. Practice leaders must find ways to get the administration performed (with quality) without consuming all of their precious time.

Virtually every practice leader should have a high-powered administrative officer to whom administrative and financial matters can be delegated. In almost all cases, such a person is self-funding, since the time freed up for the practice leader to apply to high-valued tasks is worth much more than the cost of an administrative officer. Any practice leader spending more than 10 percent of his or her time on administrative or financial matters is being an administrator, not a manager.

What of doing professional work (i.e., staying personally billable)?

Is this a necessary activity for a practice leader? To a certain extent. Managers, in order to have the credibility to lead, must continue to earn the professional respect of those they are hoping to influence. They must also ensure that they are not completely isolated from the market. And yet it is clear that performing personal billable work on his or her own clients is not a highly leveraged use of a manager's time. There is only a limited opportunity to help and influence others in the office when doing this.

How much of this must the manager do in order to retain the respect of colleagues and remain in close contact with the market? Answers may vary by profession and by firm, but it could be argued that, if it is the right kind of work, a manager can continue to demonstrate "value as a professional" by being no more than 10 to 20 percent chargeable. Doing professional work is fulfilling and fun, and coaching others is not always so, but one must recognize which is the true "building" activity.

A similar line of reasoning applies to new business development or selling. The manager must be involved in this to earn the respect of the senior professionals. Yet a manager adds the most value not by selling, but by teaching others how to sell. *There* is the leverage. There are forms of business community activities and new prospective relationship building that the senior professionals cannot do as well alone and the manager is needed to help—but not to be a substitute. A manager's role is to be a teacher first and a "doer" second. Both are needed, but the priorities must be clear.

Time spent dealing with senior professionals is, as we have discussed above, a very high-value activity, if done well: helping others solve *their* problems, helping them keep *their* priorities straight, helping them set stretching goals for themselves. These are the activities that produce results *beyond* what the people would accomplish if left to their own devices. The best coaches devote significant time to this area, anywhere from 30 to 60 percent of their work-week.

What of client relations? It is important to note that, as used here, client relations is a separate category from both business development and personal professional work. Instead, we are referring to the activity of visiting clients of other partners in the practice to discuss the client's satisfaction with the firm's services, their emerging business issues, and the like. Of course, these visits are not intended to go behind the backs of the partners responsible for those clients and would usually be done in conjunction with those partners.

This activity is immensely valuable. Spending time with existing client executives on top of what the professionals are already doing goes a long way in cementing relationships, assuring client satisfaction, and uncovering new business issues with decision makers. Of course, the visits also act as a powerful quality assurance function. If a manager can use time and position to support senior professionals in this area, it will have a highly leveraged impact and deserves 20 to 40 percent of the manager's time.

The percentages given above are not, of course, absolutes. For example, a manager in a very large practice may have so much opportunity to make an impact in the client relations and coaching areas that it is sensible for him or her to reduce his or her personal billable hours to zero, establishing and retaining credibility solely through assisting others with their client work and client relations activities.

Some managers reviewing the five categories of activity might ask "Where is the time for doing strategy and planning, for sitting alone and thinking?" I believe strongly that a manager sitting alone is not managing. Strategy and planning are not distinct from the activities described above. If the manager is active in visiting clients to discuss their emerging issues, and active in meeting with partners individually or in small groups, then the strategic task will be well executed.

WHO SHOULD COACH?

It should be clear from this discussion that, except in the smallest of firms, one person cannot possibly coach all other partners. Accordingly, coaching should be the responsibility not only of the managing partner, but of each and every one of the departmental practice heads in the firm. Unfortunately, while departmental practice leaders often understand the importance of their role, they don't always act upon it. When working with practice group leaders, I often ask the question: "If you had an extra day per week to spend on increasing the success of your practice group, what would you do with that day?" The most common answer is "Spend more time with my partners." "Doing what?" I ask. The replies to this question include much of what we have discussed above: following up on planned initiatives, motivating partners, cheering them on, solving problems and conflicts such as staffing or scheduling, holding small-team meetings to develop action plans, and discussing strategies. They readily agree that performing these activities would make a significant difference to the success of the practice. "Then why don't you spend that day a week?" I ask. "Too busy," comes the reply, "We've got to stay billable."

Let's do the arithmetic on this argument. Let's examine a practice leader who is responsible for a group containing ten partners, with total billings of $8 million and a profit of $3 million. (Naturally, you should substitute your own numbers in this example.) One day a week represents 20 percent of the practice leader's time. Let's assume a 2,500-hour year. This translates into 500 fewer billed hours. (We'll assume the practice leader keeps up all other activities, including business development, but just reduces his or her billable time by 500 hours.) Now assume that the practice leader's billing rate is $400 per hour. This means a cost of $200,000. What is the probability that with one day a week available (week-in, week-out, throughout the year) to focus on managing an $8 million practice generating $3 million in profit, the practice leader could recoup an investment of $200,000? If the practice leader has *any* managerial skill, the probability should be very high, perhaps over 99 percent. It might even be worth considering having the coach manage for two days a week!

What this analysis attempts to show is that it is clearly more economic for the practice leader to help *other* people become successful—or even more successful than they already are—rather than focusing on his or her own activities. The practice leader's job is not to be the most successful practitioner in the group, nor its best salesperson. Instead, the job is to help others succeed as practitioners and salespeople.

EVALUATING THE PRACTICE LEADER

Since the job of the practice leader is to help the group succeed, practice leaders should be judged on how well they accomplish this task. They should never be evaluated on their individual performance (i.e., their personal numbers on such things as billings, business generation, etc.), since this sets up an irreconcilable tension between what they are being asked to do, and how they are measured. Instead, practice leaders should be explicitly judged on the aggregate performance results of the group they manage (i.e., total group billings, total group business generation).

In addition, practice leaders should receive feedback. Like every partner, a practice leader has clients. However, a practice leader's main clients are not those outside the firm, but the partners within the group. To ensure that practice leaders are fulfilling their role, some firms have instituted a feedback system from the partners in the group to the practice leader. Each of the partners anonymously rates the practice leader on questions such as those shown in Figure 19–1. The results are tabulated by a third party, and the practice leader (and, in some cases. firm management) receives the aggregate results.

Although many firms break this rule, it is also important that practice leaders do not receive "position pay," that is, they should not automatically be compensated more highly for taking on the coaching role. Like everyone else, they should be paid for performance—their group's performance. Such a reward system should help the practice leader in performing the role since all the team members will know that the only way for the practice leader to succeed is by helping them succeed. This should make them more ready to accept the practice leader's direction and suggestions.

THE MANAGEMENT STRAIN

Naturally, it takes a talented person to be able to do well on the criteria shown in Figure 19–1, and an even more special kind of person willing to be held accountable for performing against those criteria. Not everyone has what it takes to be an effective practice leader. The more I spend time with professional service firms, the more I realize how different the required skills are between being an outstanding professional and being an effective manager, and how stressful the manager's role can be.

On an average day, the typical professional can concentrate his or her attentions on one or two major projects, staying focused and probably ending the day with visible signs of progress. For the typical manager of professionals, the day is broken up into numerous small chunks of amazing diversity: dealing with a disgruntled client, handling the personal problems of a staff member, analyzing financial reports, interviewing a potential new recruit, approving various administrative arrangements, working on a new business presentation, and a thousand other matters, each of which must, in rapid succession, command the manager's full attention. The ability to change mental gears rapidly is one of the manager's most important talents, as is the ability to continuously evaluate and reshuffle priorities.

FIGURE 19-1

Evaluation of the Practice Leader

To evaluate the practice leader, please complete the following questions. Indicate your agreement or disagreement, using the following scale: 1 = Strongly disagree; 2 = Somewhat disagree; 3 = Neither agree or disagree; 4 = Somewhat agree; 5 = Strongly agree

THE PRACTICE LEADER . . . . .

Is more often encouraging than critical	1	2	3	4	5
Is accessible when I want to talk	1	2	3	4	5
Keeps informed about what I am doing	1	2	3	4	5
Is fair in dealings with partners	1	2	3	4	5
Causes me to stretch for performance goals	1	2	3	4	5
Is concerned about long-term issues, not just short-term profits	1	2	3	4	5
Conducts team meetings in a manner that breeds involvement	1	2	3	4	5
Is consultative in his/her decision making	1	2	3	4	5
Is sufficiently involved with nonpartners and their issues	1	2	3	4	5
Provides constructive feedback that helps me improve my performance	1	2	3	4	5
Is a source of creative ideas about our business	1	2	3	4	5
Gives me the freedom to set my own goals	1	2	3	4	5
Makes me feel that I am a member of a well-functioning team	1	2	3	4	5
Acts more like a coach than a boss	1	2	3	4	5
Helps me understand how my tasks fit into the overall objectives for the firm	1	2	3	4	5
Keeps me informed about the things I need to know to perform my role properly.	1	2	3	4	5
Actively encourages me to volunteer new ideas and make suggestions for improvement of the practice	1	2	3	4	5
Helps me to grow and develop	1	2	3	4	5
Encourages me to initiate tasks or projects I think are important	1	2	3	4	5
Is publicly generous with credit	1	2	3	4	5
Is prompt in dealing with underperformers	1	2	3	4	5
Is good at keeping down the level of politics and "politicking"	1	2	3	4	5
Encourages innovation and calculated risk taking	1	2	3	4	5
Relates the total reward system (compensation, recognition, etc.) to job performance, rather than such things as position or seniority	1	2	3	4	5
Emphasizes cooperation as opposed to competitiveness between work groups	1	2	3	4	5
Is effective in communicating with partners	1	2	3	4	5

The manager must also learn to live with a higher level of ambiguity and risk than the typical partner. whose success or failure, for better or for worse, is in his or her own hands, dependent on what he or she does. The manager must accomplish goals through others, and his or her success is less under his or her personal control. The results of the typical partner's work are often clearly visible, and the client feedback frequently prompt. However, for the manager, the very definition of what "success" means is less clear, and the feedback on whether it has been achieved is more circuitous and ill-defined. Rarely can a manager go home knowing that something concrete and substantial was accomplished today.

The manager of professionals must also possess a great deal of "bounce-back ability." As David Ogilvy put it in his *Ogilvy on Advertising*,[1] the CEO of the professional firm must be a good leader of frightened people and resilient in adversity. Professionals look to their managers for inspiration, enthusiasm, and confidence (never so much as when things are tough). Rather than indulge the inevitable emotions that accompany daily triumphs and disasters, the manager must maintain an even keel. Paul Alvarez of Ketchum Communications says the hardest and most important lesson that he had to learn on taking over the managerial reins was that he had to operate on the principle of "No Good Days, No Bad Days."

To be successful, the coach must also be able to suppress his or her own ego needs, since the very nature of the job is to make other people feel successful and important. The job of the manager is to build a team, not an empire. The best leaders of professionals are quick to give credit to others, and to play down their own role in successes—a behavior trait that many superb professionals have to work to acquire at some personal psychological cost.

The coach's job contains other stresses: Since few professionals like to be *told* what to do, the manager must act through persuasion and cajoling, even where the manager sees the way clear. Living with the frustrations of building consensus and resisting the temptation to just *act* are a permanent struggle. This is particularly true in resisting the temptation to intervene in the professional work of others. Managers must allow professionals to make their own decisions (and perhaps mistakes) in order to allow them to develop. Since the manager's job is to *teach*, he or she must have patience with those still trying to learn. For many, taking on the manager's role means giving up a significant degree of the personal fulfillment that comes from practicing one's professional craft.

Since there are no surer paths to the decline of a professional firm than the absence of honest, constructive criticism and the failure to confront nonperformers, the coach must also bear the emotionally hard tasks of giving and justifying performance feedback and, on occasion, termination notices. Managers must also be responsible for reconciling conflicts, especially on the use of resources. In their management of group resources, they must routinely arbitrate between partners on who gets what staff member, who chases what lead, who is given what opportunity.

Coaching takes time, patience and ingenuity. It is often frustrating and only occasionally rewarding. The practice leader must have the ability to interact with others in such a way that critiques are accepted as welcome assistance, not as interference. The practice leader must be able to ask people to stretch without making them resentful or defensive. It requires a style that results in the practice leader being seen as a personal resource to them, not as a nit-picking supervisor, nor as a boss. Good practice leaders create motivation in others by communicating and demonstrating their own enthusiasm. Cynicism and excitement are both infectious—which of the two the practice leader communicates is critical.

A crucial requirement of leadership in a professional firm is the ability to earn the trust of others. To trust a leader does not necessarily mean that one always agrees with him or her. Trust is the conviction that the manager means what he or she says, that the manager *cares*. That what is being done is not self-serving or driven by ego, but because he or she is truly serving the long-term firm purposes. The people they coach must believe that the coach's motives are pure—the coach is not being authoritarian, but is really trying to *help*. A coach must make people believe that they are being asked to change not to make the coach look good and not just to benefit the greater glory of the firm, but because the coach has helped them see what is in it for *them*.

In many firms, regrettably, being appointed as a practice leader is some form of "reward." The position goes to the most eminent, or the most senior, or the best business-getter among the partners. None of these criteria is appropriate. Practice leadership should be seen as a role or a responsibility, not a title, a promotion, or a reward. There is a highly specialized and difficult job to be done here. Naturally, practice leaders cannot be effective if they do not have the professional respect of their colleagues. They must have a history of being able to do what they ask others to do. They must be good professionals. But, as in sports, the coach does not have to be the *best* player in order to coach well.

Finding good coaches in a professional firm is tough. There are few individuals who "naturally" possess the skills described here. There are even fewer who are eager to give up a portion of their practice to accept the responsibilities discussed. However, given the desire to learn them, coaching skills can be developed—and therein lies the opportunity. Given both the scarcity and the power of good coaching, it is entirely possible that a firm's competitive success can be built on a superior ability to get the best out of its people.

CHAPTER 20

HOW TO CREATE
A STRATEGY

A few years ago, I was given the opportunity to examine the strategic plans of most of the major competitors in a given professional service marketplace. Each had performed a thorough analysis of the marketplace and had identified which client industries were most attractive, based on such factors as growth, profitability, need for services, and so on. Each had analyzed carefully the most attractive clients in these industries, and had identified the most desirable target prospects. Each had analyzed which services and specialties were most in demand among these target clients.

The result of this analytical endeavor (on which each firm scored a perfect ten) was that each firm wrote a strategic plan which read "Our strategy is to target the following clients in the following designated industries and serve them with the following key services."

Nothing wrong with that. Except that each competitor had exactly the same list of target clients, industries, and key services: They all had got their arithmetic right. Their strategic plans could have been reshuffled and redistributed, with firm names replaced, and no one would have been the wiser.

Rather than finishing their strategy development task, these firms had just reached the starting point. In the jargon of business schools, strategy development is the search for ways to " build a competitive advantage through distinctive capabilities." Stripped of its grandiose terminology, this is a straightforward idea: the development of a set of actions that will make the firm's services *more valuable to clients* than the services of competing firms.

When the most desirable markets to compete in have been identified, the firm must then turn to the more difficult task of deciding *how* it will compete. This next stage of the strategy development effort is clearly less about marketing tactics than about internal, operational matters: how to change the firm's methods of delivering services so that clients derive additional benefits from its approach compared to that of the best competitors.

Viewed in this light, developing a strategy is fundamentally a *creative* activity, not an analytical one. It's about finding *new ways of doing things* that provide an advantage over the competition. How can this be done? Table 20–1, while not exhaustive, lists some of the major alternatives.

The challenge for an individual firm is not to find a positive answer to each of the questions posed: It would be unrealistic to expect any single firm to excel on each dimension listed. Rather, the strategy challenge is to pick two or three of these alternatives and be sufficiently innovative in finding ways to achieve the extra value for clients in those areas.

WHAT SHOULD YOU STRATEGIZE ABOUT?

There is a natural, but regrettable, tendency for professional firms, in their strategy development processes, to focus on new things: "What new markets does the firm want to enter? What new clients does the firm want to target? What new services does the firm want to offer?" This focus on new services and new markets is too often a cop-out. A new specialty (or a new office location) may or may not make sense for a firm, but it rarely does much (if anything) to affect the profitability or competitiveness of the vast bulk of the firm's existing practices.

On the other hand, an improvement in competitiveness in the firm's core businesses will have a much higher return on investment since the firm can capitalize on it by applying it to a larger volume of business. Unfortunately, enhancing the competitiveness of the existing practice will inevitably require changes in the behavior of the existing partners.

TABLE 20-1

Possible Strategies for Being More Valuable to Clients

---

a. Can we develop an innovative approach to *hiring* so that we can be more valuable to clients by achieving a higher calibre of staff than the competition?

b. Can we *train* our people better than the competition in a variety of technical or "counseling" skills so that they will be more valuable on the marketplace than their counterparts at other firms?

c. Can we develop innovative *methodologies* for handling our matters (or engagements, transactions or projects) so that our delivery of services becomes more thorough or efficient?

d. Can we develop systematic ways of helping, encouraging and, above all, ensuring that our people are skilled at *client counseling* in addition to being top technicians?

e. Can we become better than our competition at accumulating, *disseminating, and building on our firmwide expertise and experience*, so that each professional becomes more valuable in the marketplace by being empowered with a greater breadth and depth of experience?

f. Can we *organize and specialize* our people in innovative ways, so that they become particularly skilled and valuable to the market because of their focus on a particular market segment's needs?

g. Can we become more valuable to our clients by being more systematic and diligent about *listening to the market*: collecting, analyzing, and absorbing the details of *their* business than does our competition?

h. Can we become more valuable to our clients by investing in *research and development* on issues of particular interest to them?

As Table 20-1 suggests, it implies new methods of operating, new skill development, new accountabilities. In the real world of professional firms, these changes are potentially disruptive, uncomfortable, contentious, and political.

How much easier to take a view of strategy which in essence says, "Existing partners will carry on as before, and we'll solve our strategy problem by adding laterals to develop a new specialty or opening a new office in another city!" I describe such reasoning as "adding pimples to the elephant."

Of course, new specialties and locations must be considered. A firm must have strategies both for new things and for the core: One without the other is insufficient. But it should never be forgotten what strategy is really all about: changing current methods of operating in order to render more value by existing partners on existing services to existing market segments.

WHO SHOULD DEVELOP THE STRATEGY?

One of the most unfortunate myths about the strategy development process is that it is the responsibility of the firm leadership, or a firmwide committee, to develop a strategic plan and then persuade or "sell" the rest of the partnership on following that vision.

There are a number of problems with this approach to developing strategy. First, most professional firms are made up of subgroups providing significantly varying services to different groups of clients. Consequently, any attempt to address the questions shown in Table 20–1 becomes impossible to achieve if considered at the level of the whole firm.

For example, the best way for a litigation group in a law firm to achieve a competitive advantage may be completely different from what the real estate group in the same firm needs to do to differentiate itself from its competitors. The consulting division of an accounting firm may require a completely different strategy than what the same firm's audit group must do to distinguish itself. Figuring out how to make the firm's services more valuable to clients logically belongs at the level of each service line, that is, at the practice level.

One would be hard pressed in most professions to identify whole firms that are perceived in the marketplace as differentiated *as firms*. Clients will readily talk about the strengths and weaknesses of different practice groups within firms, but rarely can they perceive differences between whole firms (unless the entire firm is built around well-defined specialties). Accordingly, any attempt to develop a strategy from the top, and striving for actions that will differentiate the whole firm, will be doomed to failure.

There is a second problem with top-down, firmwide strategic planning. If a central group (however formed) develops a vision of how to compete, then, as noted above, there remains the task of "persuading" the rest of the partnership to implement the prescribed course of action. It is on this rock that most professional firm strategic initiatives falter. Partners, as we all know, value their autonomy and resist hierarchical direction. They cannot be "instructed" to practice differently; they can, at best, be *convinced*. However, presenting the final conclusions of a strategy developed by others is not a particularly persuasive tactic for obtaining "buy-in."

Any new strategic initiative concerning the existing practice will inevitably require new modes of behavior on the part of large numbers of people, especially partners. Predictably, many traditional patterns of behavior will be challenged, reward systems will frequently have to be modified, and roles and responsibilities reassigned. Accordingly, any strategy development process must be consultative, one in which individual partners can become convinced that the benefits *to them personally* of achieving the goals will be worth the personal "costs" of doing new things or different things.

For these reasons, it is *essential* that the professionals in the firm perform the strategic planning activities themselves. They must "own" the recommendations if they are to be implemented, and this is hard to achieve if the recommendations are those of a staff group, a management committee, or an outsider.

Since strategy is not just about *what* the firm wants to achieve, but *how* the firm is to achieve it and *who* is going to do it, an action plan must be devised, and the best people to do that are those who are going to be responsible for implementing it. Therefore those people must be involved early. In fact, they should be primarily responsible for developing and proposing the strategy. People always feel more committed to self-selected goals than to goals and plans imposed from above.

The best way to structure the strategy development process in firms is to do it as much "bottom-up" as possible. What this means is that each practice group (or area) should be asked to develop a strategy for *their* practice area. They should be presented with a set of "challenging" questions (see Table 20–2) about how *they* plan to improve the competitiveness of their practice area. A date should be scheduled for the firm's management to listen to a presentation of their plan, and the management (this is important to the process) should act as "friendly

TABLE 20–2

Some "Friendly Skeptic" Questions to Appraise a Strategic Plan

---

What special capabilities do you plan to have that your best competitors cannot match?

Why can't they match them?

What actions will you take to put these capabilities in place?

In what way are your investment priorities likely to be different from those of the competitors?

How do you know the clients will like what you're planning? What field testing have you done? What client input have you obtained?

Who will be in charge of executing each component of the plan?

Who was involved in the development of this plan? Is everyone in agreement? (Who was not consulted? Do they have a role in executing the plan?)

On whom will you be dependent for the execution of this plan? Do they have sufficient incentive to do their part? Is it in their interests to do what you want? Do you have to modify your reward systems to make this happen?

Specifically, which 5 or 10 clients, by name, represent your most *likely* source of expanded business for the next few years? What actions do you plan to take to get closer to these clients?

Which new clients are at the top of your priority list? Why? What makes you think you can get their business?

What is the one most significant thing that each of the main competitors is doing that will affect you? What do you plan to do in response?

In what way do you plan to take advantage of the firmwide network? How do you plan to get the cooperation of others?

How do you plan to contribute to the firmwide network? How will what you are doing benefit them?

What are the staffing implications of your plans? Where will you get the staff from?

What are the main assumptions on which your plan is based? Which is the most "risky"? (i.e., if it can go wrong, where will it go wrong?)

How will we know if the plan is working? What indicators can we agree on, and when shall we review them?

What early warning signals will there be if the plan is not working? What contingencies have you put in place?

---

skeptic": challenging, questioning, asking for evidence on specula-
tions, questioning the reasoning, always asking "Who's going to *do*
it? How do you plan to pull it off? How are the best competitors going
to respond? What is your practice area going to do to promote/assist
other groups in the firm?"

Usually, the team will be sent away from the first such meeting to
revise its thinking, and return for a second presentation. In most cases,
this process will result in a clear plan of action and a request for some
form of investment. When the management has listened to (and challenged) the plans of each of the groups, it will now be in a position to
develop a strategy for the firm. It has heard the "best shot" of each
group in describing the opportunities available, and can now decide
on the aggregate level of investment it thinks prudent to make, which
opportunities seem the best investment and which will make the firm
strongest. Management can then negotiate with each practice head
any modifications for action plans not fully approved or funded.

In some firms the formal management group might choose to involve other senior people in either the "friendly skeptic" critique process or the final resource allocation decisions, rather than doing it
alone. In part this choice will be based on considerations of whether
firm harmony will be promoted or compromised by doing this.

The results of this strategy process at the firm level should be a set
of "contracts" between the firm management and the leaders of the
various practice groups. The contract should spell out the measurable
goals the group is aiming for, the action steps they plan to take, the
investments they require, and the support they need. It is also a good
idea to ask for some "milestone" points: "When will we review
progress and how will we measure whether it's working?"

What is important about this strategy development process is that
it represents not just a one-time event, but a shift in the ongoing management processes of the firm. It puts in place a "conscience" mechanism which forces each practice area to consider (and, over time,
reconsider) how it is operating, where it is going, and how it plans to
compete.

In too many firms, the strategy development process is a discrete
activity, wherein the firm attempts to predict where the market is going and then prepare for that future. This approach is fatally flawed.
Professional marketplaces are too changeable and fluid to "bet the

firm" on a single vision of the future. Besides, as noted above, most analytical exercises on "where the market is going" tend to result in firms reaching the same (obvious) conclusions as their competitors.

The strategy development task is not an exercise in forecasting. Rather, the goal is to *create the responsive organization*; to put in place a set of operating procedures which force the practitioners to listen to their marketplace on an ongoing basis, not as a one-time piece of market research; to require them to reexamine their methods of operation periodically with a critical eye on the search for improvement; to commit to actions that benefit the firm in ways that do not necessarily show up in the monthly profit-and-loss statements of the firm.

The strategy process described here is not an exercise in budgeting or goal setting. Many strategy development "exercises" fail because groups underestimate the practical managerial difficulties of translating strategic ideas and analyses into *action*. In their strategy development activities groups should spend a small proportion of their time (say, no more than 20 percent) figuring out what goals they want to achieve, and the rest on devising action plans that will get them there.

Paperwork should be *minimized*. Managers should not ask for a written strategic plan; rather, they should ask for an interactive presentation, with only a few overheads or exhibits. The benefit of the process lies in the thinking and reasoning about the issues that takes place, and the development of (and commitment to) a concrete action plan. Too many strategic plans lie unchallenged and unread, and hence unimplemented. The only piece of documentation that matters in this process is that listing action commitments: who will do what and by when.

The view of strategy espoused here can be summarized as follows: It is *not* the responsibility of the firm's management to develop and enforce a strategy for the firm. However, it *is* their responsibility to ensure that strategy development is done. It is *not* their job to do the thinking and scheming about competitive issues on behalf of the rest of the partners; it *is* their job to ensure that partners go through the thinking and scheming process. This does not represent an abandonment or delegation of management's responsibility. Rather, it substitutes a vision of the manager as a (demanding) coach, a conscience, instead of the manager as boss, decision maker, or overlord.

This approach is certainly counter to the way strategy is developed in industrial companies. But then, professional firms are not like industrial companies. An industrial company CEO, once a course of action has been identified, has the power and authority to make it happen. Not so the managers of a professional firm. In an industrial company, the same (or similar) products are made again and again: One group can validly consider the "best" way to make the product on behalf of everyone. Not so the professional firm. In a world of autonomous partners, each with his or her own differing kind of practice, "bottom-up" strategy development is the only way to go.

PERSONAL STRATEGIC PLANNING

The concept of bottom-up strategy development can, and should, be pushed further. In the most successful firms I know, all of the individual partners act as if they have personal strategic plans for their own careers—they have each thought through what their special value on the marketplace will be, what will make them more than just one more practitioner in their specialty, how they plan to achieve this vision of personal career progress.

In such an environment, the overwhelming bulk of the strategy development task is done. The firm's strategy, if it exists, serves solely as the icing on this cake of individual energized, directed efforts. Unfortunately, in too many firms (even in, or perhaps especially in, those with well developed firmwide strategic plans), the individual partners have no such commitment to a personal development plan. The strategy of the firm (or even the practice area) is not *theirs*; it is someone else's responsibility.

A firm will have achieved little if it has developed a formidable strategy but has partners who have no vision of their personal development goals, career strategies, designated specialties, or individual vision of excellence. Again we can note: The job of management in a professional firm is not to develop a strategy for the partners, but to ensure that they develop one for themselves.

To institute this system of personal strategic planning takes nothing more than practice leaders engaging in private closed-door meetings with each partner and asking "What, precisely, is it that is going to make you special (or even more special) in the marketplace over the next few years? Would you like to develop a specialized expertise in a particular technical area, in certain types of transaction, in the problems of certain types of clients? You probably can develop cutting-edge expertise in any one of these, but not all of them simultaneously. The choice is yours. All the firm asks of you is that you *focus* and *stretch*; that you pick a career-building goal and work towards it."

By posing this question (and requiring an answer) practice leaders are ceding to partners, as they should, the autonomy to determine their own professional lives. However, by requiring an answer, they ensure that partners' efforts are energized and directed.

In theory, such an approach could lead to a practice area becoming unfocused as each individual partner pursues a personal vision of excellence. In practice, this is rarely the case. The practice leader posing this question does not just accept whatever the partner says, but instead plays the friendly skeptic role. For example, he or she may point out that a partner has chosen something that no other partner wants to pursue, and ask "Do you really want to try to develop that specialty alone? There are some of your colleagues committing themselves to developing a practice in a related area: Would being a part of that team fulfill your ambitions?"

In the course of such negotiations viable teams are likely to emerge. Perhaps the teams will not be as neat as they would have been if the practice leader, in his or her wisdom, had chosen the strategy for the department, but the likelihood of successful implementation is far higher. As noted frequently, the critical stumbling blocks in strategy development are making it happen, follow-up, and action implementation. By basing the process on the personal enthusiasms and ambitions of the individual partners, this problem is greatly alleviated.

THE ROLE OF FIRM MANAGEMENT IN STRATEGY

Apart from encouragement (and monitoring) of strategy development at the practice and individual level, a major question that firm management should wrestle with is: What can and should the *firm* be doing to assist the practices and ensure the firm's competitive success?

The management of the firm has two key roles to play in the strategy development process: It must establish policies concerning the "rules of the game" (firm policies) and "expenditures" (firm-level investments and funding).

It is part of management's job to ask: "How will we get others to behave differently (more competitively) than in the past? Are we sure that our people have the incentive to execute the designated activities? Are some important things not getting done because people perceive it is not in their interest to spend time on them?"

An example may illustrate the point. Many firms (or practices) include as part of their competitive strategy the goal of marketing to existing clients. Yet in these same firms partners will often report that the rewards (financial or cultural) are far greater for bringing in a new client than for bringing in an equivalent amount of revenue from an existing client. Similarly, firms may preach the benefits of increasing leverage, yet continue to evaluate partners primarily on their personal billability rather than on the volume of business they are responsible for. Examples of this "folly of asking for X while rewarding Y" abound among professional firms.

Accordingly, firm management should examine whether they have provided the best "context" for individual partners and practices to compete successfully, today and in the future. They must question whether the right incentives and rewards are in place. It is only with some exaggeration that one can assert: "Tell me how you measure and reward partners, and I'll tell you what your strategy is, because I'll be able to tell you what choices the partners will make in running their practices."

In executing its strategy responsibility, the firm's management should review policies ("rules of the game") such as the following:

Performance appraisals (For what do we hold people accountable?)
Profitability and other measurement systems (How do we keep score?)
Systems for salary, bonus, and profit allocations
(What incentives drive the behavior of our people?)
Selection, role definition, and evaluation of practice leaders
Quality assurance procedures

An example of a strategic move in this area is provided by the accounting firm that has committed itself to mandatory client feedback on all engagements above a certain size, in order to create an internally visible scorecard on service quality. This is a move more profoundly strategic in achieving service quality than any amount of training programs and retreat speeches could accomplish. Or, to take another example, the multioffice actuarial firm that has committed itself to annual staff satisfaction surveys, the results of which are to be used in the performance appraisal of office managers. Again, changing the "scorecard" will be infinitely more powerful in changing behavior (and achieving strategic improvement) than preaching the importance of "human resource management" or including "professional fulfillment" in the mission statement of the firm.

The second responsibility of firm management in the strategy process is to set the ground rules for investment of firm funds. Strategy development is fundamentally an *investment* notion: A competitive advantage doesn't come free. Accordingly, if the firm is to be better "positioned" tomorrow, the firm must spend *something* today. It might not be out-of-pocket cash: the firm may have to invest its (otherwise billable) time. Since the firm's ability to make investments, whether of time or money, is obviously limited, the firm must establish some priorities.

As noted above, those best positioned to *suggest* or *propose* specific investments are those responsible for executing the strategy: the practice groups. However, it is the responsibility of the firm management to set the ground rules for how investment proposals will be treated. Perhaps more important, it is the role of firm management to stimulate and elicit investment proposals.

One of the unfortunate quirks of professional firm accounting is that most of the critical strategic activities (such as training, allowing selected individuals reduced chargeability in order to develop new specialties, developing new project methodologies to achieve efficiencies, engaging in new service development) do not show up as "investments" in the firm's accounts. Rather, they show up as reduced billability, that is, lower net income. As the saying goes, "One person's investment is another person's loss." Accordingly, individual partners, subject to the ongoing financial control systems of the firm, tend to postpone or avoid investment activities for fear of being judged as missing their income targets.

It is therefore an important responsibility of firm management to create an opportunity for investment proposals to be brought forward, considered outside the normal accounting procedures of the firm, and approved or disapproved in advance on the merits. The "bottom-up" strategy development process described here is just such a process.

GETTING STARTED

In launching a strategy development process, I have found two questions to be of particular value. Posing them either to the management committee, the practice areas, or (better) to the partnership at large, I seek answers to these questions:

a. If you could invest $X million in the next year (above and beyond our current level of investment) with the goal of improving the competitiveness of the practice and making its future more secure, what would you spend it on?

b. If you could improve our competitiveness by changing one aspect of the firmwide management practices and policies (measurements, reward systems, organization, compensation policies, selection and appraisal of practice leaders, etc.), what would you change?

The answers to these questions usually provide an excellent starting point for the essential debate that is the crux of strategy: How can we get *better* at what we do?

CHAPTER 21

FAST-TRACK STRATEGY

Here's how it's done. You divide the firm into small teams or practice groupings (by location, by discipline, by industry). Go for the smallest subgroupings you've got, keeping the teams as small as possible. You give each team four sheets of paper (Figure 21–1) which have four key objectives, one to a page.

The four key objectives are to:

- Raise client satisfaction
- Increase skill building and dissemination of skills
- Improve productivity (not just production)
- Get better business

Beneath the objective listed on each page are five columns:

- What actions are proposed
- Which individual will take responsibility for each action
- How much time will be spent on each action
- When each will be done by
- How we'll know each action's been done

You tell each group that a "coach" (either a managing partner or a member of the executive committee) will meet with them for two to three hours in four to six weeks' time to discuss what actions they are prepared to commit to do over the next three months to make progress toward the four objectives.

FIGURE 21–1

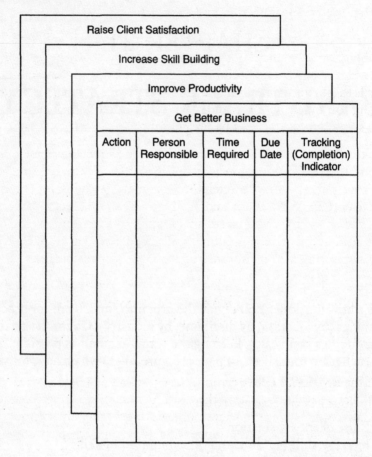

They are informed that only *actions* will be accepted, not goals. Thus, it is not permissible to write "Raise our market awareness"—that's a goal. Instead, they must choose something like "Put on three seminars on topics X, Y, Z." They can't put "Train juniors better"—that's also too vague. They must put something like "Hold weekly discussion sessions with staff including presentations by senior partners on their respective specialties."

Each action, it will be noted, must be the responsibility of a specific person: This is not meant to discourage teamwork (different actions may be part of an integrated plan), but is required to ensure a specific focus of responsibility. Many people may be involved in putting on a seminar, but some specific someone must be "on the hook" for ensuring that it all comes together and takes place.

During the discussion of the action plan, the coach will "test" the feasibility of the plan. Will the proposed actions really make a difference? Has enough time been budgeted to complete each action properly? Is there enough nonbillable time available to do it all? Is the team leaning too much on a few individuals? Are there other people who have some time who could be brought into the effort?

Like all good coaches, the coach will alternate between encouraging ambition ("Couldn't you accomplish a little more in three months? Can't we put a bit more stretch into this plan?") and dampening excessive enthusiasms ("Let's take it a step at a time. I recommend you limit yourselves to what you really think you can get done. Remember we're asking for solid commitments"). If necessary, the coach might offer some suggestions (not instructions) for possible actions.

The coach will try to guide the team (gently) to actions that are likely to have a payoff, to work. What the coach wants is what the team wants—the early successes that breed not only optimism and enthusiasm, but also the morale and commitment to do more—to try it again.

At the end of this conversation, the surviving plan becomes a "contract" between the coach and the team. Before the meeting concludes, a specific, ironclad meeting date is chosen approximately three months hence to review the execution of the plan, and its impact—what worked, what didn't, what proved easy to pull off, what is more complicated than it first looked. At that meeting, in addition to the look-back review, a new action plan covering the next three months (using the same planning forms) will be discussed and agreed to. And so on, and so on, until the process becomes a routine part of the management control systems of the firm.

That's it—that's fast-track strategy making.

WHAT'S DIFFERENT ABOUT THIS

What's different about this approach to strategy is that it doesn't waste a lot of time talking about the objectives of the practice. The objectives of the practice are the same as the firm's—the same as **every** firm's. If you're making progress on client satisfaction, skill building, productivity, and getting better business, you've got all the strategy you need. And if these **aren't** your objectives—well, it's hard to imagine what you are up to.

Most, if not all, other strategic topics can fit within these four categories. Take, for example, that of technology—where does it fit in this system? The answer is that some teams may see technology as a way to enhance profitability. Others may identify practical opportunities to use it to further the goals of client satisfaction or skill building. If it furthers none of the four goals, then what's the point of technology? Or consider another "hot topic" nowadays: globalization. Some practice groups may be involved with international clients and will list tactics addressing this area in the name of client service, profitability enhancement, or getting better business. Staff morale and retention will be addressed in the skill-building category.

This approach to strategy cuts through all the hoopla and hocus-pocus that goes on in the name of strategic planning and goes directly to actions—actions for which there is a finite horizon, an identifiable accountability, and most of all, a high degree of confidence that something will actually happen. It's not grand scheme, inspirational vision, analysis-paralysis strategy making. There are no great volumes of paper, nothing to be filed on a shelf, no "Business Unit Planning Methodologies," no "Analysis of Strengths and Weaknesses," no "Competitor Analysis," no boring presentation to sit through: just action steps which people commit to. It's strategy through activity: Try something, anything, but *act—now*!

The action steps are not meant to be transformational, home run ideas that take months to get organized for, and broad consensus to implement (such as "Let's form a committee to develop a new human resource model for the firm"; "Let's turn all our partners into business advisors"). These things almost always fail to be implemented. The action steps are a first set of ideas that can be done within three months (no long "planning horizons" please). They're not a complete strategy, but they *are* the first of an ongoing series of actions, reconsidered, reanalyzed, and readjusted every three months. If what we thought of doing first doesn't work, we'll do something different in three months time, but *let's get started*!

This approach takes strategy out of the realm of being a periodic ("Once every X years") exercise, and builds strategic thinking ("How can we improve from where we are") into the regular operations of the firm. It is a system to institutionalize continuous improvement, and create the "constantly learning organization." It fights complacency, because each three months it asks, ". . . and what are you going to do next?"

This approach is *not* a budgeting process—it's a complement to financial budgeting. Practice group budgets describe what firms aim to accomplish with their billable time. The fast-track strategy process provides a framework for practice groups to make wise use of their nonbillable time. What a group does with its billable time determines its income for the year. What it does with its nonbillable time determines its future.

Unlike uniform firmwide planning systems, this approach doesn't impose the same force-fit solutions on every practice. There's no centralized plan handed down from on top to be followed by everyone regardless of circumstances. What one part of the firm needs to do to improve profitability may be different than some other part of the firm. That's OK—as long as they both do something. Some may approach client satisfaction through technical approaches, others by focusing on client service. That's OK too—as long as they all accept their obligation to contribute in some way in this area. This approach to strategy maximizes the chance that each practice does what is right for its circumstances. It automatically accommodates the needs of small offices and large offices, mainstream practices and emerging practices.

This brings us to the next virtue of this approach to strategy: Each group is given the freedom and autonomy to plan its own activities—the plan is theirs. They are not being asked to execute the ideas of others (with which they may or may not agree). The group is being asked to plan as a team: Together they must develop the action lists to be discussed with the coach. Planning together and making their own decisions increases the likelihood of enthusiasm in implementation.

In this approach, everyone has a role in strategy development. The message is sent and reinforced every three months—what happens to this firm is what you come up with. Each one of you is a strategic planning committee member—except there's no such committee.

THE ROLE OF THE COACHES

Coaches (usually firm management) get to play a key role in this approach to strategy—not by telling people what to do, but by encouraging them to take responsibility for their practice's success (and the firm's success). They must make the process work by giving as much attention and seriousness to reviewing the action plans as they do to the monthly financials. If they do not, the system will wither away as yet another bureaucratic exercise.

One part of this system is critical: Follow-up. The system is about negotiating "contracts for action." What makes it work is the fact that the coach will be coming round to see how things have worked out. Not a year from now, but in three short months (the short cycle is essential to breed the sense of urgency that leads to action). If the follow-up meetings do not take place as scheduled, then the whole approach falls to the ground. If management doesn't take the process seriously by visibly monitoring what has been agreed to, the level of activity will grind to a halt.

The coaches have a final, perhaps most important role in making the system work. They have the responsibility and the duty to cross-fertilize ("Group X has tried this: Do you think it can work for you?") and to find new linkages ("You guys seem to be thinking along the same lines as one of our other teams—why don't you talk to them and develop some joint activities?"). By capturing and sharing the best ideas from each team, they can, over time, develop the firm's accumulated experience on "what works." By encouraging and supporting continued experimentation in each of the four key areas, they will help to breed a flexible, adaptable, responsive organization—one that is constantly trying new things and responding to the marketplace.

PART FIVE

PARTNERSHIP MATTERS

CHAPTER 22

PARTNER PERFORMANCE COUNSELING

Of all the ways of improving a professional firm's success, partner performance counseling is one of the most powerful. Done well, it can help ensure that all professionals are making the most of their talents and capitalizing fully on their potential. Unfortunately, the process rarely works this way in practice. In many firms, partner performance reviews are a rushed (and often poorly executed) step in a larger compensation process.

In these firms, reviews tend to focus overwhelmingly on the "look-back" *appraisal* function (in order to serve as an input to reward decisions) and contain only a minimal "look ahead" *counseling* component. Partners frequently complain about ineffective goal setting, ambiguous performance criteria, a lack of feedback (of any sort), and a process that is not well understood. A common complaint is "I can tell from my compensation award what you think of my performance, but I can't tell *why* you think that; and I've no idea what you want me to change."

The performance counseling process can (and should) be designed to *help* partners, creating the opportunity for them to:

- Reflect on and learn from the past year's accomplishments
- Receive constructive feedback, positive or negative
- Receive personalized advice on how best to advance their career

- Receive guidance in setting realistic but stretching personal goals for "growing their asset" and making a contribution to the firm

In what follows we shall describe a process designed to accomplish these goals.

STEP 1. SPECIFYING PERFORMANCE CRITERIA

The first essential element of any effective performance counseling system is a shared understanding of what aspects of performance the firm wishes to stress. There is often much ambiguity here. In my view, the key performance indicators, for which all partners would be held accountable, should be made up of the following six categories:

1. Profitability of work supervised
2. Client satisfaction on work supervised
3. Coaching on work supervised
4. Contributions to practice development
5. Contributions to the success of others
6. Personal growth (career strategy)

The first three categories, it will be noticed, relate to the partner's performance in managing and supervising client work. Taken together, they signal that any partner handling a client matter has three responsibilities: to the client (client satisfaction); to the firm (profitability); and to those who worked with the partner on the assignment (skill building). Not coincidentally, these three performance indicators coincide with the three traditional goals of most professional firms—(client) service, (professional) satisfaction, and (financial) success. (See Chapter 1, A Question of Balance.)

Note that the financial measure being proposed relates to the *overall profitability of the client assignments* that the partner is responsible for, not just his or her *personal* billings. Systems that stress a partner's personal numbers (rather than the aggregate of what he or she is responsible for) tend to lead to "hoarding" of work and a lack of attention to efficiency and productivity. There is little virtue in partners managing engagements so that their own numbers look good if this leads (as it often does) to poor management of the efforts of other professional staff involved. (See Chapter 4, Solving the Underdelegation Problem.)

Even in firms that *do* focus on the total client billings rather than personal numbers, there is frequently a problem. In many firms' reward systems, one frequently sees reference to performance indicators such as "supervising an extraordinary volume of fees." This indicator can be dangerous, since it is not result oriented or performance oriented. The issue should less be one of what *volume* you manage than what results you accomplish with that volume—profitability, client satisfaction, or skill building.

To avoid this problem, firms should calculate a full profit and loss statement for each client assignment, specifically calculating the costs of the resources, partner and nonpartner, that were consumed in conducting the assignment. At the end of the year, these can then be aggregated to provide a figure on the total profitability of each partner's work. (See Chapter 3, Profitability: Health and Hygiene, for a discussion of profitability measures.)

Client satisfaction can be measured on a systematic basis by using feedback questionnaires. If done routinely, these can be aggregated annually, to provide a "score" on client satisfaction, by partner. (See Chapter 8, A Service Quality Program.) Similarly, the use of routine "upward feedback" questionnaires from junior professionals on all client assignments can provide a metric on each partner's performance in coaching. (See Chapter 4, Solving the Underdelegation Problem.) Through the use of these systems, quantitative indicators of all three engagement performance areas can be obtained.

It should be noted that this system of simultaneous accountability for profitability, client satisfaction, and coaching explicitly discourages hoarding of "client responsibility." In some firms, particularly those where emphasis is given to volume, partners compete for client responsibility because it increases the "bulk" of their practice. Under the system proposed here, volume is no guarantee of good performance. A partner who accepts responsibility for a client assignment also accepts an accountability to perform in three measurable areas. Accordingly, partners will accept (or keep) this responsibility if and only if they think they can execute and supervise the work well. This should give the firm greater flexibility in making sure that work is assigned to appropriate partners.

The remaining three performance categories (practice development, helping others, and self-improvement) need to be judged, not measured. This is particularly true of the "contributions to practice development" category. Many firms attempt to quantify this performance by assigning "origination" credits to specific individuals who brought in specific pieces of new business. Such systems are fraught with problems.

First, origination credit systems tend to reward the *volume* of business brought in (i.e., the top line) rather than either its profitability (the bottom line) or its strategic desirability. Consequently, an incentive is created to bring in any work, rather than the types of work that will truly develop the practice. A second flaw of quantified origination credit systems is that they interfere with (if not destroy) teamwork in practice development. Credit usually goes only to those who "sell and close," leaving little incentive to participate in other necessary practice development activities such as writing articles, participating in seminars, and so on. (See Chapter 12, Managing the Marketing Effort.)

In the typical professional firm, it is usually easy for an executive or compensation committee to tell who has contributed to and been effective in practice development, even if there are no hard statistics on this. By making the system judgmental, there will be a greater likelihood that individual partners will find a way to contribute to the overall effort, and that rewards for practice development activities can take into account not only the volume of business won but also its value to the firm. By explicitly including this criterion in the performance counseling system for *all* partners, a signal will be sent that, one way or another, all partners should contribute to developing the practice. Some may never "sell," but they may write articles, give speeches, nurture existing clients, or any of a myriad of other activities which support the growth and development of the firm.

The fifth performance category described above was "contributions to the success of others." One of the eternal risks in any performance appraisal and counseling system is that it encourages an excessive focus on individual performance and destroys teamwork. To counteract this, each partner should be asked to point to specific ways in which he or she has contributed to the success of others. A partner who cannot meet this criterion should be deemed as having failed to meet his or her obligations as a member of a firm.

The final category is self-improvement. Every partner should (on a look-back basis) be able to show some way in which he or she has grown as a professional, and (on a look-forward basis) have a plan for growing his or her asset.

STEP 2. DESIGNING THE COUNSELING PROCESS

SELF-EVALUATION

The process should begin with the firm sending to each partner the quantitative information it keeps on partner performance (preferably including financial and nonfinancial scorecards, as described above) with a note saying:

> Please prepare a self-evaluation of your accomplishments this year. As you prepare your review, please examine the enclosed quantitative information on your activities. If you believe any of this is in error, or in any way misleading, please feel free to comment.

The firm should include the "official" statistics that it collects on that partner (perhaps also a listing of new business that the partner assisted in winning). It is important that data be provided not only for the latest year, but also for at least one preceding year. This is necessary to ensure that "good performance" is taken to mean *improvement* and not just sustaining a given level of result. To do otherwise will only encourage "cruising." Counseling discussions should focus upon year-on-year changes, not just the latest year.

The firm should also send the goals and action plans from the partner's previous counseling session. It is remarkable how frequently past plans are filed and forgotten. This undercuts the credibility of the performance counseling process. The simple gesture of saying "We haven't forgotten the goals you set two years ago, here's what you said and what we agreed to" conveys a powerful message about the seriousness of the process.

Figure 22–1 provides a format for the partner self-appraisal. It will be noted that the partner is invited to comment on all six performance areas.

STEP 3. IMPLEMENTING THE PROCESS

The partner is now ready to meet with the counselor. But who should this be? In a small firm, all partners could be counseled by a single compensation committee chosen for that purpose. In larger firms, this

FIGURE 22–1
Partner Self-Evaluation

Please describe and review your principal accomplishments in the past year. Your review should focus more on accomplishments (results achieved) and less on a description of activities (what you did). If specific goals were agreed on in a previous counseling session, please relate your comments to those goals. You should address the following performance categories:

1. PROFITABILITY
Please comment on your contributions to firm profitability through wise engagement management, control of billings, accounts receivable, work-in-process, and other financial matters.

2. QUALITY OF CLIENT RELATIONS AND SERVICE
What special accomplishments have you achieved in providing outstanding service to clients, either through technical achievement or relationship management?

3. COACHING AND OTHER CONTRIBUTIONS TO SKILL BUILDING
Please comment on your contribution to building skills in others through your supervision of more junior professionals on your engagements.

4. PRACTICE DEVELOPMENT
Describe your accomplishments in contributing to the development of our practice, through assisting in developing new work from existing clients, new clients obtained, or any other activities advancing the reputation of the firm. Include here your accomplishments in community activities, any speeches, participation in seminar panels, publications, etc., and any civic service, social club, or other outside activity which you wish to include.

5. GOOD CITIZENSHIP
Please comment on any achievements in the area of firm, office, or practice contributions, such as participation in firm recruiting, committees, or other nonbillable assignments you have performed. You may also want to refer to ways you have contributed to the success of the firm not otherwise covered above. In particular, please identify what you have done in the last year that the rest of the partnership has benefited from. The following list of possibilities may help:

1. *Made intellectual/technical contributions used by others*
2. *Transferred my skill to other partners and/or juniors*
3. *Made methodology improvements used by others*
4. *Increased market awareness of our practice*
5. *Brought in work for others to work on*
6. *Successfully cross-sold my partners to my clients*

6. PERSONAL DEVELOPMENT
Review the ways you judge that you have improved your knowledge and skill in the past year. What has made you a more valuable professional? You may wish to comment on:

- *Increase in technical knowledge and skill*
- *Industry knowledge*
- *Supervisory and management skills*
- *Client counseling and relationship management skills*

is impossible, and the counseling must be done by practice leaders—those in charge of a discipline, an office, or a practice area. In fact, this approach is preferable. The job of being a practice leader carries with it the responsibility of helping other partners in the group to succeed. Indeed, that's almost the definition of the role. Counseling and performance appraisal are, therefore, central to the practice leader's function. A compensation committee may be appropriate to take the results of the counseling and translate them into compensation awards, but the counseling itself is a *managerial* function.

FORCED RANKING

Obviously, the counselor must also prepare for the meeting. A good discipline is for the reviewing partner to form a *tentative*, beginning opinion on where the reviewed partner falls *relative to all other partners* on each of the six performance categories. An effective way to do this is to place the partner in one of four levels in each category: superior (top 25%), good (upper 50%), acceptable (lower 50%), and needs improvement (lower 25%). This "forced ranking" is often emotionally difficult (no one wants to tell others that they are below average) but the courage to be honest is the essence of good counseling.

The partner should also be invited to rank himself or herself on this scale for each of the six categories. In the meeting between that partner and the counselor they would discuss and compare their evaluations. Differences in the partner's self-perception and the reviewing partner's evaluation would be discussed *and documented* (for review by the compensation committee).

The virtue of documenting the two ratings (one by the partner, one by the counselor) is that the partner has a right to know as soon as possible if the reviewing partner's judgment is different from the partner's own self-evaluation. Although it might appear potentially confrontative, the documentation of ratings means that the partner being reviewed has the comfort that what he or she has been told in the counseling session is the same as what is being forwarded to the compensation committee. Any differences in perception that remain after the counseling session, if put in writing, become valid input to the compensation committee. This process has the virtue that it guarantees the partner feedback on his or her performance and it forces differences in perception to be brought out for discussion.

If the firm uses a structured form for counseling sessions (in general, a good idea), it can be productive to include a section which rates not only accomplishments but specific skills. For example, the form could include the following skills:

- *Communications skills (ability to express thoughts in a logical, fluent, and concise manner)*
- *Counseling skills (tact, the ability to explain, to persuade others in a nonconfrontative style, see the other person's point of view, keeping client informed, listening well, etc.)*
- *Creativity and innovativeness*
- *Planning and organization (ability to get things done)*
- *Leadership (motivation of subordinates, effectiveness in delegation)*
- *Cooperativeness and team play*
- *Drive, self-motivation*

Both a self-rating and a feedback rating could then be made on these items as well as the six categories described above. If a counseling session is to be constructive, the suggested areas for improvement need to be as specific as possible. By providing the opportunity to point out the need for improvement in specific skills, the partner can only benefit.

An overall evaluation category should be included on the form. This is a reasonable expectation for a partner to have and is needed to ensure that no misperceptions remain about what the performance review implies for the remainder of the compensation-setting process. It should serve to reduce (but never eliminate) the number of "surprises." (Great performance review, no compensation increase!)

CAREER PLANNING

The next stage of the counseling discussion is the "career planning" portion. Career planning ("What's my role in the firm?") cannot and should not be separated from the performance evaluation process ("How am I doing?"). Rather these need to be two portions of the same process. One way of doing this is to include a section in the partner counseling process that explicitly asks the partner being reviewed (and the reviewing partner) to engage in career planning for that partner, that is, to identify which "career" track offers that partner the greatest opportunity to make a contribution to the firm.

This is seeking an answer to the question "What, specifically, do you wish to be famous for?" Possible options that could be included as career tracks are:

- Technical expert in a particular service area
- Industry expert
- Superior client counselor
- Superior ability to get things done through others
- Special abilities in practice development
- Special ability to work with certain types of clients (e.g., Fortune 500, entrepreneurs, high net worth individuals)
- Superior ability to transfer skills to others

Together, the counselor and the partner can think through what that partner could do to make himself or herself "special in the marketplace." Forcing a discussion on career plans will make the counseling process more long-term, and will signal to all partners the need for them to develop some form of special skill or focus that will make them different.

GOAL SETTING AND ACTION PLANNING

The final, and most important phase of the counseling process is goal setting and action planning. This could be enhanced by including in any documentation a section that establishes clear priorities for improvement among the possible goal categories. Firms have had great success with rating systems that "force" a ranking among possible goals and success criteria. For example, the forms could ask partners to do the following:

> For the 6 categories of achievement place a "1" by the strongest category and a "6" by the category most in need of improvement. Then place a "2" by the next strongest category and a "5" by the category needing the next most improvement. Place a "3" and a "4" in the remaining categories. Use these rankings to choose priorities among your goals.

It is important to force the discipline of designing (and documenting) concrete action plans by requiring that every action item must show a due date, a tracking measure (i.e., a milestone to show whether the action has been performed or not), and an estimate of time required. This discipline helps to highlight ambiguous goals ("become better known") and also to reveal actions that might be infeasible because of time limitations. The objectives and plans thus created form the beginning of the appraisal system for the following year.

CONCLUSION

The test of successful counseling is simple: Does the partner being reviewed know *specifically* and *precisely* what to do to improve his or her performance in the coming year? If so, then the counselor has done the job properly. If not, then the counseling has failed, and so has the counselor. Accordingly, I consider it a good discipline for the counseling process to end with a statement signed both by the partner and the counselor affirming that the partner does know where to go from here.

The design of an effective counseling and appraisal process is not a difficult task. Good implementation is difficult because counseling is a relatively time-consuming activity that requires a significant commitment (and no little skill) from those charged with managerial responsibility. They (and the firm) must accept (and believe) that the job of a manager is to help other people succeed—and that the counseling process is a major instrument in making this happen.

CHAPTER 23

THE ART OF PARTNER COMPENSATION

Partner compensation is the most troublesome topic in professional service firm management. A firm may live happily with its system for a long time, but when the topic comes up—and it inevitably does—the ensuing debate can be the most bitter and divisive the partnership ever faces.

The issues are indeed profound. In the division of profits, what is an appropriate balance between recognizing current performance versus long-term contributions? Who should get more: the big business getter or the most creative professional? The partner who trains associates well or the one who works the most billable hours? The leader of a large department or a pioneer in a new practice area? Most important, who, in a partnership of supposed peers, should make these decisions? Partners, after all, are owners, not employees.

At least as important as dollars and cents are the signals communicated, or at least perceived to have been communicated, through compensation decisions. These messages—about what gets rewarded and about the relative status and respect accorded each partner—affect not only the firm's culture and atmosphere, but also, by influencing how partners choose to spend their time, its strategic direction.

Many firms postpone evaluations of their compensation system as long as possible, attempting to handle problems case by case. In my

255

view this is dangerous and unwise. When working with professional service firms on *other* management issues such as marketing, client service, or coaching of junior staff, I continually encounter one major stumbling block in improving effectiveness in these areas. At some point in every discussion, one or more partners will say, "Yes, I can see we would be better off if we did these new things. But how will that affect my compensation? If I get paid for doing other things, I'm not going to give much attention to these new topics." As a result of this reaction and reasoning, the firm finds it hard to make progress on important business issues. All too often, because of the obsolescence or rigidity of the compensation system, conservatism prevails, and the firm finds it hard to implement strategic initiatives.

THE SENIORITY SYSTEM

Historically, in most professions, partner compensation has been closely tied to seniority. Some firms do this explicitly, using a lockstep model: Increases are set by a formula in which the only variable is how long an individual has been a partner. Other firms may say they decide compensation on a number of factors, but seniority nevertheless often dominates the process. (I have analyzed compensation results for numerous firms, and more often than not the weight statistically given to seniority is *much* higher than generally acknowledged or intended.)

There are two ways to justify a seniority-based system: First, the senior partners' past efforts have contributed to the firm's current profitability, and second, their greater experience makes them more valuable to the firm now. Both are testable propositions, however, and should not be *assumed* to be true. Some partners' past contributions may long ago have ceased to benefit the firm, and the incremental value of extra years may be slight.

Moreover, past contributions and greater experience are two quite distinct rationales. The former is an "equity" claim, with equity ownership having been built up by past contributions, while the latter asserts the greater *current* worth of a senior partner. The latter, if adequately demonstrated, is more readily acceptable to younger partners. The equity interpretation is harder. In a corporation, equity is built by making contributions to support certain fixed financial assets. In a professional firm, equity contributions primarily mean building up the assets of goodwill, skill, and reputation. In a competitive, transactional marketplace, these assets depreciate rapidly, and claims for "equity returns" are less valid.

Perhaps the greatest benefit of the seniority system is that, by de-emphasizing year-to-year performance, it avoids the whole problem of trying to weight the various forms of performance. It thus has the virtue of being easy to administer—as we shall see, an important consideration. Its most commonly cited weakness is that, in failing to reward superior professionals, the firm risks losing these productive people. In a competitive environment, in which lateral moves of partners are commonplace and younger professionals are less willing to wait for (increasingly uncertain) future rewards, the danger is particularly acute.

While this may be the most visible problem of the seniority system, it is *not* the most important. Far more significant, in my experience, is the fact that the system fails to recognize and reward differences in performance among partners of *equivalent* tenure (at all levels) and thus creates an environment that can be extremely discouraging to a number of partners. "Why," they ask, "should I strive for outstanding performance, when such efforts are neither rewarded nor even acknowledged?" Such reactions are particularly likely in firms in which, because departures from the seniority system are avoided, poor performance is not confronted.

In the world of professional services, there is a fine line between the good and the excellent. It is, however, upon such distinctions that reputations and profits are built. Once partners stop striving for excellence and settle for competence, the firm has entered a period of inevitable decline.

In spite of the problems of the lockstep system, some of the most prestigious and successful professional firms continue to use it. Such firms assert that by avoiding discussions of partners' relative contributions, they preserve collegiality and can focus attention externally, on winning and serving clients, rather than internally, on intrafirm politics. Instead of financial incentives, these firms depend on such mechanisms as firm culture and "social control" to motivate partners to work at their peak and to accept various roles in promoting the long-run health of the firm. If a partner's slice of the pie is predetermined, all that remains is an incentive to work to increase the size of the pie—a welcome coincidence of individual and firm interests.

Lockstep systems appear to have survived mostly among firms that have not suffered declines in overall profitability. When there is more than enough to compensate everyone well, there is less pressure to compare and evaluate individuals. Few firms, however, have the twin blessings of a bountiful environment and a homogeneous group of bright workaholics.

PERFORMANCE-BASED COMPENSATION

As many firms have discovered, the path to a performance-based compensation system is fraught with difficulties. Not the least of these is a general discomfort about assessing each partner's performance. Partners, it is felt, should deal with each other as peers; performance appraisals are something one engages in with employees, not with those who are, in a real sense, owners. I believe this view is misguided. As the manager of a successful professional service firm observed to me:

> You have to be tougher on partners than nonpartners. If you believe that partners' performance is more critical to the firm than juniors', then you must hold the partners at least as accountable. Most firms have elaborate performance appraisal and reward systems for their young professionals. Why not for partners? To believe that all partners can be trusted to perform well forever without being held accountable flies in the face of reality, particularly in a large firm. And if you are overpaying one partner, it comes straight out of the pocket of another partner, and therefore it is not to be treated lightly.

Even firms attempting a performance-oriented compensation system often try to minimize its explicit appraisal aspects. This is a serious mistake. Once one departs from a strict lockstep system, performance assessment and compensation decisions are inextricably intertwined: They are two sides of the same coin. The issue is not whether performance appraisals can be avoided—they cannot —but whether they are done thoroughly or superficially.

MEASUREMENTS AND JUDGMENTS

In order to avoid "subjective" assessments of partners' work, some firms divide partnership profits solely according to measurable criteria: business origination, hours billed, total hours or dollars supervised, percentage of time or dollars written off or uncollected, and so on. Even more extreme, some firms attempt what might be termed a "profit center" approach, whereby all expenses are allocated among the partners, creating a "profit and loss" statement for each partner, compensation awards being made accordingly.

Such methods almost always lead to the sacrifice of mutual cooperation among partners and fail to recognize that many important contributions can't be measured. Consider the partner who is diligent in referring business to other partners at a cost to his own billable-hours total. What of the partner who spends time training juniors? Or the partner who solves troublesome administrative problems? As sophisticated as accounting methods have become, no system can successfully capture and encourage all of the kinds of behavior required. Measurement-oriented (or "formula") approaches also work against the efficient delivery of professional services. Partners who are too busy or overqualified should pass on work to others, using younger partners or associates where appropriate—but if numbers are all that count, there are real reasons to hoard work rather than delegate it.

Measurements are inherently short-term oriented. How do you account for the partner who develops a new practice area that will add to firm profits for years to come, or who established the firm's strong reputation in certain types of matters, or who strengthens the firm by being an excellent coach? Each has contributed more than will show up in this year's numbers. Whenever compensation is based too heavily on current contributions, investments in the firm's future will suffer. Partners will strive to "look good" today. Yet as the professions become more competitive, the future must be planned for, invested in, and worried about. Clients are less loyal, and time and effort must be spent in developing new specialties and penetrating new industries and geographic areas—at the expense of today's billable hours and origination credits.

It follows that, like most important decisions in a professional service firm, decisions about compensation must result from a *judgment* process, not a *measurement* process (although, to be sure, judgments should be formed with knowledge of whatever statistics are available). The ways to improve a measurement system are usually obvious. How does one improve a judgment system?

THE CHARACTERISTICS OF A JUDGMENT SYSTEM

In systems involving judgments there are always winners and losers. When complex trade-offs are made, someone inevitably disagrees with the results. (One managing partner asserts that "you know you've got a good set of compensation decisions when everybody feels a little hard done by.") What is more, no system is perfect: In any judgmental process, errors will occasionally be made.

If such is the case, where should one look to make improvements? As in the courts, attention should be directed at the judgment *process*, not the decisions. If the process is thorough, unbiased, and equitable—and is perceived to be so—then good judgments will result and, just as important, be accepted. Using the judicial metaphor, we can identify a number of essential characteristics:

- If the people being judged do not trust the judges, the system won't work.
- The laws governing the decision must be consistent and well understood.
- Judgments should not be made until a sincere effort has been made to collect all pertinent information, and the defense has been allowed to make its case.
- Judgments that are explained are more readily understood and accepted than those that are not.

With these propositions as a starting point, how does one run an effective compensation-setting process?

SELECTING THE JUDGES

In firms ruled by their founding partners or some other group of acknowledged leaders, there seem to be few fights over compensation. Pie-splitting disputes often follow on the heels of governance disputes. As one managing partner puts it, "A partner's satisfaction with his compensation and that of others largely depends on his perception of the legitimacy and integrity of the group deciding compensation."

Problems arise particularly when there is confusion over the respective roles of the executive and compensation committees. The executive committee of the firm must play an important role in setting compensation. Its members are, after all, most likely to know about every partner's activities. But theirs should not be the sole voices. The credibility of the committee is much enhanced, I have learned, when the compensation committee has both representation from the executive as well as additional compensation committee members elected or appointed for the sole purpose of providing for "checks and balances" on the (already considerable) power of the executive. These "supplemental members" of the compensation committee should be chosen for objectivity, fairness, diligence, trustworthiness, and commitment to the firm as an institution.

In order to select wise, virtuous, and *objective* judges, some firms choose compensation committee members from the ranks of senior partners—those already receiving the maximum share of profits allowed. This works well only as long as these partners continue to share the same values and sense of direction as the rest of the firm; once their values differ, they will lose trust. Other firms use an electoral process in an effort to ensure legitimacy, but this is no panacea: In a firm divided over values and direction, no judiciary, elected or appointed, will ever be fully trusted. Strategy, governance, and compensation are inextricably intertwined, and lack of consensus in any one spills over into the others.

Compensation decisions need to be made in an atmosphere free of politicking, lobbying, and sectional interests. My research has convinced me that a compensation committee should be small: three to five partners is ideal, seven may be tolerable. Tough compensation decisions *can* be made by democratically elected judges, but not through the direct democracy of open debate among all of the firm's competing factions. Voting and compromise (common practices in large committees) do not tend to produce fairness in results. A small group must decide. A larger oversight group (say, for example, a board of partners) can accept or reject, but if it rejects, it should send back the entire set of decisions, rather than tinkering with a few.

SETTING CRITERIA

An inevitable part of being a judge is interpreting conflicting laws and precedents, but there must be laws. The rules by which partners are appraised—the varying forms of contribution to the firms' success that will be recognized and their order of importance—must be clear. It is neither fair nor sensible to evaluate performance against criteria that are ambiguous or change without notice. A written statement of compensation policy, including a detailed description of the information-collecting process, should be updated and circulated every year.

However, in contrast to what seems a widely held view, the committee need not give different criteria the same weight in every partner's case. Indeed, I would argue, it cannot. As professional firms mature, individuals and groups contribute in different ways. One group may be looked to specifically for generating business; another to specialize in a new area in which billable hours and revenues are small in the short term; another may act as a service department to the rest of the firm. Looked at another way, the form of contributions can be expected to change with time, with, for example, more emphasis on billable hours earlier in a partner's career and more on business getting or management later on.

In such an environment, a rigid formula—"hours count 60 percent, new business 30 percent, and profitability 10 percent"—is unworkable. The firm may believe that business development and billable hours are more important than development of associates and should indicate that, but it would be a mistake to apply the rule uniformly—no one would bother with associate development. What is required is a process of "management by objectives," whereby each individual, in consultation with the executive committee, agrees to a set of objectives for the forthcoming year, and is assessed accordingly. This approach clarifies what is expected and, by forcing each partner (and hence the firm) to contemplate goals, encourages active planning rather than opportunistic, reactive behavior. In a professional world that increasingly requires strategic thinking, this is no small thing.

The management-by-objectives approach also allows the compensation committee to evaluate every activity. If a partner is responsible for recruiting, then his or her performance can be evaluated in that context. If a branch manager devotes a lot of time to managerial duties, then the evaluation depends on how well those duties were executed. In this way, a firm can avoid "position pay," that is, increasing compensation to reflect a job title. A manager's job is to make others productive and the firm profitable. If he or she succeeds, then he or she should be rewarded handsomely; if not, the reward should not be automatic. (Incidentally, one of my guiding principles is that any professional firm paying its managers more than its top producers is in trouble. Top producers shouldn't be attempting to become managers to increase their pay and status. Glory, and dollars, should always flow to those who excel at client work.)

Compensation adjustments should be based on relative *improvements* in performance, not on absolute levels. A partner whose clients were billed $2.3 million this year, down from $2.9 million the year before, probably deserves less of a raise (if any) than one whose clients were billed $1.5 million, up from $700,000. To do otherwise would encourage "coasting." While this may seem obvious, in numerous firms I have studied, a partner with high billings is highly rewarded, regardless of changes from the previous year. (In part, this happens because compensation committees are flooded with numbers and thus fail to analyze past years' statistics thoroughly.)

Finally, it is essential to note that in any firm, an inflexible compensation structure is likely to become moribund over time. In one era, business getting may be particularly important; in another, the priority may be improving the profitability of the firm's existing work. As the partnership's strategy changes, so should the weighting of performance criteria. As long as the changes are announced and discussed before they are implemented, reevaluation is to be commended rather than avoided.

GOOD JUDGMENTS ARE INFORMED JUDGMENTS

One of the most common complaints about judgment systems is that the judges are incapable of arriving at an equitable decision because "they just don't have the facts" or they misinterpret those they do have. In compensation systems, this is often a valid cause for complaint—and certainly the single greatest cause of mistrust of judges. Fortunately it is easily addressed. The compensation committee must be vigorous in collecting as much information as it can, from as many sources as it can, seeking not only the "hard," measurable facts (which frequently are less hard than they appear) but qualitative descriptions as well: what each partner has accomplished during the year, what help he has provided to other partners, how useful he has been as a coach, and so on. The committee should not be afraid to solicit opinions, so long as they are treated as such.

There are a number of ways to accomplish this. First, send every partner a summary of his or her statistics and invite comment on any possibilities for misinterpretation. What should the committee members know about that partner's significant triumphs and regrets?

While face-to-face meetings between partners and members of the compensation committee are not unusual, many firms do this only on the individual's initiative or target those in trouble. Such meetings should not be so restricted: The committee should conscientiously ensure that *every* partner meets with one of its members. Not only can partners provide explanations, they can also reflect on the past year, discuss what they had set out to do and frequently adjust plans for the coming year. Among firms that adopt this practice, I never fail to hear praise for it.

Another important source of information on a partner's performance is the opinions of other partners. In a small, homogeneous firm, where partners practice in similar areas with similar types of clients, the compensation committee can easily assess all partners accurately. However, in a large multidepartmental or multisite firm, it is not surprising that partners worry that the small group of committee members may not be qualified to judge every partner's contributions. The greater the distance between the judges and the judged, the less trust and confidence exists.

Certainly the assessments of departmental and branch office heads should be solicited; this is a common practice. Yet judgment by informed peers can be far more extensive. At a number of well-run firms I have studied, the committee invites, either by memo or in interview, all partners to answer the following: "With which other partners have you had professional contact in the last year? For each, based on your involvement, how would you rate his or her performance and contribution to the firm? In what ways does he or she excel? In what ways that we may not otherwise know about has he or she contributed to the firm's success? For what should he or she be complimented? If you could encourage this person to do one thing differently, what would it be?"

This approach may be daunting to firms that have never tried it, but it gives the judges an accurate reading of how a partner is perceived by his or her peers and it uncovers essential information, favorable and unfavorable. Knowing that all opinions will be treated as confidential in the committee and that no one opinion will be accepted without cross-checking, partners are likely to offer sincere opinions on the merits, strengths, and weaknesses of others. It is a time-consuming process, but well worth the cost.

ARRIVING AT DECISIONS

Equity requires that, whatever a firm's rules are, they need to be applied in a consistent manner throughout the firm. This is often more difficult to accomplish than it would seem. In a mid-sized firm of, say, thirty partners, a compensation committee may be faced with a spreadsheet with ten to fifteen columns of data (origination, hours, etc.) for each partner, and must somehow absorb all of this data to arrive at thirty decisions that reflect consistent treatment of each of the factors of interest.

In my research and consulting experience, I have found that many firm committees will attempt to process this vast amount of data in a very "impressionistic" way, attempting to absorb simultaneously the confusion of messages contained in hundreds (if not thousands) of numbers, in addition to trying to bear in mind important qualitative considerations. Even with the best of intentions, this rarely results in complete consistency or an observable logic in the overall set of decisions. Because of the unstructured approach taken to the analysis of the information, it also tends to be more time consuming than it needs to be. Decisions of this importance and complexity cry out for a more formal analytical approach.

In fact, quantitative tools are available to analyze such data. (See Chapter 24, Patterns in Partner Compensation.) Many firms state that, in arriving at compensation decisions, they consider more than a single year's performance and reward superior performance over a period of time. However, it has been my experience that, because of the unstructured decision-making process, few firms in fact reexamine past performance statistics and rely instead on what is often an imperfect, impressionistic memory of previous years' performance. It should be stressed that a formal approach to analyzing the measurable aspects of performance does not preclude the application of important qualitative judgments. It merely ensures that this is done in a conscious, consistent manner.

EXPLAINING THE DECISIONS

Having gone through this thorough performance-appraisal process, the compensation committee would be foolish not to let the partners know how they fared. To conclude with the simple announcement of each partner's take is to invite discontent. Feedback must be given and decisions must be explained (preserving, of course, the confidentiality of specific opinions expressed to and within the committee).

This cannot be overemphasized: If the reasoning behind a judgment is explained, it is more likely to be accepted. Moreover, feedback encourages excellence. Even where compensation awards are accepted as equitable, a natural follow-up question is, "What do I have to do to do better next year?" At firms that provide no feedback, partners are left to guess at—and, possibly misinterpret—the compensation committee's intended message.

DISCLOSURE

Despite what is becoming common practice, I believe disclosure of every partner's compensation to all other partners has as many risks as benefits. It is understandable that firms choose to do this: These are, after all, partnerships of owners, in which democracy and collegiality are highly valued. Yet if everyone's compensation is disclosed, the temptation to compare is well nigh irresistible. And this game, as everyone readily concedes, is destructive. Andrew Grove, in his book *High Output Management*,[1] observes that if people are concerned about their absolute level of compensation, then they can be satisfied. However, if their focus is on relative standing, then they can never be satisfied.

Disclosure certainly discourages the cooperative behavior required in most professional practice. Opportunities for misunderstandings and resentment are high. The process by which qualitative judgments were reached is hard to explain simply, yet if only measurable data were disclosed, partners might interpret decisions solely in those terms. Another difficulty is that justifications are frequently sought not only about oneself but about others—"Why did he get more than I?"—and this might require disclosing the personal circumstances of others or opinions given by third parties.

Disclosure also makes it difficult to implement the hardest decisions—dealing with the less-than-productive partner or one with personal problems. Compensation awards can become symbolic of status, of a place in the pecking order. Thus, reductions in compensation affect the partner's public image—an unnecessary compounding of punishments.

Owners *can* be kept informed without knowing *everything*. A summary, aggregated by broad age groupings, specialty, or some other category, can give partners a full understanding of the range and distribution of compensation and where they stand within it. (See Chapter 24 for one method of doing this.)

Clamors for disclosure are themselves symbolic: What is really being sought is reassurance that the judges are objective, fair, and consistent. Along these lines, there is one aspect of disclosure that must not be overlooked: How the compensation committee has dealt with itself. Here, some disclosure *must* take place, in either aggregate or detailed form.

BALANCING PAST AND PRESENT

I argued above that seniority, per se, is a poor and increasingly untenable basis for awarding partner compensation. This should not be interpreted to mean that past contributions to the firm's success should be totally discounted. Indeed, firms must be very careful not to become too short-term oriented in compensation. One of the most common misunderstandings I have found among professional firms is a belief that the alternative to a seniority-based system has to be a cut-throat "last year's performance only" approach.

This is an overreaction. In the professions, superior performance is evident only over an extended period of time, and should be so appraised. A given year's compensation decision should be seen as one of a *series*, not as a game to be won or lost each year, with no view to past or future. Rapid changes in anyone's compensation, except where there is a clear consensus that they are merited, are extremely disruptive—as are, at the other extreme, fine distinctions made on the basis of small differences in a single year's performance.

One way to balance past and present is to think of compensation awards as a smoothed, moving average of performance, updated every year as new evidence comes in. In order to accomplish this, a firm may choose to make compensation decisions on the basis of statistics covering a three-year period rather than a single year's time. Each year the three-year cumulative totals for each partner are updated by adding in the most recent year's results and dropping those from four years ago. Thus, a good year will continue to show up in the data for an extended period of time, but not forever. Similarly, the impact of one good (or bad) year will be dampened when added in with four average years. If performance improves each year, the partner will have a gradually rising share. If it consistently declines, so will his share. (Incidentally, this device thus deals naturally with the gradually retiring partner.)

A second device—one gaining favor among the professions—is what I have come to call the "two-pool system, in which some large percentage of the profits is distributed (prospectively) based upon long-term considerations, while a smaller pool (say, 5 or 15 percent) is distributed (retrospectively) in recognition of outstanding contributions in the current year. These special awards are clearly outside the long-term compensation structure, so that a single year's "bonus" does not become part of the recipient's longer-term expectations.

COMPENSATION AND STRATEGY

In spite of the tactical and pragmatic advice offered above, there is ultimately only one test of a compensation system: whether or not it encourages the full range of behavior needed for the firm's success. If partners are spending their time wisely and energetically on things that benefit not only themselves but also the firm, then the system is working. If an individual's best interests don't coincide with the firm's, the system needs an overhaul. To apply this acid test, one first has to understand what makes the firm succeed. What *are* its best interests? As many firms have discovered, this requires careful thought. Compensation decisions cannot be made in a vacuum: They are an integral part of what defines the firm. Sorting out these complexities is an art, and is likely to remain so.

CHAPTER 24

PATTERNS IN PARTNER COMPENSATION

It is remarkable how frequently professional firm compensation systems fail to accomplish a simple goal—motivating partners to focus on those aspects of performance that will make the firm successful.

The problem is not that the firm's compensation committee necessarily rewards the wrong things (although some do that). The issue is that the typical partner often doesn't know what is being rewarded, or doesn't believe what is said by the compensation committee about what has been rewarded.

Official declarations of policy don't solve the problem. Most firms have a statement of compensation principles of the form "Among the numerous factors taken into account are . . ." (followed by a laundry list of quantitative and qualitative performance indicators). These declarations are uniformly ambiguous and rarely meet the partners' need to know what factors were actually used and with what weights.

It is perhaps a sad fact, but nonetheless true, that most partners are not prepared to take on faith that the compensation committee has done what it says it has done. When it comes to compensation, issues of trust, credibility, and confidence abound in professional firms. This is a serious business issue. If the partners misperceive what is being rewarded, then they will focus their attention and efforts only on the things they think are rewarded, and fail to focus on other important performance areas that will affect the success of the firm.

So how can the compensation committee convincingly communicate what it has done? Simple disclosure of compensation results alone will not do the job. Even if I know what each and every partner in my firm made this year, it is not a simple task for me to deduce what has been rewarded unless I am intimately familiar with each and every partner's performance. This is difficult in a small firm, and impossible in a large firm. Even if, as a partner, I am given a spreadsheet (or, more likely, a thick, bound document) containing all the information used by the committee, it will be difficult to detect patterns in the numbers by staring at voluminous columns of data.

What is needed is an approach that demonstrates unequivocally what has been rewarded, clearly reveals how much reliance has been placed on quantitative factors, and how much on qualitative factors, and yet can preserve (where necessary) the confidentiality of specific individual partner data.

Fortunately, such an approach exists—a "Compensation Committee Report" that makes use of graphs and some basic statistics. To illustrate the approach, let's examine a fictional firm of thirty-two partners that collects quantitative (descriptive) data on its partners in six areas:

a. Age (an indicator of seniority)
b. Personal billing rate
c. "Grade" for contribution to business development
d. Total dollars billed as client partner
e. Percentage of standard fees billed and collected ("realization rate")
f. Personal billable hours

Of course, numerous other qualitative factors are taken into account by the committee of our fictional firm, but it is only for these factors that there is quantitative data. With this information in hand, the committee goes off into its deliberations and, using its best judgment, develops a schedule of "points" (or profit shares) for each partner. The committee then issues a report showing the graphs illustrated here. We, along with the partners in our fictional firm, will examine them one at a time.

Figure 24–1 shows the relationship between points (profit share) and age. (On this, as on all of the graphs, each "dot" represents an individual partner.) Did seniority play a role in the committee's decisions? As any reader can see from the graph, there is a general rising trend—older partners tended, on average, to get more points. However, it can also be seen that there is a significant degree of "scatter." This factor was not treated by the committee in a formulaic way.

A partner who cares to examine the evidence carefully might note that the "seniority effect" (the upwards trend) is quite marked between the ages of, say 35 and 41, but after that age there is no clear pattern. What the committee has appeared to do is give attention to seniority in the first few years of partnership, but rely on other (performance?) factors after that.

Is this pattern appropriate? That's for the committee and the partnership to decide, according to their compensation philosophy. However, by showing the graph, the partners can at least see what has been done.

The statistic at the top of the graph is a measure of the strength of the relationship, that is, how tight a fit can be seen between the two factors (points and age). A figure close to 0 percent would mean that there is no observable relationship between the two factors. A figure close to 100 percent means that the two factors tend to be highly correlated. The specific number (known formally as the "R-squared statistic" and a standard feature in most spreadsheet programs) can be used to answer the question, "How much of the variation in one factor (e.g., points) can be "explained" by the other factor (e.g., age)?"

In this case the answer is 39 percent, which means that age seems to "explain" 39 percent of all differences in point holdings, leaving 61 percent to be explained by other factors. This may overstate the case. It could be that what's really going on is that (say) it is billings that really drives point holdings and since older partners have higher billings, the "age (or experience) effect" is deceptive. Fortunately, we have more than one graph, and can test that hypothesis. We can state with confidence that the "age effect" is not more than 39 percent.

Of course, this analysis says nothing about the *actual* reasoning process used by the compensation committee. In saying that there is a correlation of (up to) 39 percent between age and points, we are say-

FIGURE 24–1

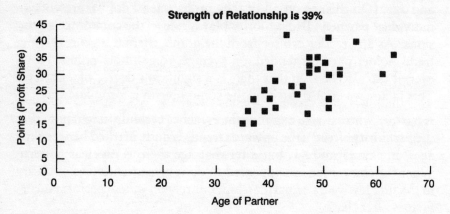

FIGURE 24–2

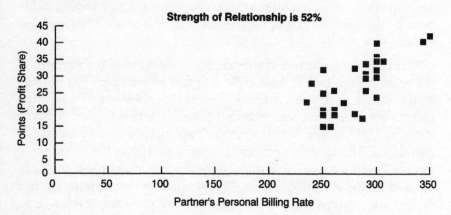

FIGURE 24–3

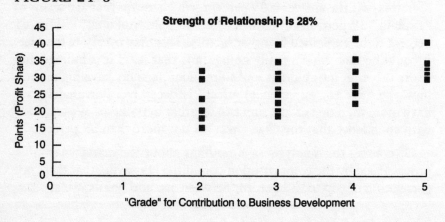

FIGURE 24–4

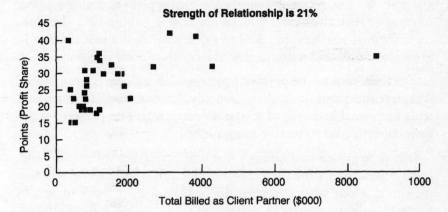

FIGURE 24–5

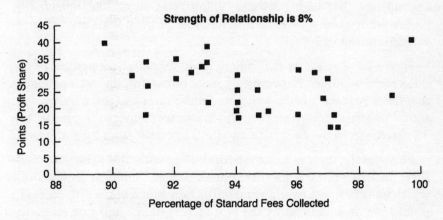

FIGURE 24–6

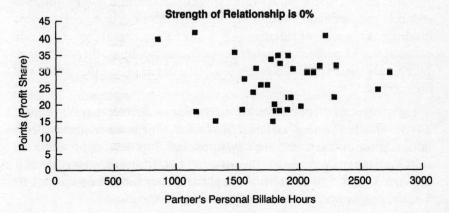

ing that the committee has acted *as if* the weight given to age was this amount. We are not analyzing their decision process, but the *consequences* of their decisions. We can say nothing about their decisions on individual partners, but we can say a great deal about the trends, generalizations, and patterns that emerge from their decisions.

Next, we turn to the partner's personal billing rate (Figure 24–2). Again, readers can draw their own conclusions. I see a clear trend, with a reasonable degree of scatter. Clearly, high-rate partners in our fictional firm tend to receive more points.

Is it appropriate that billing rate be so correlated with point holdings? Again, that's for the firm to decide. Our purpose here is simple—to disclose what has been done. However, if the firm sets its partners' billing rates by the market (i.e., individual billing rates reflect the value of the partner in the marketplace) then it is entirely appropriate that high personal billing rates should be reflected in higher point holdings—the most valuable professionals are being rewarded more highly.

Figure 24–2 suggests that billing rates "explain" 52 percent of the differences in points. However, we must be careful, since it is probable that older partners also have higher billing rates and there is therefore some "overlap" going on. For this reason, we cannot add together the 39 percent from the age graph and the 52 percent from the rate graph.

Fortunately, there is a method for dealing with this. In most spreadsheet packages there is another statistic (called "multiple regression") which will eliminate overlap and tell us how much of the differences in points can be explained by the two factors of age and rate taken together, without double counting. In this case, the answer it gives is 59 percent, meaning that after eliminating overlaps, age and billing rate together can "explain" a total of 59 percent of the differences in point holdings. One way of interpreting this is to say that if age alone can account for 39 percent of differences in point holdings, then adding in billing rate can explain an additional 20 percent (59 minus 39) of the differences.

Let's turn to "contributions to business development" (Figure 24–3). This is a "quasi" quantitative factor. Our fictional firm collects information on each partner's business development efforts and results and assigns a grade for their overall contribution, on a scale of 2 through 5, with 5 being the highest grade. (They intended to use a 1 to 5 scale, but in practice never assign a 1.)

As can be seen, there is also a rising trend here. On average, a higher "score" for business development will result in higher points. As always, we must look not only at the trend but the amount of scatter around the trend. There is a significant amount of scatter, revealing that the business development grade influenced compensation, but did not determine it. By itself, it appears to "explain" 28 percent of differences in points.

As before, we must be careful of overlaps. It is possible that high-billing-rate partners are also the best at business development. The "multiple regression" statistic referred to above can be applied again and, this time, reveals that taking the three factors of age, billing rate, and grade for business development into account simultaneously will "explain" a total of 74 percent of all the differences in points. This is up from 59 percent for age and billing rate alone, implying that business development performance explains 15 percent of the differences in points that age and billing rate cannot explain.

Figure 24–4 shows that "Total Dollars Billed as Client Partner" played some role in compensation setting (there is somewhat of a rising trend), but that it was probably not a dominant influence (there is a lot of scatter). While the relationship seems to have a strength of 21 percent, there is a lot of overlap with other factors: Adding this factor to those we have already considered only adds (according to the nongraphical analysis) an incremental 2 percent to the 74 percent we have already explained.

The last two graphs are revealing. Figure 24–5 shows that there is a barely observable relationship between points and the percentage of standard fees collected (the "realization rate"). (If anything, it seems as if there is a slight trend downwards.) It would appear that "good profitability management" was not applied across the board as a factor in determining points. This does not prove that the compensation committee did not take into account this factor in individual cases. It does show that they did not apply a consistent pattern across the range of partners.

Finally, Figure 24–6 reveals that our fictional firm did not, for better or for worse, place much reliance on a partner's personal billable hours in setting compensation—there is no observable trend. (While unusual, this may be an appropriate finding. If too much emphasis is given to individual partner hours, there might be an incentive to hoard work that should more appropriately be done by others.)

We have examined each of our available quantitative factors. Can anything be said about the *qualitative* factors used by the committee? At least this: If one takes together simultaneously all of the six quantitative factors, then a total of "only" 76 percent of the differences in points can be explained. (This result comes from the "multiple regression" statistic referred to earlier.) Therefore, we can conclude that the compensation committee relied on qualitative factors for 24 percent of its decision making. We cannot tell whether these other factors were sensible (quality of work, associate training, cooperativeness, etc.) or not (politicking, arbitrariness, etc.) But we have shown that our fictional firm's system is not purely a formula driven one. Is 24 percent weight given to judgment too much or too little? As always, that's for the firm to decide. But at least the partners know.

For better or for worse, the ambiguity of "What's rewarded around here?" has been significantly reduced. Of course, it has not been eliminated. There is still that 24 percent judgmental component that we cannot explain. (Although it is worth noting that the device used in awarding a "grade" for business development can be applied in other judgmental areas such as associate coaching, thereby turning a judgmental factor into a quasi-quantitative one.)

There is also a degree of ambiguity left because of the overlap between performance factors. If, for example, "billings as client partner" and "personal billing rate" tend to move together, which is really being rewarded? It's not easy to say precisely.

However, progress has been made. With six simple graphs (and a few statistics) we, and the partners of the firm, have a pretty good fix on what's been done in this firm. I can easily tell, as a partner in this particular firm, that I'd be better off focusing on my billing rate and my contribution to business development as a means of getting more points, and should worry a little less about my billable hours. I may not like those conclusions, but I now know what is given attention and what is not. And I don't have to rely on believing or trusting the compensation committee.

It should be pointed out that the graphical/statistical approach to disclosure of compensation awards still permits a significant degree of confidentiality to be preserved if the firm so wishes. The "dots on the page" do not identify which partner is which. Accordingly, the approach can still be used by those firms with policies against disclosure of individual partner compensation. (There will be the potential for a breach of confidence in a small firm where one or two partners are "away from the pack" and hence show up as readily identifiable on a graph.)

However, many firms who do follow a nondisclosure policy do so because they fear misinterpretation of the results (i.e., questions of the form, "Why did X get more than me?"). If they provided the type of analysis recommended here, where the overall patterns of compensation are made clear, there would be fewer disadvantages to disclosure of compensation.

Naturally, any compensation committee would want to review this analysis before disclosure to the partners. I can hear the conversation now: "Did we really intend to give little or no weight to the profitable management of matters (the realization rate)? Of course not! That's not the signal we intended to send. We thought we were taking it into account in our individual decisions. Yet when you put it all together, there is no pattern. Perhaps we should review the decisions again!" In this fashion, the graphical (and statistical) analysis, used on a "trial balance" basis, can become a useful decision-making tool within the committee to ensure that the pattern of its decisions sends the right signals to the partners.

Naturally, there are many possible enhancements to this approach. Some firms may wish to analyze how the percentage change in points relates to performance factors, not just the absolute level of points. Others will want to examine performance data over a period of time (say, a three-year average) rather than just the latest year. Many such enhancements are sensible. The key issue, however, is sharing the analysis with the partners. A compensation committee has not done its job until it can show (not just tell) the partners precisely "what is rewarded around here."

CHAPTER 25

PIE-SPLITTING

In 1983, I decided to conduct a simple study of compensation practices among law firms to see how different firms would deal with different types of partners. Although the results are both old and from a single profession, I still get comments from clients about the survey and hear that they still use it to test views within their firms. So I have decided to include it here.

With the assistance of Steven Brill, the editor of *The American Lawyer*, and Bruce Heintz, a law firm consultant, I invented seven archetypal partners of a fictional firm and provided statistical and descriptive information on each (see Table 25–1). Those who participated in the study were asked to indicate for each archetype what the likely range of compensation (high and low) would be in their firm relative to the compensation of an average partner.

Each of the archetypes can be given a brief label:

A is the average partner,
B is the rising young superstar,
C is the unproductive older partner,
D is the individualistic solo operator,
E is the hardworking "back-room" lawyer,
F is the executive committee member actively maintaining a practice,

279

TABLE 25–1

The Archetypes: Eight Partners of a Fictional Firm

	Partner A	Partner B	Partner C	Partner D	Partner E	Partner F	Partner G	Partner H
	The typical lawyer	*Young and entre-pre-neurial; has built a loyal group of as-soci-ates around him.*	*Seems to have run out of gas; suspect some per-sonal prob-lems at home.*	*A prima donna solo oper-ator; likes high visi-bility cases; a little too glib.*	*"Journey-man" lawyer; works hard, but brings in little busi-ness; relies on oth-ers; a "partner associ-ate."*	*Execu-tive com-mittee member; tries to do ev-erything; major force in the firm.*	*Man-ages branch office, which has poor profit-ability.*	*Major rain-maker; passes on cli-ents and work for others to han-dle.*
Billable Hours Worked	100	141	74	105	115	92	95	35
Nonbill-able Hours Worked	100	152	51	92	60	243	156	150
Dollars Managed	100	198	33	45	55	129	90	112
Write-off Performance	100	120	50	102	101	150	63	132
Unbilled Dollars	100	105	59	40	93	121	80	108
Collections Per-formance	100	110	72	50	95	115	83	103
Business Getting	100	200	25	73	15	175	74	312
Billing Rate	100	64	129	104	103	112	108	139
Age	38	34	55	42	41	49	49	60

TABLE 25–1 (CONT.)

Department	Corporate	Real estate	Probate	Tax	Litigation	Corporate	Corporate	Corporate
Quality of Legal Work	Average	Excellent	Average	Excellent	Average	Above Average	Slightly Above Average	Average
External Respect in Community	Average	Excellent	Not Known Outside	Very Visible	Not well-Known	Very Well-Known	Thought to be Well-Known	Superb
Cooperative-ness with other partners	Average	Not Good: Somewhat Territorial	Very Cooperative	Not Very Cooperative	Very Willing	Very Well-Liked	Not Perceived as Cooperative	Not Cooperative
Ability to Develop Associates	Average	Outstanding	Poor	Poor	Average	Outstanding	Not Enough Evidence	Not Good
Committee Work & Firm Management	Average	Not Much	Willing But Rarely Chosen	None	Will Serve Whenever Asked	Extensive	A Great Deal	Used to be Involved But Not Anymore
COMPENSATION	100	?	?	?	?	?	?	?

All numbers shown (except for age) are expressed as percentages of the average for all the firm's partners. Figures above 100 represent superior performance: Thus, for example, Partner D worked 5 percent more billable hours than the firm average, but 8 percent fewer nonbillable hours. When it came to the amount of work performed for his clients but not billed (unbilled dollars), Partner D's performance was only 40 percent, far less than the firm average. Similarly, his performance on collections was 50 percent: He took twice as long to collect as the average partner.

G is the struggling branch manager, and

H is the major rainmaker who doesn't put in many billable hours.

Table 25–1 gives a more developed picture of each. Before reading on, you may wish to complete the survey, by filling in what compensation each archetype would receive at your firm, compared to the average. Alternatively, you may wish to circulate the survey among all of your partners, to determine the degree of consensus that exists concerning what should be rewarded at your firm.

In my survey, forty-six firms sent usable responses, a response rate of approximately 20 percent, which is low but not unreasonable for surveys of this kind. The responses yielded some provocative findings.

In spite of low billable hours and textual hints of noncooperativeness, partner H, who combined seniority and major business-getting ability, would receive the highest compensation in most of the respondent firms (Figure 25–1). This is understandable: Bringing in business is often the most highly valued characteristic in awarding partner compensation.

But the message contained in the survey responses is more complicated: While most firms would award partner H more than the other archetypes, they differ drastically in how much more. The median award for partner H was 175 percent of the average partner's compensation, but a quarter of the firms would give H less than 25 percent more than the average partner's compensation, and a tenth would give less than 10 percent more than the average. Three firms even reported that they would assign *less* than the average partner's compensation to partner H! At the other extreme, a tenth of the firms would assign partner H more than 210 percent of the firm average and, for a quarter of the firms, the share would be more than two-and-one-half times the average partner's compensation.

The range expressed in these results is truly astounding. Ignoring the bottom and top tenths of responses, we see that partner H could receive anywhere from 110 to 250 percent of the firm average.

FIRM SIZE DOESN'T MAKE A DIFFERENCE

How partner H (or any of the other partners) is treated does not appear to be related to the size of the respondent's firm. Analyzed by firm size, the survey responses showed the same basic pattern as they did when

FIGURE 25–1
What You Make Depends on Where You Work

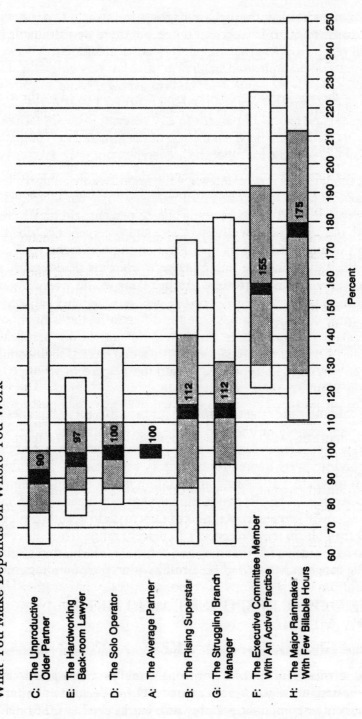

C: The Unproductive
   Older Partner

E: The Hardworking
   Back-room Lawyer

D: The Solo Operator

A: The Average Partner

B: The Rising Superstar

G: The Struggling Branch
   Manager

F: The Executive Committee Member
   With An Active Practice

H: The Major Rainmaker
   With Few Billable Hours

Percent

taken as a whole. Within each size group, the awards to partner H centered on the 160 to 190 percent range, but there were dramatic swings within each group that swamped any statistical differences between the groups. For example, one small firm (fifty lawyers or less) would give partner H only 62 percent of the firm average, while another would award 262 percent. Among the largest firms (150 lawyers plus), answers ranged from 115 percent to 250 percent. (The absence of a statistical relationship between the size of the firm and the compensation decision holds true for all of the archetypes, not only partner H.)

A similar story is revealed when the responses are analyzed by form of governance. Of the firms responding, 72 percent identified themselves as electoral democracies, while 22 percent said they were ruled by an oligarchy of powerful partners and 6 percent described themselves as benign dictatorships. For none of the archetypes could a statistical difference be found between what the democracies would award as compensation and what the others would award. Again, the main message from the data was one of huge variability between firms. The same conclusion holds true for different methods of choosing a compensation committee: There were no statistically significant differences between the 68 percent of firms that elected their committee, the 15 percent that appointed it, and the 17 percent whose compensation committee was hereditary.

Could the wide range of answers for the different archetypes be due to an uncertainty on the part of the respondents as to what each archetype would receive in their firm? It appears not. For each archetype. respondents were invited to indicate a "high" and a "low" figure, to allow for factors affecting compensation that were not accounted for in the exercise. The vast majority of firms gave estimates that ranged no more than 20 percent from the high figure to the low, and very few firms (less than one in ten) exceeded a 30 percent range. Thus, it seems that most respondents felt that they had sufficient information to place the archetypes reasonably and accurately within their own systems.

THE OTHER RESPONSES: WHO GETS HOW MUCH?

We have discussed partner H. What of the remaining partners ?

As anyone familiar with law firms would probably guess, the partner most highly rewarded after partner H was deemed to be partner F: the executive committee member who works close to the firm average on billable hours, more than double the average on nonbillable hours, and has "origination credits" 75 percent above average. The median award given to this individual by the forty-six firms was 155 percent—50 percent of the respondents would give less than this, and 50 percent more. As with partner H, the range of treatment of this hardworking executive committee member by different firms was dramatic. One-quarter of the firms would award less than 130 percent of the firm average, while one-quarter would assign partner F more than 190 percent. Ignoring the top and bottom 10 percent of responses, we find a compensation range of 120 to 225 percent of the firm average. Even though firms might have significantly different averages, this is again an incredible range.

It is interesting to compare the relative treatment of partners H (the "big rainmaker") and F (the "major force of the firm"). Even though the median awards to F and H vary by only 20 percent, there was significant disagreement among the forty-six firms surveyed as to which of these two should receive the higher compensation: 54 percent gave more to partner H, but 46 percent gave more to partner F. The exercise was designed to explore these different reactions. Business getting is important, and partner H excels at this (as well as being more senior). However, billable hours and firm management, partner F's relative strengths, are also important, and he has a respectable business-development statistic. As expected, the different firms split about evenly on the matter of who is more valuable to the firm (if, indeed, a single year compensation award can be interpreted in that light).

Most firms agreed that the older rainmaker and the middle-aged executive committee member would receive significantly more than any other of the archetypes. However, the same trade-off between business getting, firm management, and seniority was revealed at the next level. After H and F, the next two most highly rewarded partners were B and G. Partner B was our fictional firm's rising young superstar, with billable hours 41 percent above firm average, origination credits (and supervisory responsibility) double the firm's norm, and nonbillable hours 52 percent higher than average—all at the tender age of 34. In contrast, partner G, the branch manager, underperformed all of the firm's norms except two: nonbillable hours (presumably management activities) and age (49, compared with the average of 38).

Who gets the greater share? Half of the firms in the survey chose the superstar, and half the more senior branch manager. In each case, the median award was 112 percent of firm average, although as before, the variation exhibited among the forty-six firms was large. The young superstar would earn more than the average compensation at 29 percent of the firms surveyed, while another 29 percent would give her or him in excess of 140 percent of average (with some ranging up to the 190 to 200 percent range). Similarly, more than one-quarter of the firms would give the branch manager less than the firm average, and an equivalent percentage would award him or her more than 135 percent.

Moving down the rankings, we find D and E our next interesting pairing, both of whom were awarded compensation close to firm average. Partner D—the "prima donna solo operator"—worked an average number of billable and nonbillable hours but had origination credits some 27 percent below firm average. By comparison, one would expect A, the average lawyer, to be more highly valued because of A's superior business development record. However, 55 percent of the firms would give partner D at least 100 percent of firm average (partner A's reward), 34 percent would give at least 10 percent more than A, and 17 percent would award at least 25 percent more than A. Presumably, D's age (42, compared to A's 38) accounts for this difference.

Most firms ranked partner E, the journeyman back-room lawyer, significantly below partner D. The majority of the firms would award E less than firm average, and 15 percent would give less than 87 percent of firm average. Another 25 percent, however, would give E 110 percent or more. Partner D's comparative strength is business getting, although he is below average in this and exhibits a poor collections performance; E works more billable hours, has better collections and write-off performances, but has significantly fewer origination credits. As noted, most firms would give D more than E, but not much more. The median compensation for D was 100 percent of firm average for E, 97 percent.

Finally, the majority of firms in the survey agreed that the lowest-rated partner was archetype C, the 55-year-old lawyer working only 74 percent as many billable hours as the average partner and scoring below the average on every measure except age and billing rate. The median firm in the survey would award this partner only 90 percent of the average partner compensation. (So much for seniority!) However, as in all previous cases, the range of awards among the forty-six firms was dramatic. A tenth of the firms in the survey would award less than 65 percent, while another tenth would award at least 170 percent (presumably due to seniority). Almost half the firms would give partner C at least as much as partner D or E, and (to my eyes) an amazing one third of the firms would give C more than the young superstar, archetype B!

NO CONSENSUS

Clearly, the most significant lesson to take away from this study is the single word "confusion." The most important parts of the table of results are not the relative rankings of H, F, D, or E, but the amazing differences exhibited in the pie-splitting practices of different firms, in particular the relative weights they give to the factors of seniority, business getting, billable hours, management responsibilities, and collections performance.

Variations in the criteria firms use in splitting the partnership pie are understandable and, indeed, desirable. Different strategic positions in the marketplace require different compensation systems. A firm with a large institutional client base and with multidisciplinary matters will probably need to give less weight to business origination and more to billable hours and supervisory and management responsibilities. A firm dependent on small transactional matters will need to have a broad base of business getters and will therefore tend to rate origination credits higher. A diverse, multisite firm will have a greater need for management skill and will tend to reward this more highly than a relatively homogeneous, single-site firm would.

Compensation system experts note that any compensation scheme, if it is to stand up over time, must pass two tests: that of internal equity and that of external equity. Internal equity requires that, whatever the rules are, they be applied in a consistent manner. Even when internal consistency has been achieved, there remains the test of external equity: Do the compensation rewards in the firm reflect the economic realities of the open market? In the past, law firms have not had to confront this issue because, until recently, there has been no appreciable market in law firm partners. It is clear from the results of this survey, however, that, as this market develops, many firms will be forced to make significant shifts in the relative rewards they allocate to different types of partners.

CHAPTER 26

PARTNERSHIP GOVERNANCE

The design of a governance system for a professional partnership is an exercise in constitution forming, and the lessons of history and political science in this area are instructive. Two models of governance have historically been in contention: the aristocratic (in which appointed leaders have significant power to make decisions on behalf of citizens) and the democratic (which emphasizes the autonomy of the citizenry).

The aristocratic model is applicable where strong leadership is crucial to the success of the organization and where the requisite skills for leadership can be readily defined and identified. However, it runs into problems when the standards of skill, wisdom, and virtue are unclear. Who, after all, is to judge the judges, and on what criteria? Popular election does not appear to screen for skill, virtue, or wisdom. More important, how, in an aristocratic system, can we ensure that the chosen leaders receive the consent of the governed?

The problems of democracy are no less clear, no less damning. Is it *really* possible to maintain equality of influence and power over government? Does not power tend to concentrate in the hands of a minority with great wealth, political skill, or determination? If everyone is to have an equal say, how can decisions be made with sufficient knowledge? How can a popular government act with vigor, speed, and decisiveness, particularly in crisis? How can a democracy handle the twin problems of the tyranny of the majority and the obstruction-ism of the minority?

One solution is to adjust our view of what democracy entails. In early Greek society, particularly in Athens, democracy meant the equivalent of a permanent town meeting—all decisions of conse-quence were made in public assembly. As many professional service firms have rediscovered, this view of democracy tends to result in much wasting of time, slowness of response, and extreme conserva-tism in action. The consensus decision making that such processes imply is only feasible, Rousseau argued, among small, highly homo-geneous bodies of people. (Even in Athens, disruptive citizens could be banished from the town meeting.) As they grow, all societies be-come more diverse, and consensus democracy increasingly infeasible. Accordingly, the world has changed its view of democracy, allowing elected representatives accountable to the populace to act according to their conscience and their greater knowledge of the facts surround-ing a specific situation. Between elections, the government is free to act without repeated referenda; it is judged on its long-term perfor-mance.

WHAT MAKES PROFESSIONS DIFFERENT?

In spite of the success of this model in national life, all kinds of pro-fessional service firms continue to struggle with the tension between the desire for autonomy and for the benefits of government. Why should this be so? Why is Athenian democracy so eagerly defended among the professions, when that battle was lost decades or even centuries ago in other commercial enterprises?

The explanation is in part economic. Democracies flourish when the nation is at peace and the harvest is bountiful—as, historically, was the environment of the professions in the post-World War II era. However, when war is declared or the crops fail, even the most ardent democracy selects a government that will direct the troops and tell factories what to produce. The style, if not the structure, of govern-ment changes. The national purpose calls for more centralized power, more authoritative (if not authoritarian) behavior. Since the peaceful, bountiful environment the professions enjoyed in their peak is no more, Athenian democracy is increasingly inappropriate. Yet the tran-sition is a difficult one, largely due to the nature of professional work and those who choose it.

It is a common complaint that professionals are unmanageable. In every profession I have studied, managing partners say theirs is an impossible task because of the independent nature of the "prima donnas" they are supposed to lead. Samuel Butler, the presiding partner of Cravath, Swaine & Moore, has likened his role to that of the only fire hydrant on a street with fifty dogs. Another managing partner, well informed about a variety of professions, observes that "professional service firms are managed in one of two ways: badly or not at all."

In my experience, the problems of the ill-managed firm frequently derive not from a lack of skills on the part of the manager, but from the unwillingness of others to allow the manager freedom to act. This pattern—common in law, medicine, architecture, indeed in all the professions—suggests that there are forces in professional work that cause this "unmanageability."

One of the most salient psychological characteristics of those who choose professional careers is a strong need for autonomy. People choose professions (rather than, say, corporate careers) *because* the work is not routine or rigidly structured. Thus, the professions have more than their share of people with an aversion to taking directions. One of the most important features of partnership is the seeming absence of hierarchy among partners. Of course, there usually is a hierarchy, but the game of equal status is played on the surface. The decision-making process is as much a device for certifying status—the right to participate—as for getting things done.

A final attribute, I believe, contributes to the unmanageability of professionals: their daily roles as "experts." In many professions, especially the advisory professions, clients need trust and reassurance, and, to be successful, professionals must project an air of omnipotence and omniscience. Naturally enough, this manner carries over into other areas of the professional's life and breeds a sense of self-confidence, of mastery, that can seduce the top professional into believing that he or she can handle anything. Hence, every partner has an opinion on how the firm's affairs should be conducted and believes that no decision should be made without his or her input.

STRATEGY AND GOVERNANCE

The prevalence of participatory democracies in professional partnerships can be explained by more than the economic and psychological factors given above. Perhaps most important of all is the nature of professional work itself.

In a service in which the "technology" is well established, which can be delivered with a reasonably routine set of actions, specialization and division of labor are possible (and demanded by the marketplace); organizations that deliver this type of service tend to be bureaucratic, hierarchical, and "managed." Where a service is so customized or complex that its execution remains more of an art than a science, organizations tend to be more free-form, less hierarchical, and less bureaucratic. Sociologists of business refer to these two extremes as "mechanistic organizations" and "organic organizations."

Part of the turbulence affecting professional-service-firm governance, I would argue, is that a growing portion of the work is becoming less of an art and moving more toward the science end of the spectrum. In all areas of practice, services that begin as the domain of the creative, experienced professional inevitably "mature" and can be delivered by using more junior personnel and relatively well-specified procedures. Accordingly, as the proportion of such services increases, professional service firms are becoming less "organic" and more "mechanistic." If they wish to avoid a bureaucratic future, they must strive to get work that truly demands a high proportion of creative, artlike approaches. Routine work, though temptingly profitable because past experience can be leveraged to cut costs, inevitably results in a routinized work environment—anathema to those who choose professional careers.

Partners' autonomy has been justified in the professions because of the need to customize work activities to fit each client's needs. Professionals have demanded (if not always retained) the right to practice as they see fit, subject to minimal constraints: Only the service provider knows a particular client's circumstances and needs; no one can second-guess. This view, however, was more valid in the days of the generalist than in today's marketplace of specialization. Partners are more interdependent than when each served his own stable of clients: Now, coordination of a number of specialists is a requirement, bringing with it a demand for leadership.

THE EMERGING NORM

While it remains true that there are a broad variety of governance systems among the best professional firms, it can nevertheless be stated that there is an emerging norm, which has the following components:

a. An elected board of partners, whose function is to discuss and resolve matters of firm policy, meeting three to four times a year. This board is not an executive body, running the firm, but instead focuses on long-run policy issues.

b. A managing partner who devotes a significant proportion of his or her time to the executive function (50 to 100 percent). This individual is either elected by the partnership at large or appointed by the board, most commonly the latter.

c. A high-level business manager (or chief financial/administrative officer) who serves as the "right-hand man (or woman)" to the managing partner, to free him or her from administrative duties and business analytic tasks.

d. An executive committee, formed from the (appointed) heads of practice areas and offices, who serve as part of the management team headed by the managing partner.

e. A compensation committee formed from the executive committee, supplemented by additional members either directly elected or appointed by the board.

Like the nation state, these elements can be divided into three groups. The board (and occasionally, the partners as a whole) represents the legislative branch whose duty it is to approve or disapprove the policies under which the polity will operate. The managing partner, together with the executive committee and the business manager, form the executive branch. Finally, the compensation committee represents the judiciary.

THE BOARD

The ultimate "approval" body in a professional firm is, of course, the partnership, which reserves the right to approve major policy decisions on such matters as mergers, new partners, and the like. However, among the largest firms, a distinction is made between a "decision-making" role and an "approval" role for the partnership. Sheer numbers (and, increasingly, geography) prevent the partners, en masse, debating every policy decision. In consequence, most large professional firms *elect* a board of partners whose task it is to examine policy issues and either decide or present decisions to the partnership for ratification.

This board of partners corresponds closely to the corporate model of a board of directors representing the interests of the "shareholders" (in this case, partners). Like a corporate board, a primary function of this body is to oversee and monitor the activities of the executive (the managing partner) to ensure that the shareholders' interests are being served. Some professional firm boards meet monthly, but, as with corporate boards, a more common pattern is three or four times a year.

In most large professional firms, members of the board are elected by the partnership for terms typically ranging from two to four years, sometimes with restrictions on the number of consecutive terms an individual may serve (i.e., three two-year terms, two three-year terms, etc.). This last constraint is more often harmful than helpful, since it may force a valuable board member who has the support of his or her colleagues to step down. The opposite argument, that individuals may serve too long, can be accommodated through the electoral process.

Most multisite large professional firms make some efforts to ensure that the board is broadly representative of the practice. This is accomplished most usually by each operating unit directly electing its representative. Occasionally, heads of practice units (offices or disciplines) become de facto members of the board, although this is less common, due to the fact that these heads (see below) are frequently appointed by the managing partner, who is, in turn, appointed by the board.

It should be stressed that a significant shift has taken place in the roles and responsibilities of the board. Historically, many firms asked the body described here as the board to run the firm, that is, serve an executive, rather than a policy, function. However, a number of forces have led to a shift. First, many firms have observed that where the firm's highest committee serves both a policy and an executive role, the day-to-day minutiae tend to dominate the committee's deliberations and real policy debates are neglected. Accordingly, most firms have found it wise to separate the policy and executive functions. This same conclusion is generated by a "division of powers" consideration. By separating the policy and executive functions, the firm avoids having too much power located in one body. Finally, most firms have recognized that the managerial task, involving the day-to-day running of the professional firm, requires a distinctly different set of skills and abilities than those required at the policy level.

THE MANAGING PARTNER

The skills necessary to fulfill the prime managerial role (the managing partner, the chief executive officer, or chairman of the executive committee) are a combination of both "business skills" and "personal skills." (See Chapter 19, How Practice Leaders Add Value.) The manager's role involves a great deal of time spent working with individual partners, helping them resolve their issues and dealing with conflicts, in all senses of the word.

Much of good management in a professional firm depends on persuasion, interpersonal dealings, dealing with delicate and often private matters with and for the partners. The best manager is often neither the most outstanding professional, the best business getter, nor even the best "financial brain." Rather, it requires someone who is skilled at building consensus, and able at resolving disagreements. Such skills do not always come to the fore in open, contested, direct elections. Specifically, it is wise to empower the board with choosing the firm's managing partner. However, it should also be said that to obtain the credibility to lead, this selection (or nomination) should be ratified by the partners through a vote. In this way, the partners retain the right to veto an unwise selection, and the "manager" will receive a mandate to exercise his or her function.

Most commonly, the managing partner position is for a term (typically two to five years), thereby subjecting the managing partner to the discipline of receiving the support of partners (or their representatives, the board) in order to retain his or her position. While this formal reappointment of the managing partner on a periodic basis is typical, it is increasingly the case that once an effective managing partner is found, the person tends to retain the position for a significant period of time. Among major professional firms, the days of "rotating" the managing partner's function appear to be on the wane, if not gone.

Some firms have continued the practice of having the executive function shared by an executive committee, with the managing partner, as chair of this committee, being no more than "primus inter pares" in relation to the other committee members. There are dangers in this model of succumbing to "committee-itis." If too many people are jointly responsible for the execution of firm business, the chances that implementation will be deferred increase exponentially. Accordingly, most professional firms are evolving to a model of governance whereby executive committees, where they exist, serve an "advise and consent" role to the managing partner of the executive committee, but managerial responsibility is focused in that individual.

In structuring a governance system, it is important to note that there is a potential trade-off between *structure* and *process*. For example, if those charged with a responsibility adopt the *process* of extensive prior consultation, then the need for *structural* guarantees (such as representative committees) can be diminished. Increasingly, professional firms are reducing their dependence on committees to get things done. Rather than appoint a group with "shared responsibility" (which all too often turns into no one's responsibility), firms appoint a single individual to take responsibility for a given area, *subject to the condition* that the individual is expected to be consultative, involve others in the reasoning process, and build consensus before acting. Thus the virtues of involvement and implementation are achieved in a time-conserving manner.

A similar process solution to the problem of participation is the habit of effective managing partners of holding regular partnership meetings at which the managing partner can report latest developments, let partners know what topics are to be addressed at forthcoming board meetings, and answer questions. This approach, done well, allows those outside the official power structure to participate. Of course, done poorly, this process can become a meaningless pro forma exercise at which nothing is accomplished. However, this only serves to illustrate the point that simple structural solutions ("mandatory partner meetings" or "circulation of board minutes") rarely solve governance issues by themselves. It is the *style* with which they are implemented that determines their success.

THE MANAGEMENT TEAM

More important than any executive committee is the group of individuals who are charged with running the practice day-to-day. Practice unit heads, together with the managing partner, form the management team, a distinct entity from the executive committee, but one which must truly function as a team in the running of the firm. The managing partner should use the management team as a sounding board for ideas and as his or her "eyes and ears" on issues that should be addressed.

In most firms, the designated heads of offices and practice areas are chosen by the managing partner (often subject to the approval of the board). They should be chosen less for their prominence, technical ability, or business-getting talents than for their managerial skill in running a practice unit. (Since this skill is relatively scarce, and the duties often onerous, direct election by practice unit members is fast fading as a means of identifying these individuals.)

In many firms, the role of practice head (responsible for an office or discipline) is a significant role in making things happen and affecting the future of the firm. As the creation of the board of partners, the management team is directly accountable to the board, and, through them, to the partners.

THE BUSINESS MANAGER

In most professional firms today, a high-powered chief financial officer supports the managing partner and serves as his or her right hand.

Such a person should (and, in well-run firms, does) shoulder the burden of numerous activities that often consume the time of the chairman of the executive committee, including:

- Reviewing financials, operating statistics
- Supervising the preparation of budgets
- Dealing with leases, contracts, computers, etc.
- Analysis of new strategic initiatives

This frees up the managing partner for more high-value activities such as:

- Conducting formal and informal performance reviews
- Having informal (unscheduled) interactions with other partners
- Assisting partners on client matters
- Assisting partners on their personal professional matters
- Visiting client's firm or office and other client relations activities

It is the norm today that administrative matters and the *analysis* of major business issues are delegated to a business professional. Such a person does not make decisions, nor (far less) deal with partner issues. However, this person does free up the managing partner to make these decisions and deal with partners by serving as a high-powered resource to the managing partner. Experience has shown that as much as 25 percent of the managing partner's time (i.e., something on the order of five hundred hours) can be freed up with the support of a sufficiently skilled business officer. If these five hundred hours were to be applied to the higher value tasks on the list above the value created would be sufficient to justify a significant investment in the business manager position.

THE COMPENSATION COMMITTEE

In most well-run firms, the compensation committee is made up of two parts: all or part of the executive committee, supplemented by other members separately chosen. Three equally appropriate approaches appear to be equally common in selecting these supplementary members:

a. The non-executive members of the board play this role
b. Supplementary members are appointed by the board
c. Supplementary members are chosen by direct election

The presence of the executive committee (or at the very least its managing partner) on the compensation body is essential to ensure that consistency is established between the "signals" issued by the executive in the day-to-day running of the firm and the annual performance review conducted by the compensation committee. However, the principle of separation of powers leads many firms to conclude (correctly in my judgment) that the executive function should not be completely coincident with the (judicial) compensation function.

It is rare that any special compensation arrangement is made for board members, other than reducing their targeted workload by the number of hours consumed by their board responsibilities. (If board activities take 10 percent of their time, for example, then their other performance indicators such as personal billings, etc., would be adjusted pro rata.)

The managing partner cannot be assessed in this way. As already noted, the task of the managing partner is to help make the firm successful, and he or she should be assessed on results in this area. (Not, it should be stressed, on the hours he or she puts into the job, or on personal practice results. The former rewards "make-work" and the latter ignores any contribution or weakness in performing the managerial function).

It is most functional if the managing partner's reward is closely tied to aggregate firm results. If the firm does well, the managing partner has the most to gain; if it does not, it is the managing partner whose reward is most affected. In a good year, the managing partner should receive the highest compensation in the practice. In a bad year, it will be the first to be cut.

EVALUATING A GOVERNANCE STRUCTURE

The governance structure described here is not perfect, and effective variations do exist. However, this structure does pass some important tests that any governance structure must meet.

- By having an elected board appoint, or at least nominate, the executive (managing partner and office heads), it maximizes the chances that *people with the right skills are placed in positions of authority*, and that *they work together as a team*.
- The Board, as the highest-level committee, *provides a place for "heavy hitting" partners who may not be good managers* to nevertheless hold important positions of influence.
- *Policy functions are effectively separated from executive functions*, and a place is provided for people of different skills to make their respective contributions.
- There should be a *clear, shared sense of who is responsible for what*, thereby eliminating the chances of gridlock.
- The structure allows, even if it does not ensure, *speedy decision making*.
- There is a clear *procedure to remove those no longer effective*.
- The structure makes it possible to set *clear goals, and hold people accountable* for them.
- The people charged with executive functions should, within this system, *have the time to carry them* out.
- There is a vehicle, or forum for dissatisfaction to be expressed, and *those outside the official channels can participate*.
- Governors have the *consent of the governed*.
- Perhaps most important, *committee-itis in decision making is avoided*.

This list represents a not inconsiderable group of virtues: a list that many alternate governance structures would be hard pressed to meet.

PART SIX

MULTISITE MATTERS

CHAPTER 27

THE ONE-FIRM FIRM

What do investment bankers Goldman Sachs, management consultants McKinsey, accountants Arthur Andersen, compensation and benefits consultants Hewitt Associates, and lawyers Latham & Watkins have in common? Besides being among the most profitable firms (if not *the* most profitable) in their respective professions? Besides being considered by their peers to be among the best *managed* firms in their respective professions? The answer? They all share, to a greater or lesser extent, a common approach to management that I term the "one-firm" system.

In contrast to many of their competitors, one-firm firms have a remarkable degree of institutional loyalty and group effort that is clearly a critical ingredient in their success. The commonality of this organizational orientation and management approach among each of these firms suggests that there is indeed a "model" whose basic elements are transferable to other professions. The purpose of this article

---

Note to the reader: This chapter was written as an article in 1985. The information on specific firms contained in this article was gleaned from a variety of "public domain" sources, as well as selected interviews (on and off the record) at a number of professional service firms, including but not restricted to those named herein. However, none of the information presented here represents "official" statements by the firms involved.

In the years since this piece was written a number of changes have taken place in some of these firms. I have chosen not to update my "reporting" since my primary purpose was (and is) to describe an effective management model, and not to make comments about specific firms.

is to identify the elements of this model of professional firm success, and to explore how these elements interact to form a successful management system.

WHAT IS MEANT BY "WELL MANAGED"?

The firms chosen for discussion were identified in the following way. In the course of my research and consulting work, I have made it my practice to ask repeatedly the question, "Which do you consider the best managed firm in your profession?" The question is, of course, ambiguous. In any business context, "well-managed" can be taken to refer, alternatively, to profitability, member satisfaction, size, growth, innovativeness, quality of products or services, or any of a number of other criteria. The difficulty in identifying "successful" firms is particularly acute in the professions because many of the conventional indicators of business success do not necessarily apply. For example, since there are few economies of scale in the professions, neither size nor rate of growth can be taken as unequivocal measures of success: Many firms have chosen to limit both. Even if "per-partner" profit figures were available (which they are not), they would also be unreliable measures, since many professional firms are prepared to sacrifice a degree of profit maximization in the name of other goals such as professional satisfaction and/or quality of worklife. Finally, since "quality" of either service or work product is notoriously difficult to assess in professional work, few reliable indicators of this aspect of success are obtainable.

In spite of these difficulties, it has been remarkable how frequently the same names appear on the list of "well-managed" firms in the professions, as judged by their peers and competitors. The firms discussed here were on virtually everyone's list of admired firms, often together with the comment, "I wish we could do what they do." It should be noted that other firms, not discussed here, were also mentioned frequently. However, as expressed earlier, what makes Arthur Andersen, Goldman Sachs, Hewitt Associates, and Latham & Watkins worthy of some special attention is not only that they are successful and well respected, but that, in spite of being in different professions, they appear to share a common approach to management (the one-firm firm system) that is readily distinguishable from many of their competitors. This approach is clearly not the only way to run a professional service firm, but it is certainly *a* way that is worthy of special study.

THE "ONE-FIRM" SYSTEM

LOYALTY

The characteristics of the one-firm firm system are institutional loyalty and group effort. In contrast to many of their (often successful) competitors who emphasize individual entrepreneuralism, autonomous profit centers, internal competition, and/or highly decentralized, independent activities, one-firm firms place great emphasis on firmwide coordination of decision making, group identity, cooperative teamwork, and institutional commitment.

Hewitt Associates (described along with Goldman Sachs in a recent popular book as one of "The 100 Best Companies in America to Work For")[1] says that, in its recruiting, it looks for "SWANs": people who are Smart, Work hard, are Ambitious, and Nice. While emphasis on the first three attributes is common in all professional service firms, it is the emphasis on the last one that differentiates the one-firm firm from all the others. "If an individual has ego needs that are too high," notes Peter Friedes, Hewitt's managing partner, "they can be a very disruptive influence. Our work depends on internal cooperation and teamwork."

The same theme is sounded by Geoffrey Boisi, the partner in charge of mergers and acquisitions at Goldman Sachs: "You learn from day one around here that we gang-tackle problems. If your ego won't permit that, you won't be effective here."[2] By general repute, Goldman has achieved its eminence with a minimum of the infighting that afflicts most Wall Street firms. In contrast to many (if not most) of its competitors on the Street, Goldman frowns upon anything resembling a star system.

DOWNPLAYING STARDOM

The same studied avoidance of the star mentality is evidenced at Latham & Watkins. As Clinton Stevenson, the firm's managing partner, points out: "We want to encourage clients to retain the firm of Latham and Watkins, not Clint Stevenson."[3] Partner Jack Walker reinforces this point: "I don't mean to sound sentimental, but there's a bonding here. People care about the work of the firm."[4] The team philosophy at McKinsey, one senior partner explained to me, is illustrated by its approach to project work: "As a young individual consultant, you learn that your job is to hold your own: You can rest assured that the team will win. All you've got to do is do your part."

Above all else, the leaders and, more important, all the other members of these firms view themselves as belonging to an *institution* that has an identity and existence of its own, above and beyond the individuals who happen currently to belong to it. The one-firm firm, relative to its competitors, places great emphasis on its institutional history, broadly held values, and a reputation that all actively work to preserve. Loyalty to, and pride in, the firm and its accomplishments approaches religious fervor at such firms.

TEAMWORK AND CONFORMITY

The emphasis on teamwork and "fitting in" creates an identity not only for the firm but also for the individual members of the firm. This identity, for better or for worse, is readily identifiable to the outside world. References by others in the profession to members of one-firm firms are not always flattering. Members of other large accounting firms, particularly those where individualism and individual contributions are highly valued, often make reference to "Arthur Androids." The term "A McKinsey-type" has substantive meaning in the consulting profession—sometimes even down to the style of dress. In the 1950s, I am told by a McKinsey-ite, a set of hats in the closet of a corporation's reception room was an unmistakable sign that the McKinsey consultants were in. The hats have disappeared, but the mentality has not. Goldman Sachs professionals are referred to by other investment bankers as the "IBM clones of Wall Street."

LONG HOURS AND HARD WORK

For all the emphasis on teamwork and interpersonal skills, one-firm firm members are no slouches. All of the firms discussed here have reputations for long hours and hard work, even above the norms for the all-absorbing professions in which they compete. Indeed, the way an individual illustrates his or her high involvement and commitment to the firm is through hard work and long hours. Latham & Watkins lawyers are reputed to bill an *average* of 2,200 hours apiece, with some heroic performers reaching the heights of 2,700 hours in some years. This contrasts with a profession-wide average of approximately 1,750. At Goldman Sachs, sixteen-hour days are common. It has been said: "If you like the money game, here's [Goldman's] a good team to play on. If you like other games, you may not have time for them."[5] James Scott, a Columbia Business School professor, has commented:

"At Goldman, the spirit is pervasive. They all work hard, have the same willingness to work all night to get the job done well, and yet remain in pretty good humor about it."[6] Similarly, McKinsey, Hewitt, and Arthur Andersen are all hard-working environments, above the norms for their respective professions.

SENSE OF MISSION

In large part, the institutional commitment at one-firm firms is generated not only through a loyalty to the firm but also by the development of a sense of "mission," which is most frequently seen as client service. *All* professional service firms list in their mission statement what I call the "3 Ss": the goals of (client) service, (financial) success, and (professional) satisfaction. What is recognizable about one-firm firms is that, in their internal communications, there is a clear priority among these.

Within McKinsey, a new consultant learns within a very short period of time that the firm believes that the *client comes first*, the firm second, and the individual last. Goldman Sachs has a reputation for being "ready to sacrifice anything—including its relations with other Wall Street firms—to further the client's interests."[7] At Hewitt Associates, firm ideology is that the 3 Ss must be carefully kept in balance at all times; however, client service is clearly number one. None of this is meant to suggest that one-firm firms necessarily render superior service to their clients compared with their competitors; nor that they always resolve inevitable day-to-day conflicts among the 3 Ss in the same way. The point is that there *is* a firm ideology which everyone understands and which no one is allowed to take lightly.

CLIENT SERVICE

The emphasis at one-firm firms is clearly one of significant attention to managing client relations. In these firms, client service is defined more broadly than technical excellence: It is taken to mean a more far-ranging attentiveness to client needs and the quality of interaction between the firm and its clients. Goldman Sachs pioneered the concept on Wall Street of forming a marketing and new business development group whose primary responsibility is to manage the interface between the client and the various other parts of the firm that provide the technical and professional services. In most other Wall Street firms, client relations are the responsibility of the individual professionals who do the work, resulting in numerous (and potentially conflicting) contacts between a single client and the various other parts of the firm. Hewitt Associates, alone in its profession, has also pioneered such an "account management" group. At McKinsey, in the words of one partner, "Everyone realizes that the (client) *relationship* is paramount, not the specific project we happen to be working on at the moment."

The high-commitment, hard-working, mission-oriented, team-intensive characteristics of one-firm firms are reminiscent of another type of organization: the Marine Corps. Indeed, one-firm firms have an elite Marine Corps attitude about themselves. An atmosphere of a special, private club prevails, where members feel that "we do things differently around here, and most of us couldn't consider working anywhere else." While all professional firms will assert that they have the best *professionals* in town, one-firm firms claim they have the best *firm* in town, a subtle but important difference.

SUSTAINING THE ONE-FIRM CULTURE

Up to this point, we have been talking about a type of firm culture, a topic much discussed in recent management literature.[8] Our task now is to try to identify the management practices that have created and sustained this culture. Not surprisingly, since human assets constitute the vast majority of the productive resources of the professional service firm, most of these management practices involve human resource management.

A good overview of the mechanisms by which an "elite group" culture, with emphasis on the *group*, can be created is provided by Dr. Chip Bell,[9] a training consultant, who suggests that the elements of any high performance unit include the following:

- Entrance requirements into the group are extremely difficult.
- Acceptance into the group is followed by *intensive* job-related training, followed by team training.
- Challenging and high-risk team assignments are given early in the individual's career.
- Individuals are constantly tested to ensure that they measure up to the elite standards of the unit.
- Individuals and groups are given the autonomy to take risks normally not permissible at other firms.
- Training is viewed as continuous and related to assignments.
- Individual rewards are tied directly to collective results.

- Managers are seen as experts, pacesetters, and mentors (rather than as administrators).

As we shall see, all of these practices can be seen at work in the one-firm firms.

RECRUITING

In contrast to many competing firms, one-firm firms invest a significant amount of *senior* professional time in their recruitment process, and they tend to be much more selective than their competition. At one-firm firms, recruiting is either heavily centralized or well coordinated centrally. At Hewitt Associates, over 1,000 students at sixty-five schools were interviewed in 1980. Of the seventy-two offers that were made, fifty accepted. Each of the 198 invited to the firm's offices spent a half-day with a psychologist (at a cost to the firm of $600 per person) for career counseling to find out if the person was suited for Hewitt's work and would fit within the firm's culture. At Goldman Sachs, 1,000 MBAs are interviewed each year; approximately thirty are chosen. Interviewing likely candidates is a major responsibility of the firm's seventy-three partners (the firm has over 1,600 professionals). Goldman partner James Gorter notes, "Recruiting responsibilities almost come before your business responsibilities."[10] At Latham & Watkins, all candidates get twenty-five to thirty interviews, compared to a norm in the legal profession of approximately five to ten interviews. As a McKinsey partner noted:

> In our business, the game is won or lost at the recruiting stage: We take it very seriously. And it's not a quantity game, it's a quality game. You've got to find the best people you can, and the trick is to understand what *best* means. It's not just brains, not just presentability: You have to try and detect the potentially fully developed professional in the person, and not just look at what they are *now*. Some firms hire in a superficial way, relying on the up-or-out system to screen out the losers. We do have an up-or-out system, but we don't use it as a substitute for good recruiting practices. To us, the costs of recruiting-mistake turnover are too high, in dollars, in morale, and in client service, to ignore.

TRAINING

One-firm firms are notable for their investment in firmwide training, which serves both as a way to add to the substantive skills of juniors and as an important group socialization function. The best examples of this practice are Arthur Andersen and McKinsey. The former is renowned among accounting students for its training center in St. Charles, Illinois (a fully equipped college campus that the firm acquired and converted to its own uses), to which young professionals are sent from around the world. In the words of one Andersen partner: "To this day, I have useful friendships, forged at St. Charles with people across the firm in different offices and disciplines. If I need to get something done outside my own expertise, I have people I can call on who will do me a favor, even if it comes out of their hide. They know I'll return it."

Similarly, McKinsey's two-week training program for new professionals is renowned among business school students. The program is run by one or more of the firm's senior professionals, who spend a significant amount of time inculcating the firm's values by telling Marvin Bower stories—Bower, who ran the firm for many years, is largely credited with making McKinsey what it is today. The training program is not always held in the United States but rotates among the countries where McKinsey has offices. This not only reinforces the one-firm image (as opposed to a headquarters with branch offices), but also has a dramatic effect on the young professionals' view of the firm. As one of my ex-students told me: "Being sent to Europe for a two-week training program during your first few months with the firm impresses the hell out of you. It makes you think: 'This is a class outfit.' It also both frightens you and gives you confidence. You say, 'Boy they must think I'm good if they're prepared to spend all this money on me.' But then you worry about whether you can live up to it: it's very motivating." All young professionals are given a copy of Marvin Bower's history of the firm, *Perspectives on McKinsey*, which unlike many professional firm histories, is as full of philosophy and advice as it is dry on historical facts.

"GROWING THEIR OWN" PROFESSIONALS

Unlike many of their competitors, all of the one-firm firms tend to "grow their own" professionals, rather than to make significant use of lateral hiring of senior professionals. In other words, in the acquisition of human capital, they tend to "make" rather than "buy." This is not to say that no lateral hires are made—just that they are done infrequently and with extreme caution. "I had to meet with the associates (i.e., not only the partners) before the firm [Latham & Watkins] took me on," Carla Hills, former Secretary of Housing and Urban Development, recalls. "Lateral entry is a big trauma for this place. But that's how it should be."

AVOIDING MERGERS

A related practice of one-firm firms is the deliberate avoidance of growth by merger. Arthur Andersen, unlike most of the large accounting firms, did not join in the merger and acquisition boom of the 1950s and early 1960s, in an attempt to become part of a nationwide accounting profession network. Instead, it grew its own regional (and international) offices. Similarly, the decade-long merger mania in investment banking has left Goldman Sachs, which opted out of this trend, as one of the few independent partnerships on the street. In contrast to many other consulting firms, McKinsey's overseas offices were all launched on a grow-your-own basis, initially staffed with U.S. personnel, rather than on an acquisition basis. With one recent exception, all of Latham & Watkins's branch offices were all grown internally.

It is clear that this avoidance of growth through laterals or mergers plays a critical role in both creating and preserving the sense of institutional identity, which is the cornerstone of the one-firm system.

CONTROLLED GROWTH

As a high proportion of the professional staff shares an extensive, common work history with the one-firm firm, group loyalty is easier to foster. Of course, this staffing strategy has implications for the *rate* of growth pursued by the one-firm firm. At such firms (in contrast to many competitors), high growth is not a declared goal. Rather, such firms aim for *controlled* growth. The approach is one of, "We'll grow as fast as we can train our people." As Ron Daniel of McKinsey phrases it: "We neither shun growth nor idolize it. We view it as a by-product of achieving our other goals." All of the one-firm firms assert that the major constraint on their growth is not client demand, but the supply of qualified people they can find and train to their way of practicing.

SELECTIVE BUSINESS PURSUITS

Related to this issue is the fact that one-firm firms tend to be more selective than their competitors in the type of business they pursue. It has been reported that an essential element of the Goldman culture is its calculated choosiness about the clients it takes on. The firm has let it be known, both internally and externally, that it "adheres to certain standards—and that it won't compromise them for the sake of a quick buck."[12] At McKinsey, the firm's long-standing strategy is that it will only work for "the top guy" (i.e., the chief executive officer) and, as illustrated internally with countless Marvin Bower stories, will only do those projects where the potential value delivered is demonstrably far in excess of the firm's charges. Junior staff at McKinsey quickly hear stories of projects the firm has turned down because the partner did not believe the firm could add sufficient value to cover its fees. Similarly, while Andersen has been an aggressive marketer (a property common to all the one-firm firms), Andersen appears to have taken a more studied, less "opportunistic" approach to business development than have its competitors.

Consequently, one-firm firms tend to have a less varied practice-mix and a more homogeneous client base than do their more explicitly individualistic competitors. Unlike, say, Booz, Allen, McKinsey's practice is relatively focused on three main areas: organization work, strategy consulting, and operation studies. In the late 1970s (the hey-day of "strategy boutiques"), many outsiders commented on the firm's reluctance to chase after fast-growing new specialties.[13] But McKinsey, like all of the other one-firm firms, enters new areas "big, or not at all." Andersen's strategy in its consulting work (the fastest growing area for all the large accounting firms) has been more clearly focused on computer-based systems design and installation than has the variegated practices of most of its competitors. Goldman has been notably selective in which segments of the investment market it has entered, and has become a dominant player in virtually every sector it has entered.

OUTPLACEMENT

One of the fortunate consequences of the controlled growth strategy at one-firm firms and the avoidance of laterals and mergers is that these firms, in contrast to many competitors, rarely lose valued people to competitors. At each of the firms named above, I have heard the claim that, "Many of our people have been approached by competitors offering more money to help them launch or bolster a part of the practice. But our people prefer to stay." On Wall Street, raiding of competing firms' top professionals has reached epidemic proportions; yet, this does not include Goldman Sachs. It is said that one of the rarest beasts on Wall Street is an ex-Goldman professional: Very few leave the firm.

Turnover at one-firm firms is clearly more carefully managed than it is among competitors. Those one-firm firms that do enforce an up-or-out system (McKinsey and Andersen) work actively to place their alumni in good positions preferably with favored clients. McKinsey's regular alumni reunions, a vivid demonstration of its success in breeding loyalty to the firm, are held two or three times a year. In part, due to the caring approach taken to junior staff, one-firm firms are able to achieve a very profitable high-leverage strategy (i.e., high ratio of junior to senior staff) without *excessive* pressures for growth to provide promotion opportunities.

COMPENSATION

Internal management procedures at one-firm firms constantly reinforce the team concept. Most important, compensation systems (particularly for partners) are designed to encourage intra-firm cooperation. Whereas many other firms make heavy use of departmental or local-office profitability in setting compensation (i.e., take a *measurement*-oriented, profit-center approach), one-firm firms tend to set compensation (both for partners *and* juniors) through a *judgmental* process, assessing total contribution to the firm. Unique among the large accounting firms Andersen has a single worldwide partnership cost-sharing pool (as opposed to separate country profit centers): Individual partners share in the joint economics of the whole firm, not just their country (or local office). "The virtue of the 'one-pool' system, as opposed to heavy profit-centering, is that a superior individual in an otherwise poor-profit office can be rewarded appropriately," one Andersen partner pointed out. "Similarly, a weaker individual in a successful office does not get a windfall gain. Further, if you tie individual partner compensation too tightly to departmental or office profitability, it's hard to take into account the particular circumstances of that office. A guy that shows medium profitability in a tough market probably deserves more than one with higher profitability in an easy market where we already have a high market share."

Hewitt Associates sets its partner compensation levels only after all partners have been invited to comment on the contributions (qualitative *and* quantitative) made by other partners on "their" projects and other firmwide affairs. Vigorous efforts are made to assess contributions to the firm that do not show up in the measurable factors. Peter Friedes notes:

> We think that having no profit centers is a great advantage to us. Other organizations don't realize how much time they waste fighting over allocations of overhead, transfer charges, and other mechanisms caused by a profit-center mentality. Whenever there are profit centers, cooperation between groups suffers badly. Of course, we pay a price for not having them: specific accountability is hard to pin down. We often don't know precisely whose time we are writing off, or who precisely brought in that new account. But at least we don't fight over it: we get on with our work. Our people know that, over time, good performance will be recognized and rewarded.

Goldman Sachs also runs a judgment-based (rather than measurement-based) compensation system, including "a month-long evaluation process in which performance is reviewed not only by a person's superiors but by other partners as well, and finally by the management committee. During that review, 'how well you do when other parts of the firm ask for your help on some project' plays a big part."[14] At Latham & Watkins, "15 percent of the firm's income is set aside as a separate fund from which the executive committee, at its sole discretion, awards partners additional compensation based on their general contribution to the firm in terms of such factors as client relations, hours billed, and even the business office's 'scoring' of how promptly the partner has logged his or her own time, sent out and collected bills, and otherwise helped the place run well."[15]

INVESTMENTS IN RESEARCH AND DEVELOPMENT

In most professional service firms, particularly in those with a heavy emphasis on short-term results or year-by-year performance evaluation, any activity that takes an individual away from direct revenue-producing work is considered a detour off the professional success track within the firm and is therefore avoided. This is not the case with one-firm firms.

As the one-firm culture is based on a "team-player" judgment-system approach to evaluations and compensation (at both the partner and junior level), it is *relatively* easier (although it is never easy) for one-firm firms to get their best professionals to engage in nonbillable, staff-like activities such as research and development (R&D), market research, and other investments in the firm's future. For example, McKinsey is noted in the consulting profession for its internally funded R&D projects, of which the most famous example is the work that resulted in the best seller, *In Search of Excellence.* This book, however, was only one of a large number of staff projects continually under way in the firm. An ex-student of mine noted that "at McKinsey to be selected to do something for the firm is an honor: It's a quick way to get famous in the firm if you succeed. And of course, you're expected to succeed. Firm projects are treated as seriously as client work, and your performance is closely examined. However, my friends at other firms tell me that firm projects are a high-risk thing to do: They worry about whether their low chargeable hours will be held against them later on."

Andersen likewise invests heavily in firmwide activities. For instance, it conducts extensive cross-office and cross-functional industry programs, which attempt to coordinate all of the firm's activities with respect to specific industries. In fact, it is rumored, although no one has the statistics, that Andersen invests a higher proportion of its gross revenues in firmwide investment activities than does any other firm.

Goldman's commitment to investing in its own future is illustrated by the firm's policy of forcing partners to keep their capital in the firm rather than to take extraordinarily high incomes. Hewitt's commitment to R&D is built into its organizational structure. Rather than scatter its professional experts throughout its multiple office system (staffed predominantly with accounting managers), it chose to concentrate its professional groups in three locations in order to promote the rapid cross-fertilization of professional ideas. Significant investments of professional time are made in nonbillable research work under the guidance of professional group managers who establish budgets for such work in negotiation with the managing partner.

COMMUNICATION

Communication at a one-firm firm is remarkably open and is clearly used as a bonding technique to hold the firm together. All the firms described above make *heavy* use of memorandums to keep everyone informed of what is happening in other parts of the firm, above and beyond the token efforts frequently made at other firms. Frequent firmwide meetings are held, with an emphasis on cross-boundary (i.e., interoffice and interdepartmental) gatherings. Such meetings are valued (and clearly designed) as much as for the social interaction as for whatever the agenda happens to be: People go to the meetings. (At numerous other firms I have observed, meetings are seen as distractions from the firm's, or the individual's, business, and people bow out whenever they can.)

At most one-firm firms, open communication extends to financial matters as well. At Hewitt, they believe that "anyone has a right to know anything about the firm except the personal affairs of another individual." At an annual meeting with all junior personnel (including secretaries and other support staff), the managing partner discloses the firm's economic results and answers any and all questions from the audience. At Latham & Watkins, junior associates are significantly involved in all major firm committees, including recruiting, choosing new partners, awarding associate bonuses, and so on. All significant matters about the firm are well known to the associates.

ABSENCE OF STATUS SYMBOLS

Working hard to involve nonpartners in firm affairs and winning their commitment to the firm's success is a hallmark of the one-firm firm and is reinforced by a widely common practice of sharing firm profits more deeply within the organization than is common at other firms. (The ratio between the highest paid and the lowest paid partner tends to be markedly less at one-firm firms than it is among their competitors.) There is also a suppression of status differentials between senior and junior members of the firm: an important activity if the firm is attempting to make everyone, junior and senior alike, feel a part of the team. At Hewitt Associates, de-emphasizing status extends to the physical surroundings: everyone, from the newest hire to the oldest partner has the same size office.

The absence of status conflicts in one-firm firms is also noticeable across departments. In today's world of professional megafirms composed of departments specializing in vastly different areas, one of the most significant dangers is the professionals in one area may come to view *their* area as somehow more elite, more exciting, more profitable, or more important to the firm than another area. Their loyalty is to their department, or their local office, and not to the firm. Yet the success of the firm clearly depends upon doing well in all areas. On Wall Street, different psychological profiles of, and an antipathy between, say, traders and investment bankers is notorious. In some law firms, corporate lawyers and litigators are often considered distinct breeds of people who view the world in different ways. In some accounting firms, mutual suspicion among audit, tax, and consulting partners is rampant. In consulting firms, frequently there are status conflicts between the "front-room" client handlers and the "back-room" technical experts.

What strikes any visitor to a one-firm firm is the deeply held mutual respect across departmental, geographic, and functional boundaries. Members of one-firm firms clearly *like* (and respect) their counterparts in other areas, which makes for the successful cross-boundary coordination that is increasingly essential in today's marketplace. Jonathan Cohen of Goldman Sachs notes that out-of-office socialization among Goldman professionals appears to take place more frequently than it does at other Wall Street firms. Retired Marvin Bower of McKinsey asserts that one of the elements in creating the one-firm culture is mutual trust, both horizontally and vertically. This atmosphere is created primarily by the behavior of the firm's leadership, who must set the style for the firm. Unlike many other firms, leaders of one-firm firms work hard not to be identified with or labeled as being closer to one group than another. Cross-boundary respect is also achieved at most one-firm firms by the common practice of rotating senior professionals among the various offices and departments of the firm.

GOVERNANCE: CONSENSUS-BUILDING STYLE

How are one-firm firms governed? Are they democracies or autocracies? Without exception, one-firm firms are led (*not* managed) in a consensus-building style. All have (or have had) strong leaders who engage in extensive consultation before major decisions are taken. It is important to note that all of these firms do indeed have leaders: They are not anarchic democracies, nor are they dictatorships. Whether one is reading about Goldman's two Johns (Weinberg and Whitehead), McKinsey's (retired) Marvin Bower and Ron Daniels, Latham & Watkin's Clinton Stevenson, or Hewitt's Peter Friedes, it is clear that one is learning about expert communicators who see their role as preserver of the "true religion." Above all else, they are cheerleaders who suppress their own egos in the name of the institutions they head. Such firms also have continuity in leadership: While many of them have electoral systems of governance, leaders tend to stay in place for long periods of time. What is more, the firm's culture outlasts the tenure of any given individual.

Of course, the success of the consensus-building approach to firm governance and the continuity of leadership at one-firm firms is not fortuitous. Since their whole philosophy (and, as I have tried to show, their substantive managerial practice) is built upon cooperative teamwork, consensus is more readily achieved here than it is at other firms. The willingness to allow leaders the freedom to make decisions on behalf of the firm (the absence of which has stymied many other "democratic" firms) was "prewired" into the system long ago, since everyone shares the same values. The one-firm system *is* a system.

CONCLUSION: POTENTIAL WEAKNESSES

Clearly, the one-firm firm system is powerful. What are its weaknesses? The dangers of this approach are reasonably obvious. Above all else, there is the danger of self-congratulatory complacency: A firm that has an integrated system that *works* may, if it is not careful, become insensitive to shifts in its environment that demand changes in the system. The very commitment to "our firm's way of doing things," which is the one-firm firm's strengths, can also be its greatest weakness. This is particularly true because of the chance of "inbreeding" that comes from "growing your own" professionals. To deal with this, there is a final ingredient required in the formula: self-criticism. At McKinsey, Andersen, Goldman, and Hewitt, partners have asserted to me that "we have no harsher critics than ourselves: We're constantly looking for ways to improve what we do." However, it must be acknowledged that, without the diversity common at other professional service firms, one-firm firms with strong cultures run the danger of making even self-criticism a pro forma exercise.

Another potential weakness of the one-firm firm culture is that it runs the danger of being insufficiently entrepreneurial, at least in the short run. Other more individualistic firms, which promote and reward opportunistic behavior by individuals and separate profit centers, may be better at reorganizing and capitalizing on emerging trends early in their development. Although contrary examples can be cited, one-firm firms are rarely "pioneers": They try to be (and usually are) good at entering emerging markets as a late second or third. But because of the firmwide concentrated attack they are able to effect, they are frequently successful at this. (The similarity to IBM in this regard, as is much of what has been discussed above, is readily noticeable.)

The one-firm approach is *not* the only way to run a professional service firm. However, it clearly is a very successful way to run a firm. The "team spirit" of the firms described here is broadly admired by their competitors and is not easily copied. As I have attempted to show, the one-firm firm system is *internally* consistent: All of its practices, from recruiting through compensation, performance appraisal, approaches to market, governance, control systems, and above all, culture and human resource strategy, make for a consistent whole.

CHAPTER 28

HUNTERS AND FARMERS

In the previous chapter (The One-Firm Firm) I attempted to describe one (not the only) success model in running a professional firm. What I hope became clear in this description is that making this "collaborative" approach to practice work requires more than just an elusive "teamwork culture." Rather, it is achieved by making some definitive decisions on "hard" business systems such as compensation, hiring, training, organization, and choice of service lines.

In recent years, I have come to call these firms "Farmers" because, like such communities, these firms deliberate about what crops to sow, arrive at a (gutsy) decision, and then "bet the farm" on that crop. In other words, one-firm firms are focused on the services they bring to market, and build their success by investing heavily in the chosen areas. They succeed through focus, muscle, and concentrated efforts in a few hand-picked areas. The collaboration and teamwork that are the hallmark of the one-firm firms or Farmers derive not from an aesthetic preference (for team spirit) but from the simple fact that since the firm has "bet the farm," the success of the community depends on whether the crop comes in (i.e., the firm has bet successfully as to what the market wants). While some individuals may sow the seeds, others mend the fences, and yet others cook the meals, all must do their part to make the farm succeed. What counts is not individual performance, but contribution to aggregate success. Teamwork comes from truly "being in this together." There is no way for an individual to do well unless the organization as a whole succeeds.

The reason for the Farming model's success should be easy to see. If we know what we are trying to bring to market, then it is easy to figure out what tools we need, what training to do, what kind of people to hire, how and where we should focus our marketing. The fact that one-firm firms are known for their training, methodology development, hiring, and focused marketing is no accident.

The Farmer's greatest virtue is also its greatest weakness. As we have seen, most of the strengths of this approach derive from focus: the fact that large numbers of professionals do the same thing or take the same approach to practice. Farmer firms enter new markets "big or not at all." However, while focus is a business virtue, it is not the only one. Successful businesses can be, and have been, built on virtues such as entrepreneuralism, opportunism, flexibility, diversity, and quick responsiveness to emerging new client needs. None of these particularly plays to the Farmer's strengths. Rather, they are virtues of what I term the "Hunter" system.

Think of it this way: You have a firm of five partners, and you must make one of two choices. The first choice is that you collectively decide to practice the same specialty, in the same way, and develop joint marketing plans. On a firmwide basis you make collective investments in the same methodologies and practice tools. Your firm will, if you succeed, become known for something very particular. Your other option is to diversify your risk. The five of you choose different specialties, thereby being able to offer your market a range of services. You will have a harder time figuring out what methodologies to develop, since each of you practices in a different area, but you will have willingly given up the benefits of focus to obtain the strength of diversity. Your success will now depend on the entrepreneurial ability of each of your five partners.

Hunter firms attempt to maximize the entrepreneuralism of their members, by creating the maximum possible degree of individual autonomy. Rather than being "constrained" by firmwide choices on what markets to serve and which services to offer, Hunter firms encourage each individual (and each small group) to respond and adapt to the local market. The benefits (and limitations) of firmwide consistency (in services, in markets, and in approach) are sacrificed in order to capture the benefits of local market opportunities.

Like the Farmer system, the Hunter approach only works when it is done properly. Very concrete management systems are required to pull this strategy off. To succeed, the Hunter firm must attract, motivate, and reward the best entrepreneurs. In contrast to the Farmer model, where rewards must be structured to emphasize teamwork and group contribution, the Hunter system requires that individuals rise and fall according to the results of their own entrepreneurial efforts.

In essence, in a Hunter firm, it is everybody's job to "chase the buffalo." If buffalo die out, individuals are free to chase deer. And if, while out hunting, they spy a flock of geese, they don't have to check back with any central committee or managing partner to see if geese are "on strategy." The message is simple: There is no central strategy—just kill meat!

In order to succeed, Hunter systems need to be more short-term focused in their rewards. Those who kill meat get rewarded. Those who can no longer kill meat—well, it would be nice to support them, but if we divert too much reward from the best hunters, we may suppress their entrepreneuralism. So, the message inevitably ends up: your're as good as your latest numbers.

A key point about the Hunter–Farmer distinction should be stressed immediately. First, while I have made it sound somewhat "brutish," the Hunter approach is, indeed, a success model. Entrepreneuralism, flexibility, responsiveness, and fast adaptation to shifting market needs are powerful business virtues. Any firm that could successfully maximize these will be a formidable competitor.

Next, it is important to note that the terms do not refer to differences in marketing aggressiveness. Similarly, the reader should not think of Hunters as "business getters" and Farmers as "doers." Farmer firms are not "wimps" when it comes to marketing. Indeed, the best Farmers are superb at marketing. The key distinction is that Farmers approach marketing as an organized, joint activity done as teams, while Hunters view marketing as a matter of individual responsibility.

We now come to the tough question. Is it possible for a single organization to capture both the Hunter and Farmer benefits? Can a single firm obtain the virtues both of focus and firmwide approaches on the one hand, and of entrepreneuralism, flexibility, and adaptability on the other?

My own conclusion would be no. As I have tried to argue, it is not enough to be "sort of " a Farmer. To capture the benefits of focus, then a very detailed set of business and management decisions must be made. Similarly, to be a good Hunter, some concrete (and very different) systems are required.

To test this proposition, I compare and contrast in Table 28–1 the main managerial choices that each of the two approaches requires. As may readily be seen, the two approaches are rarely compatible. You may want to use this listing as a diagnostic test, by circling the item on each row that best describes your firm. In my view, there is a premium to be placed on internal consistency between and among a firm's management systems. If you circle mostly items in one column, you'll be in better shape than if you circle equal numbers in either column. If you do end up mostly in one column, then you may want to give some thought to the items that appear in the other column.

Because these management practices are almost always conflicting between the Hunter and Farmer approaches, firms who attempt to capture *both* groups of benefits (individual entrepreneuralism and collaborative strategy) must make significant compromises in management practices, which usually, in my view, results in lessened performance. Accordingly, professional firms must decide (or discover) whether they are Hunters or Farmers, and learn to capitalize on the strengths of their chosen model. There is a temptation for firms to believe that the "grass is always greener" on the other side. Collaborative firms often yearn for more entrepreneuralism, while individualistic firms bemoan their lack of organization. However, in their search to have both, firms must be careful not to compromise their basic strength.

TABLE 28–1

	HUNTERS	FARMERS
	BASIC CONCEPTS	
Central Principle	Individual (or small group) entrepreneuralism	Firmwide collaboration
Key Strengths	Diversity, Flexibility	Focus Strategy
Internal Atmosphere	Competitive	Collaborative
Management Style	Bottom-line numbers focus	"Values" "Mission"
Self-Image	Streetfighters	Team players
Leader	Best hunter	High priest
Decision Making	Decentralized (autonomous)	Coordinated (interdependent)
	CONTROL SYSTEMS	
Philosophy	Results measurement (almost exclusively)	Greater use of judgments
Planning Systems	Mostly financial	Strategic
Profit Centers	Strongly used, tied to compensation	For accounting purposes only
Compensation Systems	Short-term performance only	More use of rolling averages
	Frequent year-to-year adjustments	Smaller year-to-year adjustments
	Big range high-to-low	Small range high-to-low
	Seniority counts little	Seniority more important
Compensation Based on:		
Firm Profits	20	50
Profit Center Results	30	30
Individual Results	50	20
Attitude to Overhead	Resist with vigor	Prepared to invest
Internal Structure	Loose, frequently shifting	More organized
How Risk Is Taken	In small chunks by many groups	In large chunks on a firmwide basis
Territories	Not allocated	Allocated
Internal Transfer Pricing	Formalized, "full-cost"	Less dependence
Level of R&D	Lower	Higher

TABLE 28–1 (cont.)

	HUNTERS	*FARMERS*
	OPERATIONS	
Size of Operating Groups	Smaller	Larger
Location Strategies	Many locations opportunistic	Fewer locations, well-planned
Length of Engagements	Shorter (smaller)	Longer (larger)
Observed Leverage (Junior/Senior Ratio)	Lower	Higher
Variety of Work Done for Clients	High	More focused
Use of Established Procedures on Engagements	Less	More
Where Value Added to Clients	Back-room analytics	More front-room consultation
Size of Engagement Team	Smaller	Larger
	HUMAN RESOURCES	
Recruiting	Less selective, rely on "Testing in action"	Selective, partners involved
Key Appraisal Characteristic	Revenue production	More varied roles for individuals
Use of Lateral (Senior) Hires	Extensive	Reluctant
Turnover	High, especially thru "quitting"	Also high, but more asked to leave
"Fast Track" Opportunities	High	Low
Training	On-the-job	Formal, structured
Rotation of Juniors	Infrequent	Regular, systematic
	MARKET POSITION	
Emphasis on Client Relations	Lesser	Higher
Best Marketing Opportunities	Emerging practice areas	Practice areas with scale
Typical Size of Client	Varied, but frequently smaller	Larger

TABLE 28–1 (cont.)

	HUNTERS	FARMERS
Optimum Positioning	Creative, innovative, frontier	Reliable, efficient, thorough
Reaction to Mkt. Shifts	Good at small, fast shifts	Better at getting organized for systemic change
Levels in Client Organization	Anywhere	Aim for higher levels
Mkt. Appeal	Product/industry specialists	Generalists
Attitudes to Growth	Opportunistic, prime goal	Studied, secondary goal
Use of Mergers	High	Lower
Expansion Strategy	Same service, new markets	Same markets, new services

CHAPTER 29

MAKING THE
NETWORK WORK

Many, if not most, professional firms today are multilocation operations. Accountants, consultants, advertising agencies, and others have slowly built up their international presence. In the United States and Europe, multicity firms have emerged in professions where they did not exist before. These networks seem well poised to compete in the modern marketplace. However, before they can do so, they have some significant internal managerial problems to solve: the challenge of making their networks work.

The problem can be easily described. Unlike their clients, most international firms are not hierarchical companies with a simple chain of command. With rare exceptions, most of them are, in effect, federations of local organizations trading under the same brand name. Few firms, if any, have yet been able to forge together these separate organizations to take advantage (on a regular, systematic basis) of their collective power; that is, to form a truly connected network.

Collaboration and cooperation across (internal) boundaries is preached internally, and is fervently desired, but is hard to accomplish. Not because of bad management, but because of the complex managerial task of reaching for the benefits of both local autonomy and collaborative action.

A major cause of the problem lies in the nature of professional practice. By very definition, professional work requires customization and the need to adapt the practice to the special, individualized needs of a local clientele. In turn, this implies that a major degree of local autonomy is essential to any professional practice. Unlike many of their manufacturing clients, professional firms cannot be "ruled from the center" by imposing standard operating practices to be followed everywhere. If they are to act in harmony, it will come about only from a process of coalition building among powerful, independent, and autonomous peers, not through centralized edicts from a corporate "elite."

The importance of local autonomy creates a peculiar dilemma for the multisite professional service firm. If the local practice is responsible for winning engagements from clients, solving their problems, and serving them well, then what is the role of the overall firm? What does *it* do? How does the firm (or the network) "add value" above and beyond that provided by the local practice? What value do clients get from going to the multisite firm that they could not get by going to a good local firm? What value does the local practice get from the network when it is still responsible (in the main) for generating and servicing its own business? In summary, what is the value of the network?

The potential justifications for the network fall into two categories. First, the network can be valuable if it helps the local practice perform its local tasks better, and/or if the local client receives more value because its local provider is more empowered, as a result of being part of a network. I term this the "local value" issue. Second, the network can be of value in pursuing and serving multisite (or international) clients that no one practice could pursue alone. This is the "multilocation client" issue. These two justifications represent two completely different purposes (or rationales) for the network, requiring significantly different management practices to execute.

Of the two, the most important to professional firms is ensuring that the network functions well in addressing the "local value" issue; that is, ensuring that the local practice, because of its association with the network, is better able to win and serve local clients. The reason for this conclusion is that, at least to date and for the foreseeable future, the local practice dominates, in size and importance, the marketplace for professional services. Multipractice or multinational clients are glamorous, exciting, and even, perhaps, profitable; but they are not the bulk of the business and are unlikely to become so. Accordingly, the network's best opportunity to add value is being helpful across the broad volume of the local practice.

A second line of reasoning supports this conclusion. When firms *do* pursue international business they rapidly discover that a "strong local presence" in the countries of interest is a prerequisite to winning multinational engagements. Hence, it is in the firm's interests to ensure that the network is first functioning well on the local issue before attempting to tackle the multinational purpose. A third reason might also be mentioned. Since multinational work requires collaboration, and this in turn rests on mutual trust, respect, and confidence, the likelihood of success will be promoted if the local practice has a history of deriving benefit from the network, interacting with other practices for this purpose and establishing relationships across the firm.

EMPOWERING THE LOCAL PRACTICE

What, then, can the network do for the local practice that it cannot achieve by itself? One obvious benefit of belonging to the network, both to the practice and its clients, is the power of the *brand name*. For the client, the affiliation of the practice with the international network provides comfort, confidence, and (one hopes) quality assurance: In essence the "You can't be criticized for going with IBM" effect. While this is undoubtedly powerful, it can be a mistake to rely too heavily on this justification for the network. After all, in most professions there are at least a handful of equally prominent brand names. Although a brand name might help you *begin* a relationship, it is not that helpful thereafter. Yet, in some professional firm networks I have observed, the brand name remains the main benefit that the local practice receives.

What else can the network provide? An answer often given is "client access to expertise throughout the network." Again, there is great validity to this, as long as the local client truly has a need for this. In my observation, professional firms are good at delivering this benefit on "frontier" issues, where the firm's expert is readily identifiable, and that person's involvement can be charged to the client. However, if the client (and hence the practice) is trying to tap into the firm's accumulated past experience (either on a given functional topic or in the client's industry) in order to perform the current engagement more efficiently or effectively, then this is a benefit that's harder to deliver.

Few firms in my experience have data banks on past projects, formal inventories of skills and experiences, or any other mechanisms to tap into the firm's accumulated wisdom. For a very good reason: such mechanisms are hard to maintain, require significant investment, and can rarely be charged to the client. Accordingly, when a "nonfrontier" issue does come up that might benefit from assistance from elsewhere in the firm, few practices will go to the bother of "tapping the network." In most professions, the firm that could design an *effective* knowledge and experience sharing mechanism would obtain a significant competitive advantage.

Two other devices, *training* and *sharing of methodologies* are employed by most professional firms, and used well. However, it is interesting to note that, in a majority of firms, these devices involve mostly the junior staff. In my experience, there is relatively little formal organization of training and sharing of *the latest* ideas and approaches among the senior staff. In my view, a significant opportunity exists here to take greater advantage of the network in this area.

In principle, the network could assist the local practices by compiling and analyzing the *comparative economics* of the various practices and *assisting the managers* of the practices in running their businesses more effectively. In my experience, while some firms are dabbling in this area, few local practice heads would cite this as one of the great benefits of belonging to the network.

Last, but not least, we should acknowledge the importance of *referrals*. Many local practices report that this is the greatest benefit that they receive in belonging to the network: introductions to the local operations of multinational companies served elsewhere by the firm. This is clearly a real benefit.

PURSUING THE MULTILOCATION CLIENT

The issue of referrals appropriately brings us to the question of using the network to pursue and serve multilocation clients.

The first point to be made here is that, in my experience, *every* international professional service firm has as a strategic priority the goal of serving its multinational clients in multiple countries. Even those professions where international networks are not common, such as the law, are vigorously examining this issue. This is driven by the perception that business has (as the catchphrase has it) "gone global"—that there is a new era whereby firms can win new business from a client, not just one country at a time, but in the form of multicountry engagements.

Two problems exist with this view. First, it remains to be seen how many multinational corporations will indeed purchase their professional services on a multicountry basis, and how many will continue the strongly entrenched past norm of decentralizing the purchase of professional services to their head of operations in each of the countries. No one knows for sure which way things will go, but the truly multicountry purchase is today a small percentage of most professional markets, even if it is potentially the most profitable.

Second, if firms are to win this business, they must be able to deliver what the multicountry purchaser is primarily seeking: multicountry coordination, control, and consistency. Yet this central benefit flies in the face of how most professional firms are organized—as autonomous, distinct profit centers (or separately owned partnerships or companies).

Because of this structure, organizing to serve the multicountry client places strains on the way the network has traditionally been operated. Local practices have been accustomed to controlling their client relationships. In the multicountry engagement, there needs to be, for the client's benefit, someone in charge across boundaries. Naturally, local practices fear this loss of control, and worry about being dictated to.

In addition, they worry about profitability. Who is to negotiate the fees for the engagement? How will the revenues be allocated across the various practices involved? Why should we spend time trying to obtain a multicountry engagement when we incur all the marketing cost and get only some of the revenues?

Various firms have experimented with different mechanisms to solve these issues. At least one advertising agency has assigned a worldwide supervisor to each multinational client, with authority to see that the client is served in the manner required by the client worldwide. Obviously correct in principle, this action would create significant implementation difficulties at many firms. What, precisely, does this person have the "authority" to *do* in a part of the firm where he or she does not reside (i.e., in another profit center)? Where I have seen this role work, the individual operates less through authority and more by persuasion, working through the local chain of command, and *trading favors*.

Another mechanism with which some firms have attempted to overcome the barriers to cooperation is the use of "transfer payments" (i.e., internal accounting between operating units) to recompense those individuals (and profit centers) who perform activities for the "common good" of others in the network. It is impossible to design a simple transfer payment system that will provide sufficient incentive for all the desirable behaviors, but these systems can lower barriers to cooperation (if not remove them). A problem in many firms with this solution is that, historically, work done by an individual in one office for another office in the firm is *paid at a discount from standard fees* (to encourage professionals to focus on client work). Naturally, this does not provide much incentive to get involved in work outside the base office. Where (as I have seen it applied) multinational work is paid for at a premium in the internal records, more volunteers can be found to get involved in this (supposedly) important strategic work.

A common experiment that professional firms are making is the formation of a separate multinational group, not associated with any one part of the network (i.e., solving the network collaboration problem by taking the issue out of the network). These groups perform any or all of three roles: They are a home for specially hired (or developed) multinational specialists; they fund and develop special services for the multinational market; and they serve as the multinational marketing arm.

This makes eminent sense, until one considers the internal politics of the professional firm. After all, who is to pay for the activities of this group, which is rarely self-funding? Naturally the answer is the local practices through their contributions to "overhead." As might be expected, local practices are suspicious of such overhead (which they do not control), and tend to fund it thinly, if at all. Second, who is this "elite" group going after? The same clients that the local practice is pursuing for local engagements! Third, who is going to *do* the multi-country work? The local practice will want to do that part which is relevant to its locale, but (again) who's in charge of it if someone else has the relationship with the client?

SOME IDEAS ON COLLABORATION

In my experience, no "structural" solution (such as those discussed above: changing lines of authority, transfer payments, or creating separate groups) will solve the network problem. Rather, the *real* issue must be addressed head on: How *do* you get cooperation in an environment of autonomous units?

Some basic principles about human nature may help here. The first rule I would offer is: *Groups don't cooperate, people do.* An individual in one location might not feel much fervor in doing a favor for an individual in another location. But if he or she has worked with a specific person there, there is a greater chance that help will be forthcoming. What this means is that to promote cross-boundary cooperation, firms should create as many opportunities for *individuals* to get to know each other and work together as possible. Possibilities include: rotation of staff on temporary assignments; cross-staffing of client work even when not essential; frequent meetings to discuss developments and latest techniques; and so on. Even though they may not appear to be dramatic moves, these actions will go a long way toward breeding the collaborative spirit that the new environment seems to require.

In similar spirit, the second rule I would offer is: *Start small and go for the early success.* If the firm wishes to get people eager to cooperate across boundaries, there is no better way than to find an opportunity to demonstrate that it *works* (for all parties). In other words, rather than trying to sell the whole organization on *acting collaboratively*, find a limited project that those who are willing to try can act on. For example, quietly go after a *single* multicountry engagement and prove it can work. If the collaborative benefits are there, they can be publicized and the new program "rolled out."

Finally, I would offer: *Networks get built a link at a time.* This means that responsibility lies not only with the firm, but with each individual local practice. Rather than trying to take advantage of the whole firm, local practice managers should think about which of its numerous links to other practices in the firm could be strengthened by bilateral collaboration. This task is easier to execute, and quicker in its payback.

These suggestions clearly do not solve the problems faced by professional firms in this area, but they may help. The issue of collaboration among autonomous units is one of the business world's harder managerial problems. In the next chapter, Creating the Collaborative Firm, we will delve more deeply into possible solutions

CHAPTER 30

CREATING THE COLLABORATIVE FIRM

As noted in the previous chapter, large professional service firms, divided into different departments or numerous local offices, face a constant dilemma. On the one hand, the firm wishes to induce and reward individual initiative in each department or office. On the other hand, the firm has a need for coordinated action, mutual support, and shared responsibilities. To achieve this, the firm must reward those individuals who, somewhat selflessly, contribute to the success of the firm as a whole, even when this contribution is not reflected (at least in the short term) in their individual performance measures.

The tension between individual groups and the needs of the firm are frequently revealed when individual profit centers forego activities (such as market research on a particular industry) whose benefit to the firm as a whole is large enough to warrant the cost, but whose benefit to the individual profit center is not sufficient to warrant them engaging in that activity. Even if the profit center (or individual) is assured that contribution to overall firm success will (through some judgmental process) be recognized and rewarded, such rewards are often seen as more uncertain and risky than the "hard" evidence of individual profit center profitability or individual revenue generation.

The problem exists in single-site firms as well. Virtually all multidisciplinary professional firms fervently advocate cross-selling of the firm's full range of services to clients who use only one department.

Yet, remarkably, few of these firms have made cross-selling a normal part of daily behavior. Much more common is the pattern of behavior whereby individuals focus on improving the profitability of their own group, rather than assisting other groups in order to penetrate their clientele.

This problem is a difficult one, to which there is no easy answer. Some principles can, however, be established. First among these is the essential role of *long-term repeated interaction between the same people.* Cooperation emerges when people find it in their interest to do favors for each other, to help each other out. However, these favors rarely occur simultaneously. Rather, it's a case of "You do a favor for me now, and I'll owe you one: I'll help you on your problems next time you ask." To sustain this, the future must have a large enough shadow: those who are to cooperate must have a large enough chance of interacting with, and needing, each other again.

In many ways, this view of cooperation and collaboration leads individuals and firms into a Catch-22. If I've never cooperated with X in the past, I'm less likely to cooperate with him or her in the future. Those I have collaborated with are likely to receive my cooperation again. Firms that have a history of collaboration will cooperate more in the future. Firms trying to get it started will have to seed and nurture the fragile plant before it takes on a life of its own.

The foundation of cooperation is not really trust, but the durability of the relationship. It is readily evident that firms which have grown through mergers and lateral (senior-level) hires always have less internal cooperation than those that have grown from within. As obvious as this may seem, this observation casts significant doubt on those firms that have had a strategy of trying to justify the benefits of mergers through cross-selling and cross-referral of the newly acquired services.

We have already noted that *groups don't cooperate, people do.* If cooperation is based on reciprocal favors, separated in time, an audit partner in Milan is unlikely to do a favor for the consulting department or for the Brussels office, trusting that the favor will be remembered and repaid. But he or she is more likely to believe that a favor done for a given individual will be remembered and repaid. Attempts to get the audit department (as a group) to cooperate with the consulting department or the Brussels office (as groups) are doomed to failure. Firms must create a situation where the same people from these different departments (or different geographic locations) interact frequently.

It is important to note that *cooperation must be a two-way street*: It can only evolve when both parties are in a position to be helpful to the other. If one party is always *giving* the favor, and the other receiving, the situation is unstable and unlikely to be perpetuated. The absence of this has caused many collaborative efforts to die. For example, audit partners constantly complain that "you consultants keep asking me to introduce you to my clients, but you are never able to win me an audit—I have to do that myself. So if you can't help me, why should I make the effort?" The same is heard internationally: Large-country practices get "tired" of helping small-country practices of their own firm unless they see an opportunity to receive direct benefit in return.

To overcome this, it is necessary to introduce another principle: *To get a favor you must first give a favor*. Consultants who want an audit partner to help them should first find a way to be helpful (free of charge or immediate obligation) to the audit partner whose client they are targeting. Giving favors first doesn't always work. People who do this may get "burned" a few times by those who do not return favors. But in the long run they will get more cooperation (and the benefits of cooperation) than those who refuse to be the first mover.

Once established, collaborative activity can be infectious—if cooperation is indeed worthwhile, those doing it will clearly be seen to be benefiting. However, it must get started somewhere, in a visible way, to "lure" others into trusting behavior. Accordingly, professional firm managers should look for opportunities to create small-scale but highly visible examples of collaborative behavior, so that the partners can overcome their fear, temptation, and skepticism and give cooperation a real try.

In Table 30–1, I have listed many of the "network collaboration" tactics that large multisite professional firms consider in attempting to induce more cooperation in their networks. Based both on my direct observation of these tactics at work, and on the reasoning given above, I have arranged these tactics in order of what I judge to be their effectiveness.

Because they both involve people from different groups working together on the same client project, the two best tactics for nurturing

TABLE 30–1

Tactics to Achieve Network Benefits and Collaboration
(In approximate order of effectiveness)

Cross-staffing

Rotation of staff

Generating integrated client work

Reorganization around people with whom we want to collaborate
more

Centralization of selected network decisions

Firm-level funding of collaborative activities ("free" resources)

System of cross-boundary "client relationship partners"

Appointment of practice coordinators

Rewards for collaboration in compensation system

Joint training

Joint committees

Transfer payments and other accounting devices

Information sharing

Data bases to facilitate access to expertise

Education/awareness of resources available

---

future collaboration are cross-staffing of engagements (i.e., professionals from different profit centers or departments on the same client project) and semipermanent rotation of staff (i.e., assignment of individuals in one group to work for a period of time such as a year in some other group).

In firms committed to breeding collaboration, these tactics are used even where the specific client project does not require the cross-staffing. For example, a firm may assign a consulting person to be part of an audit team, performing audit work, even though that person will be less productive on the audit engagement. This "investment" is made in the belief that future collaboration between that consultant and the audit personnel he or she worked with will amply repay the loss of efficiency in doing today's assignment. The "semipermanent" assignment of personnel from one group (e.g., one geographic location) to another follows the same logic.

A related, and powerful, tactic is to use the firm's practice development efforts to generate the type of client project that truly requires multiple disciplines (or multiple locations) on the same project. It is important to note that this is not simple "cross-selling" where different groups do different projects for the same client. That approach does not give people from the different groups common work experiences; and thus fails to provide the opportunity for them to get to know each other and hence trust each other. Instead of "cross-selling" distinct projects, the goal is to sell projects that simultaneously require an integrated staffing. (This approach also has the not insignificant benefit of being easier to sell—the client has a clear reason to want to use staff from the same firm. In a pure cross-sell, with no overlap of work teams, it is hard for the client to see what extra value is obtained from buying from one firm.)

Obviously, the tactics of cross-staffing, rotation, and selling integrated projects are both slow and costly, and for that reason are often avoided. But they remain the most effective tools for laying the groundwork for future collaboration. Many firms have learned that, if the groundwork is not laid, then the other tactics described below lose their efficacy. There are no "shortcuts" to creating collaboration: Firms must make the investment if they wish to receive the benefits.

Next on my list is reorganization. Many firms have found that the most effective way to get individuals to cooperate is to put them in the same profit center. For example, one major law firm decided to reallocate its staff so that all those practitioners serving the same industry were in the same group, regardless of their formal discipline (corporate law, tax, creditor's rights, etc.). Now, serving that industry did not require that the corporate "department" (or individuals within it) needed to do or receive favors for the tax "department": They were in the same group, working towards the same goal. A similar trend to reorganizing into (multidisciplinary) industry groups is evident in consulting firms and, increasingly, accounting firms.

In the same spirit of creating small-scale "forced" interpersonal dealings that lead to future voluntary cooperation, some firms create firmwide budgets which allow them to provide "free" resources to the individual groups (e.g., access to experts) that encourage them to draw upon firmwide resources. Alternatively, these funds are used to manage firm-level investments in R&D, market research, product development, and so on. These approaches, which have proven to be very effective, create collaboration where none existed before because they take the decision on whether to cooperate or not out of the hands of the individuals involved. Trust and confidence that favors will be reciprocated are no longer required. Instead, a single firmwide body makes the decision.

Some firms have experimented with creating greater collaboration by appointing cross-boundary (i.e., inter-profit-center) organizational positions such as "worldwide account managers" or "nationwide industry leaders." The success of these positions is varied. My experience suggests that the key to making this tactic work is (not surprisingly) money. If the person fulfilling this role has funds to spend (on market research, proposal support, methodology development, etc.), then he or she can be a source of help to individual offices. Accordingly, this person can collect IOUs for favors done, and thereby ask for favors to help another office, as well as ask for cooperation with his or her own firmwide agenda. (See Chapter 31, Coordinating Industry Specialty Groups.)

Some organizations have attempted to induce cooperation by reserving some firmwide funds to be allocated (retrospectively) to those individuals (or groups) that have exhibited *good citizenship* by cooperating in ways that do not necessarily show up in the factors that normally drive compensation (or profit-allocation) decisions. These approaches can work, but in my experience, they tend to induce only the highly visible forms of cooperation (special events) rather than the ongoing daily cooperation that is the essence of a true network. This tactic is generally a good idea, but is rarely sufficient as a stand-alone device.

Many notable firms have achieved success by making use of joint (cross-profit-center) training and committees. These achieve the collaboration result not through the substance of the training or the agenda of the committee meeting, but through the simple fact that individuals are brought together in a work environment. While not as powerful (in my estimation) as the earlier cited cross-staffing and rotation tactics, the same principle is at work.

While transfer payments (of various sorts, such as commissions for work referred by one group to another) have a certain appeal, my observations suggest that they are "blunt instruments." They are hard to fine-tune (either overrewarding or underrewarding) and hence as often fail as they succeed.

For example, if referral fees (or commissions) are paid when one group introduces a new client to another (internal) group, how does one decide what is sufficient effort to warrant the fee? Is the transfer price the same when a new client is handed over "on a plate" as when a simple *introduction* is made, and the receiving practice still has to go through a full proposal effort to win the engagement? If not, where is the demarcation line? It is on such basic issues that most transfer pricing schemes founder.

Finally, we turn to what I call the "facilitators" of cooperation: data bases; information sharing and cross-education of resources; products and skills available elsewhere in the network. I have learned that such tactics make a good last step (easing the implementation of cooperation where it has been induced by other tactics), but a poor first step.

As the discussion above has attempted to show, the problem of cooperation is not one of lack of knowledge of the opportunities and benefits of collaboration; rather, it is a managerial problem of creating the environment in which people know their counterparts in other groups so well that collaboration (the bet that a favor given will be returned) represents a fair wager.

No one of the tactics presented here will alone solve the problem of collaboration in a network. However, there are a sufficient number of tactics available to suggest that, properly addressed, the goal can be reached. But not quickly: Collaboration must be nurtured—it cannot be force-fed.

CHAPTER 31

COORDINATING INDUSTRY SPECIALTY GROUPS

In the typical multisite professional service firm, the predominant organizing principle is that of geography. The local office managing partners (OMPs) have dominant voices in the day-to-day affairs of the firm. It is they, rather than any "headquarters" group, who collectively control the firm's financial and human resources. They not only exert significant influence over the market direction of the local practices for which they are responsible, but also control the main engines that drive the firm: the assignment, appraisal, compensation, and promotion of the professional staff.

This emphasis on local office initiative and independence is readily understandable. In spite of the growing significance of standardized, "packaged" services and products, most professional work remains a highly customized, and customizing, activity with a significant need for individual initiative both in the winning of clients and the conduct of the work. It is usually necessary to adapt the firm's service offerings to the needs of the local marketplace, creating a requirement for extensively decentralized decision making. Local resources and identity are frequently as important competitively as national capabilities and image, and responsibility for the former falls naturally to the OMP. Looking internally, it is clear that the critical functions of coaching, directing, appraisal and reward of professional staff all require a detailed understanding of the specific individuals involved. Again, the local OMP is the person best situated to be in command of these critical levers.

As competition in the professions intensifies, however, firms increasingly face the need to integrate their practices across office boundaries. They must strive to ensure that professionals working in the same functional or industry specialties take a consistent approach to the marketplace and can draw upon the accumulated wisdom and experience of the firm in that practice area. Clients increasingly select their professional service providers not only on the basis of local presence and functional expertise, but also on the extent to which the provider has experience and special insight into the peculiar problems and needs of the client's industry. Now the professional firm must coordinate its activities across office boundaries not only as to functional specialty, but also its industry experience. Accordingly, one of the fastest growing titles in the professional service world is industry head, industry coordinator, or some such phrase.

The situation of these industry heads is not enviable. Typically, they bear significant responsibility for the firm's aggregate practice in their designated industry but possess little direct authority over the key resources of the firm (most importantly the people). My research, which has involved extensive study of firms in a wide variety of professions, suggests that successful implementation of industry programs remains one of the most problematic areas of management in the multisite professional service firm. In part, I have found, this is because the full complexity of the industry specialization problem in the multisite firm is frequently underestimated. In this chapter, I will explore these complexities, attempting to clarify the alternatives available for dealing with them, and make recommendations where my research has revealed examples of "good practice."

Much of the discussion that follows applies not only to industry specialty programs, but also to any form of cross-office coordination of practice areas. Many of the problems and solutions discussed here can also be applied to the departmentalized single-site firm that is attempting to coordinate its various industry activities across functional departmental boundaries, as well as to the coordination problems of firms practicing in different countries.

CLOSE CONTACT BUILDS MORALE

In theory, the potential benefits of cross-office industry coordination are many. It can bring increased synergy, leverage, productivity, and quality in both the marketing of the firm's services and their operational delivery. From the client's perspective, close contact between professionals in different offices, working on similar matters, should lead to a higher level of service, since the firm's talents, skills, and expertise can be leveraged to be made available to a broader array of clients.

The competence of the professionals working in a given practice area is likely to be more rapidly advanced if lessons learned in one part of the firm are speedily disseminated throughout all of the firm's offices. From a marketing perspective, close integration of a practice area across offices allows the firm to present a more consistent image in the marketplace and ensure that its (usually decentralized) marketing activities are working in harmony. In addition to all of this, cross-office coordination, by bringing together professional staff from the firm's various offices, can have a salutary effect on pride and morale.

Given this array of potential benefits, why is successful practice area integration so difficult to achieve? In part, it is the very breadth of the potential benefits sought that creates many of the problems. Consider, for example, this brief extract from the responsibilities of one industry head at a large consulting firm:

> The industry head shall develop and recommend, in consultation with the office heads, an overall strategy for the firm's practice in his industry. He will be responsible for the evaluation and monitoring of the market and competition in the designated industry, and the development and dissemination of practice aids and other marketing tools to be used throughout the firm. He will assist in the identification of key new client opportunities and coordinate the development of proposal and engagement teams drawn from across the firm to enhance the firm's chance of success in key engagements. He shall be responsible for the development of new products and services for his industry and ensure their adoption throughout the firm. He will identify and recruit personnel within the offices to work in his industry, and shall oversee the professional development of such people, including such training programs as may be deemed appropriate. He is also responsible for ensur-

ing that all work performed in this industry conforms to the firm's standards of work quality.

Given this array of responsibilities, it is easy to see why practice area management can be so problematic, both for the individual (or team) charged with these responsibilities and for the powerful OMPs, whose autonomy and authority might be diminished if all of these functions are exercised by some other individual or group. To accomplish all of the tasks described above, an individual would need to acquire significant power and influence within the firm.

The problem is exacerbated by the fact that so much of practice area management involves nonbillable staff work, such as market research, the updating of brochures, or investing in new product development. Unlike the industrial corporation, the professions have traditionally had lean organizations with a minimum of staff roles. The road to glory has always been bringing in and working on client engagements. Accordingly, practice area management activities are resented not only as threats to local autonomy, but also as an overhead cost burden viewed with suspicion and constantly subject to challenge.

FIVE WAYS TO SHARE KNOWLEDGE

Because of these concerns, many firms have attempted to achieve cross-office coordination without the formal designation of industry practice leaders or other organizational restructuring. Other, more basic, coordination mechanisms are sought which are organizationally more acceptable, require less administrative overhead burden, and involve less suppression of local initiative. Since they are used even where formal, organizational coordination programs have been implemented, it is worth discussing these methods briefly.

Most basic are the information-sharing approaches to coordination, such as "skills inventory data bases," involving the collection and dissemination of information on the practice area specialties of staff members, so that individuals needing assistance from others in the firm can speedily access those with the special expertise. As simple as this concept is, it can be a troublesome system to implement and keep up to date, particularly in a large firm. In addition, the mere existence of the information is no guarantee that it will be used.

Another generic approach to industry coordination is the use of a "transfer pricing" system, whereby an office can buy the services of professionals from other firm offices to facilitate sharing of expertise. Frequently, however, the transfer payment system used by professional firms has precisely the opposite effect. For example, the system may successfully account for the billable time of a senior partner working "out-of-office," but fail to recognize adequately the opportunity cost of lost revenues to the home office because of the interruption of that partner's business development activities. In consequence, local OMPs are reluctant to volunteer their best people to engage in firmwide activities. (This problem is particularly acute within firms that place a great emphasis on profit center accounting and tie individual rewards closely to profit center results.) Accounting system barriers to practice area integration are complicated by the fact that it is frequently the same (usually small) offices that are the main seekers of assistance, and the same (usually large) offices that repeatedly are the providers.

A third basic approach to encouraging coordination is the use of the compensation system to encourage cooperative behavior and reward it appropriately. Many firms include "general contributions to the firm's success" in their appraisal system of both staff and partners, and attempt to base compensation awards, at least in part, on such contributions. However, the way in which performance appraisals are actually conducted often creates disincentives for individuals to engage in firmwide activities. As previously noted above, it is typically the local office OMP who has the major voice in the appraisal and compensation of staff in his office. Accordingly, professionals are reluctant to engage in out-of-office work (i.e., working on engagements being run out of another office), for fear that their contributions will not be adequately recognized and rewarded by their home office OMP.

A fourth coordination approach is to make extensive use of "discussion" committees, bringing individuals with similar client bases together to discuss mutual interests, common opportunities and shared problems. While these are favored because they do not involve binding decisions which might infringe upon local autonomy, they are frequently ineffective for the same reason, as well as often resented because of the nonbillable time required.

A final generic approach to industry coordination is that of goal sharing: ensuring that the overall strategy of the firm is well understood and disseminated, so that local OMPs (and others) can integrate their decisions into the strategy. This, too, is frequently ineffective. In more than one firm I have heard the complaint: "We can try to tell the offices which industries we plan, as a firm, to focus upon, but we have no means of enforcing it. The offices continue to pursue whatever opportunities seem to make sense in their own area."

WHERE ACTION MUST BE CENTRALIZED

One of the common characteristics of all of the coordinative mechanisms described above is that they function on a decentralized basis: None of them requires a centralized entity which might threaten the autonomy of the offices. Most firms, however, quickly come to recognize that in spite of the importance of local autonomy and initiative, there are industry-specific activities that the local offices cannot, should not, or will not do for themselves that justify more centralized approaches.

At least six distinct justifications can be identified: First are those activities which, if left to the offices, might involve duplication of tasks. (Collection of market intelligence about an industry might fall into this category.) Next are those activities that are avoided by offices because their cost cannot be justified by the benefit that would accrue to a single office, even where the aggregate benefit to the whole firm might warrant the investment. This is, of course, the economies of scale argument. (Among numerous other activities, industry training might fall within this category.) Third are those activities that an office might avoid because of the high risk involved, such as investments in research and development of new products and services. A centralized industry group, acting on behalf of the whole firm, should be expected to have a different risk profile than an individual office, and hence could get involved in more speculative activities than those an office could justify. The fourth rationale for centralized (or at least centrally coordinated) industry activities is that a central industry practice group should be able to afford a longer-term perspective on investments in the firm's industry practice than a single office might, given the pressure for short-term results felt by the typical local office.

A central industry group could also be expected to be able to make better informed decisions as to the firm's industry practice, because of its more global access to information. For example, a local office might fail to recognize significant industry trends requiring a studied response by the firm. Centralized industry activities might also be justified on the grounds of the needs for consistency in the approach to market, a need that might arise from marketing, operational, or even (in the case of such services as audits) regulatory considerations. Finally, centralized industry decision making can be justified on the grounds of strategy: the need to maximize the chances of industry penetration by targeting the same sorts of clients with the same sorts of services.

As can be seen, the case for forming firmwide industry groupings is strong. The duplication, scale, risk, long-term perspective, limited information, consistency, and strategy arguments might be used to justify a wide range of centralized decision making. To accept these arguments fully and centralize too much might, however, risk transforming the organization into an insensitive bureaucratic operation, with too much suppression of the local office entrepreneuralism upon which most professional firms have been built. Accordingly, in most firms with established industry specialty groups, the charter of these groups is to coordinate firmwide activities, not centralize them. The group is meant to function as an *advisory* department, whose role is to assist and support line activities in the individual offices, rather than to direct them. They are meant to be facilitators, catalysts, and coordinators, not czars. In consequence, those responsible for firmwide industry activities frequently have more responsibility than authority.

THE INDUSTRY HEADS NEED CRUCIAL SKILLS

A senior officer of a large consulting firm once commented to me that the single most important determinant of the success of an industry practice area was the selection of the individual to head the practice. This conclusion has been borne out repeatedly in the course of my research and consulting work with multisite professional service firms. The reasons for this are not hard to detect: The role of practice head is an ambiguous one, requiring an individual with very special skills.

In some firms, practice head responsibilities fall either to the most prominent firm professional in the field—usually on the grounds that such a person, through his prominence, is best suited to help the firm win new clients—or to the person who is most technically skilled in the area—on the grounds that this individual is best situated to act as a "thought leader" for the practice area and keep the firm at the forefront of innovative services and products to offer to clients. My research has led me to the conclusion that neither of these approaches, which can be jointly described as the superstar approach, is the best way to proceed. Instead, I have learned, firms should select as industry practice heads those individuals who possess the greatest managerial and leadership skills, in particular, those adept at organizational politics.

Because of limited authority, a practice leader must win, through persuasion or inspiration, the cooperation of a large number of separate offices. He must persuade OMPs and others within the offices to give attention to "his" industry or practice area in their business development activities. Since he cannot conduct all of the practice area activities (such as market research, development of training programs, etc.) himself, he must get the offices (and the individuals within them) to agree to spend their time on his program. Above all else, the industry head must get individuals to participate in his area for the benefit of the firm, rather than their parochial local office needs, in spite of powerful forces leading individuals to focus on their immediate short-run objectives. He must do all of this in competition with other industry or practice area heads, who are also trying to win resources of money or professional time from the offices or the firm's managing committee.

To accomplish all this, an industry practice head requires good political skills: the ability to recognize and listen to the needs (and values) of his constituency (the local offices), the ability to inspire that constituency to share his enthusiasm for his agenda, and the ability to "horse trade" favors over time so that help and assistance is forthcoming when it is needed. A practice leader in a multioffice environment cannot use the authoritarian coercion, or reward power, to accomplish his goals. Rather, he must *achieve* influence by being instrumental in helping others achieve their goals. He must be expert at finding or creating consensus, common ground, common purposes.

A practice head must be an enthusiastic, articulate person, able to convey a vision to others in the firm who are asked to contribute their services in the name of the common good. To be successful at winning cooperation from the offices, the practice leader must be able to communicate the importance of, and the opportunities within, his specialty. He must be good at selling new ideas internally as well as externally, and have the discretion to give up on bad ideas when support for them is not forthcoming from the organization. He must be, in the words of one managing partner, a "tactical but committed zealot."

In the various professional service firms with whom I have worked on this topic, I have made it my practice to ask individual industry heads for the one activity they think they should spend more time on in order to increase their effectiveness. The responses contain frequent references to such phrases as:

- "develop a network"
- "inspire enthusiasm"
- "listen to OMPs' needs"
- "encourage participation by giving prompt and visible recognition to those who help"
- "travel a lot to stay close to the line"
- "create and nourish teamwork"
- "bring people together frequently to give a sense of belonging to something bigger than their local office"

These pieces of advice are all concerned with learning how to play organizational politics—to win the enthusiasm and commitment of others to the industry head's agenda.

KEEPING AN AFFORDABLE BALANCE

One of the dangers of appointing zealous industry practice heads is that they will continually push for more firm resources to be invested in their particular specialty. (They would not be doing their job, if they did not.) The fears among line partners that centralized industry and other practice area activities might consume more resources than they merit is based in reality. In part, this danger is due to the fact that the range of possible activities which could be justified under the name of industry coordination is large. Consider, for example the extract from the industry head "charter" given earlier. In that brief description, we can identify at least eight distinct and potentially conflicting roles to be played. Using analogies to equivalent functions in an industrial corporation, we can see that an industry group could function as a:

- *Market research* department, assembling market data and performing analyses to identify market opportunities
- *Strategic planning* department, deciding how the firm's resources in a given area can best be deployed

- *Sales promotion* department, developing brochures, articles, booklets, and other sales aids
- *Research and development* department, working on enhancing the products and services offered by the firm
- *Quality control* department, ensuring that work conforms to specifications
- *Training* department, responsible for developing both sales and operations skills
- *Sales management* department, ensuring that the firm's experts are made available to local offices to help win important engagements
- *Production scheduling* department, influencing the assignment of key people to important engagements

Not all of these activities will be needed simultaneously in every industry practice area, but if the industry specialty is to be a real strategic thrust for the firm and not just a convenient marketing label, then most will be required at one time in the life of the practice. Clearly, one of the most important elements in good industry practice area management is to establish a clear understanding of the particular needs, at a given time, of a particular practice. In the early stages of the life cycle of a new industry practice, the emphasis may be upon market research and strategic planning. In a mature practice, more attention (and funds) should probably be directed towards training and quality control.

The allocation of investment funds among these various activities and between the various industry specialties of the firm is one of the most significant strategic decisions a professional service firm can make. It is through the availability of *free* resources in favored industries that the officers of the firm can influence centrally the strategic emphases of the local offices, while preserving local autonomy in decision making. A well-funded industry program can provide a larger range of (free) services to the local offices, and hence influence the direction of their practices. A poorly funded program can provide few services and will have a greater struggle persuading local offices to participate.

Deciding on the level and allocation of industry program funding is a difficult process, largely because of the problems in assessing the effectiveness of an industry program. A firm may be able to measure the growth in its volume of work in a given industry, or even, if its cost accounting system is sufficiently sophisticated, the profits generated by an industry firm-wide. But it will still remain difficult to relate this to the level of investment made in that industry's practice area program. As a result of these difficulties, industry programs must be assessed by a procedural, judgmental process rather than a numerical, measurement-oriented system. These assessments should not be made on a short-term basis. Ultimately, industry program investments are strategic choices.

The basic elements of an effective industry program management system would include the following. First, to avoid the temptations of *empire building*, and to preserve the manageability of what is, in any event, a difficult responsibility, industry practice areas should be defined in relatively narrow terms. Large programs should be broken up to make them more manageable. Funding for programs should be based on strategic emphasis, not on size. An industry practice area that accounts for a large proportion of the firm's fees does not necessarily warrant a greater investment than a small but emerging area.

As with any investment decision-making process, a request for funds should be backed up with a detailed proposal from the industry head justifying the request. Such a proposal should clearly indicate what proportion of the funds are to be spent on each of the distinct activities listed in the beginning of this section. As a natural tie-in, a retrospective review of accomplishments should be scheduled for each program every few years. (I do not recommend that this be done every year. By their very nature, investments in industry practices are long-term, risky investments and should be appraised accordingly.) I consider it good practice to impose a "sunset" policy on industry practices, whereby they have to justify their very existence after a certain number of years. Without such a policy, there is the danger that inertia will become a major factor in the allocation of practice area investments. It is also usually a wise policy to make the industry head position a nonpermanent assignment, so that new blood and fresh thinking can be brought into an industry practice every five to ten years. (Considerations of burnout, in what we have seen is a difficult position, also affect this conclusion.)

Finally, any industry program must be tested against the rigorous criterion of acceptance by the line offices, whose appraisal of specific practice areas should be repeatedly and vigorously sought. OMPs and other line partners should be polled on the merits of the various reports, products, and services produced by the practice area. They should be asked how helpful to them, as an office, the existence and conduct of the practice area has been. Given line skepticism toward firmwide "overhead" activities, this test is a tough one. Yet it is critical. An industry head in a multioffice professional service firm, as we have seen, has something to "sell," and his customers are the line offices. Only by being adept at convincing his clients of the value of his services can he accomplish his goals and achieve success. This is never an easy task, but if the firm is to develop and market industry expertise on a coordinated multisite basis (an increasingly important requirement for success), it is always an important one.

PART SEVEN
LAST THOUGHTS

CHAPTER 32

ASSET MANAGEMENT

If there has been one major theme in this book, it is that the key to ensuring any professional firm's future is wise management of its two key assets :

    a. Its inventory of skills, talents, knowledge, and ability
    b. The strength of its client relations and reputation

Achieving a good income statement result is a necessary condition for professional firm success, but it is far from a sufficient criterion. To have been judged a good year, a firm must not only achieve its volume and profit goals, but do so in a way that both builds new skills and strengthens client relations.

What would an asset management approach look like? What follows is a summary of some of the "new" management processes discussed in this book.

APPROACH 1: A LOOK-BACK MIX EVALUATION

In Chapter 13, How's Your Asset, we argued that client work can fall anywhere along a spectrum of "asset milking" to "asset building." Accordingly, wise management of the firm would require that a firm judge its success in part on the *type* of work it was generating. However, while most firms have volume goals for their new business de-

359

velopment effort; few have a mechanism to judge the qualitative mix of business they bring in.

Accordingly, what do their people go out and sell to meet their new business targets? The familiar or the new? It is much easier to sell a project on something you are known for, have references for, have methodologies for, and can be convincing that you can solve, than it is to sell an asset-building project for which you cannot provide five references, one that will help you learn new skills or develop new methodologies. Not only is it easier, but it is more comfortable to do the familiar project: You feel more confident about being able to solve the client's problem.

If there is a temptation for successful firms to exploit their reputation, rather than use their practice to build their balance sheet, the problem is even greater for less established firms in the building stage. Hungry for work, they will (appropriately) be keen to accept whatever they can get. For them, the risk that income statement considerations will dominate balance sheet concerns is even greater. Unfortunately, there is a spiral effect at work. If a firm starts off with a weak balance sheet, it can get too hungry and need to bring in any work, whether it grows the balance sheet or not. Hence it ends up growing its balance sheet less rapidly than a firm that has already positioned itself to be able to be more selective about its projects. A less hungry firm is more likely to grow its assets faster, assuming it uses the benefits of its reputation wisely.

The solution is for firms to establish mechanisms to appraise the quality of their practice, as well as its quantity. One such method is a regular look-back mix-evaluation. Every three months (or some such period) firms should pull out the list of projects they have been working on and give each project a grade (say from 1 to 5) on each of a number of selected "balance-sheet-building" criteria. *Did this engagement:*

a. Allow us to develop new skills?
b. Expose us to an important new client?
c. Allow us to train our juniors?
d. Increase (not just sustain) an important existing client relationship?
e. Allow us to work higher in client organizations?
f. Introduce us to an important new market segment?

Done regularly, and taken seriously, this evaluation of the "quality" of the practice, not just its aggregate volume, would provide guidance for future new business development efforts, and act as a "conscience" measure. While one would not expect all engagements to score high on all measures, the assessment of the mix will give a good guide as to whether or not practice development efforts are helping the balance sheet as well as the income statement.

APPROACH 2: EXPLICITLY MEASURE AND REWARD SKILL TRANSFER

The asset management issue is not solely (or perhaps even mainly) a marketing issue. As important as what matters are brought in is the issue of how they are handled. In the short run, it is always more economic to get the assignment performed by those who already know how to do it. But if this is always the operating rule, how will the firm ever transfer and grow its skills? At some point, the firm must use its staffing system to assign people to the project who don't yet have the skills, so they can learn from project leaders. Yet how many project leaders seek out neophytes to help them with their projects? It is in the project leader's interests to get his or her project staffed with the office rising star, not the one who needs developing.

Most firms say that they reward "building skills in others" in their compensation scheme, but few senior professionals I have met within these firms believe that this consideration plays anywhere near the role played by (aggregate) revenue growth, current profitability and personal workload. It is not surprising, therefore, that it receives more lip service than execution. The issue, therefore, is how to make it credible and operational. In Chapter 4, Solving the Underdelegation Problem, we looked at a method that would introduce a strict accountability: the "upward feedback" or "Rate your Engagement Experience" system.

APPROACH 3: MEASURE AND REWARD CLIENT SATISFACTION LEVELS

There is perhaps no more valuable asset that a firm has than the satisfaction of its clients. Yet few firms have any systematic means of tracking client satisfaction levels or rewarding those who excel in this area. In Chapter 8, A Service Quality Program, we looked at a method to put in place explicit measures and rewards for this activity by mandating an inescapable client feedback system. In every case where this system has been installed, the behavior of all professionals has changed to pay more attention to these asset-building, reputation-enhancing activities.

APPROACH 4: INCLUDE BALANCE SHEET QUESTIONS IN PARTNER GOAL SETTING, EVALUATION AND REWARD

Most compensation schemes for senior professionals stress income statement measures—revenues, workload, profits. Few recognize or encourage investment in asset-building activities such as development of new methodologies or transfer of skills. The measures proposed in Approaches 2 and 3 above provide systematic scorecards on skill transfer and client satisfaction that can be used in reward systems to shift the focus to activities that have a long-term benefit.

In addition to these, we saw in Chapter 22 (Partner Performance Counseling) that it is possible to include "balance sheet" questions in the performance evaluation system for senior professionals. For example, they could be asked to address the questions "What have you done that makes us stronger for the future?" or " In what way are you personally more valuable on the marketplace than last year?"

These questions effectively constitute a system of "personal strategic planning" (see Chapter 20, How to Create a Strategy). If they become an integral part of the senior professional goal setting, performance review and reward system, they can influence the senior professionals to focus more on asset-building activities.

APPROACH 5: PLACE MORE EMPHASIS ON MARKETING TO EXISTING CLIENTS

We noted above that, in order to grow its skills, any practice needs to bring in a certain proportion of projects for which the firm does not have well established methodologies, for which it cannot provide ready references, for which it does not already have a reputation. Who is likely to award such a project to the firm? A new prospect or an existing client? With overwhelming probability, such asset-building projects are likely to come from existing clients, if they are explicitly pursued. Accordingly, as we discussed in Chapter 9, firms should develop explicit marketing plans and budgets to penetrate existing clients.

APPROACH 6: SYSTEMATIC DEBRIEFING OF ENGAGEMENTS

It is trivial to observe that most new learning (skill, talent, and knowledge accumulation) in professional firms takes place on engagements. However, it is not trivial to point out that many firms (and individuals) fail to capture and disseminate much of this potential learning.

In principle, one of the competitive advantages of large firms is that the value they can bring to market is not just the individual talents of individual practitioners, but the individual empowered by the accumulated knowledge, wisdom, systems, methodologies, and experiences of the firm. Realizing this potential value takes effort and attention. It requires systematic efforts to debrief engagements and capture (on paper or on videotape) "what we learned from this one," so that the new knowledge, however incremental, can be put to work the next time not only by the individual who did the project but by others in the same practice.

A few firms of my acquaintance are diligent in this. They make documentation of "what we learned from this one" a requirement of every project leader: as inescapable a responsibility as sending out the bill. They hold regular practice group meetings for the sole purpose of sharing latest ideas, tactics, and approaches (see Chapter 14, How to Build Human Capital). Alas, most firms of my acquaintance expect this to happen "naturally." Being a "nonbillable" activity, it gets infinitely postponed, and the capturing of knowledge is spotty at best.

APPROACH 7: INDUSTRIAL ENGINEERING STUDY OF PROJECT METHODOLOGIES.

As discussed in Chapter 2, The Professional Firm Life Cycle, all professional services go through a life cycle which requires that firms learn how to increasingly use less costly staff to deliver engagements as the service matures. A good test of whether this is happening (i.e., whether or not the firm is adding to its assets by developing valuable methodologies to deliver services at lower cost) is to compare the staffing of similar engagements performed two or three years apart. Hopefully, the firm will find that, in the intervening period, it has learned how to perform these "similar" engagements with more methodology, less senior time, and more practice tools. If not, then the firm may wish to commission a special study to analyze each of the work tasks required by the engagement, and, just as in any industrial engineering study, find ways to redefine work tasks and develop tools to allow for more effective "production" in the future.

CONCLUSION

The approaches listed here are far from exhaustive in giving ways for firms to manage their balance sheet. However, they point the way to the sort of management processes that are required if firms are to ensure a healthy future. The challenge of the future for professional firms does not lie in being good at forecasting. Rather it lies in using today's activities to ensure that the firm is strong enough to meet tomorrow's challenges. The good news is that income statement thinking does not have to be sacrificed to ensure a good balance sheet. Done right, one can make as much money on asset-building work as on work that exploits preexisting assets. One can make money through sharing and development of skills as easily as living off them. The bad news is that it doesn't happen naturally. Firms must manage for it.

REFERENCES AND SOURCES

CHAPTER 11.   ATTRACTING NEW CLIENTS

1. Gerald M. Weinberg, *The Secrets of Consulting: A Guide to Giving and Getting Advice Successfully* (New York: Dorset House Publishing, 1985).

CHAPTER 12.   MANAGING THE MARKETING EFFORT

I gratefully acknowledge the contributions of Mike Cummings and Barry Schneider of SAGE, Inc. to an early draft of this chapter.

CHAPTER 15.   THE MOTIVATION CRISIS

1. Tracy Kidder, *The Soul of a New Machine* (Boston: Little, Brown, 1981).
2. Morgan W. McCall, Jr., "Leadership and the Professional," in T. Connolly, ed., *Scientists, Engineers, and Organizations* (Monterey, Calif.: Brooks/Cole Engineering Division, 1983).

CHAPTER 19.   HOW PRACTICE LEADERS ADD VALUE

1. David Ogilvy, *On Advertising* (New York: Vintage Books, 1983).

CHAPTER 23.   THE ART OF PARTNER COMPENSATION

1. Andrew S. Grove, *High Output Management* (New York: Random House, 1985).

CHAPTER 27.   THE ONE-FIRM FIRM

1. R. Levering, M. Moskowitz, and M. Katz, *The 100 Best Companies to Work for in America* (Reading, MA: Addison-Wesley, 1984).

2. B. McGoldrick, "Inside the Goldman Sachs Culture," *Institutional Investor,* January 1984.
3. S. Brill, "Is Latham & Watkins America's Best Run Firm?" *American Lawyer,* August 1981, pp. 12–14.
4. Ibid.
5. Levering et al. (1984).
6. McGoldrick (January 1984).
7. Ibid.
8. See, for example, V. J. Sathe, *Culture and Related Corporate Realities* (Homewood, IL: Richard D. Irwin, 1985).
9. C. Bell, "How to Create a High Performance Training Unit," *Training,* October 1980, pp. 49–52.
10. McGoldrick (January 1984).
11. Brill (August 1981).
12. McGoldrick (January 1984).
13. See, for example, "The New Shape of Management Consulting," *Business Week,* 21 May 1979.
14. McGoldrick (January 1984).
15. Brill (August 1981).

CHAPTER 31.   CREATING THE COLLABORATIVE FIRM

Some of the ideas in this article were derived from an academic text (*The Evolution of Cooperation* by Robert Axelrod, Basic Books, 1984) that offers interesting insights into the problem of cooperation in a variety of fields.

INDEX

Schon, Donald, 148
Scientist, Engineers and Organizations (McCall), 171
Scott, James, 306–307
Screening, 12, 15
Secrets of Consulting, The (Weinberg), 121
Seduction principle, 122, 125, 131
Selection stage, 115
Self-evaluation, 249, 250
Self-improvement, 246–249
Seminars, 121, 135
  ballroom-scale, 122, 130
  small-scale, 122, 123–124
Seniority system, 256–258, 267, 271
Senior-level staff, 3–20; *see also* Practice leadership; Staff
  coaching and, 44–48, 157–159, 196, 203, 209–212, 215–216, 220, 241–242, 246, 247
  in experience-based practice, 25
  in expertise-based practice, 23, 24
  underdelegation and, 41–50
  work assignment system, 156–157
Senior partner visits, 54, 63, 66, 83, 84
Service quality, 69–77, 79–82, 361–362; *see also* Motivation
  program, 83–95
Skepticism, 113, 114, 122
Skill building, 93, 196, 237–240, 361, 362
  scheduling and, 177–178
  underdelegation and, 42, 48, 49
Skills inventory data bases, 348
Small-scale seminars, 122, 123–124

Small-team approach, 136–140, 212
Soul of a New Machine, The (Kidder), 167, 170
Speeches, 121–123, 125, 135
Sponsorship of cultural/sports events, 122, 130
Staff, 3, 4, 143–204
  asset building, 143–153
  efficiency-based practice, 26
  experience-based practice, 25, 26
  expertise-based practice, 23
  human capital development, 155–162
    coaching, 157–159
    teaching partners, 159
    work assignment system, 156–157
  leverage and, 6–8
  motivation, 163–174
    importance of, 165–166
    meaning of work, 171–172
    professional psyche, 168–169
    promotion and, 172–174
    recruiting process and, 166–168
    scheduling and, 178
    supervisory style, 169–171
  productivity strategies, 193–199
  reduce need strategies, 194, 197–198
  retention, 192, 198–199
  rotation of, 335, 340, 341
  scheduling, 175–184, 195
    good system, 176–178
    management of, 181–184
    related to other systems, 178–181
  substitution strategies, 194, 199–202